Lecture Notes in Computer Science

Commenced Publication in 1973
Founding and Former Series Editors:
Gerhard Goos, Juris Hartmanis, and Jan van Leeuwen

Nail Akar   Michal Pioro
Charalabos Skianis (Eds.)

IP Operations
and Management

8th IEEE International Workshop, IPOM 2008
Samos Island, Greece, September 22-26, 2008
Proceedings

 Springer

Volume Editors

Nail Akar
Bilkent University
Electrical and Electronics Engineering Department
Ankara 06800, Turkey
E-mail: akar@ee.bilkent.edu.tr

Michal Pioro
Warsaw University of Technology
Institute of Telecommunications
00-661 Warsaw, Poland
and
Lund University
Department of Electrical and Information Technology
22100 Lund, Sweden
E-mail: mpp@tele.pw.edu.pl; mpp@eit.lth.se

Charalabos Skianis
University of the Aegean
Department of Information and Communications Systems Engineering
811 00 Mytilene, Lesvos, Greece
E-mail: cskianis@aegean.gr

Library of Congress Control Number: Applied for

CR Subject Classification (1998): C.2, D.4.6, K.6.5, C.4

LNCS Sublibrary: SL 5 – Computer Communication Networks
and Telecommunications

ISSN 0302-9743
ISBN 978-3-540-87356-3 Springer Berlin Heidelberg New York

Springer is a part of Springer Science+Business Media

springer.com

© Springer-Verlag Berlin Heidelberg 2008

Typesetting: Camera-ready by author, data conversion by Scientific Publishing Services, Chennai, India
Printed on acid-free paper   SPIN: 12523801   06/3180   5 4 3 2 1 0

Preface

On behalf of the IEEE Communications Society, Technical Committee on Network Operations and Management (CNOM), Manweek 2008 Organizing Committee, and members of the IPOM Technical Program Committee, it is our pleasure to present the proceedings of the *8th IEEE Workshop on IP Operations and Management (IPOM 2008)*, held as part of Manweek 2008 during September 22–26, 2008, on Samos, Greece.

The current Internet is a large-scale distributed system whose sub-components such as addressing, protocols, algorithms, services, need to scale in time with the rapid growth of Internet traffic volumes. Moreover, there is a high level of interaction between different subcomponents of the Internet sometimes in undesired ways – for example, denial of service attacks can jeopardize the operation of a commercial network. With these challenges in place, operations and management of IP networks have become increasingly important. This necessitates a good understanding of the emerging technical and scientific problems in the current Internet, and lessons from such understanding will be particularly important for future Internet design and management. Building on the success of the previous events, we wanted IPOM 2008 to focus on network management challenges for the current Internet as well as on future Internet design.

Like the previous three IPOM workshops, IPOM 2008 was co-located with several related events as part of Manweek. The other events were the 19th IFIP/IEEE International Workshop on Distributed Systems: Operations and Management (DSOM 2008), the 11th IFIP/IEEE International Conference on Management of Multimedia and Mobile Networks and Services (MMNS 2008), the Third IEEE International Workshop on Modelling Autonomic Communications Environments (MACE 2008), the 4th IEEE/IFIP International Workshop on End-to-end Virtualization and Grid Management (EVGM 2008), and the 5th International Workshop on Next-Generation Networking Middleware (NGNM 2008). Co-locating these events provided the opportunity for an exchange of ideas among separate research communities working on related topics, and also allowed participants to forge links and exploit synergies.

This workshop attracted 30 paper submissions through an open call for papers. A rigorous review process was followed with typically three reviews per paper. The Technical Program Co-chairs decided to have a strong program with single-track sessions. With this in mind, the submitted papers were discussed based on the reviews received as well their relevance to the workshop. These proceedings present 12 accepted full-papers; thus, the acceptance rate is 40%. Authors of accepted papers are from nine different countries spanning three continents; they were invited to present their work at the conference.

We thank members of the IPOM Technical Program Committee, IPOM Steering Committee, Manweek 2008 Organizing Committee, and reviewers for their hard work that made this workshop possible. In particular, we thank Tom Pfeifer, Manweek 2008 Publications Chair, for his excellent handling of the production of these proceedings.

Finally, we thank the patrons of Manweek 2008, and the TSSG for their financial and in-kind contributions to this workshop.

September 2008   Nail Akar
                                                                      Michal Pioro
                                                               Charalabos Skianis

IPOM 2008 Organization

Workshop and Program Co-chairs

Nail Akar — Bilkent University, Turkey
Michał Pióro — Warsaw University of Technology, Poland
Charalabos Skianis — University of the Aegean, Greece

Steering Committee

Prosper Chemouil — OrangeLabs, France
Tom Chen — Southern Methodist University, USA
Petre Dini — Cisco Systems, USA
Andrzej Jajszczyk — AGH University of Science and Technology, Poland
G.-S. Kuo — National Chengchi University, Taiwan
Deep Medhi — University of Missouri-Kansas City, USA
Curtis Siller — IEEE ComSoc, USA

Publication Chair

Tom Pfeifer — Waterford Institute of Technology, Ireland

Publicity Co-chair

Luciano Paschoal Gaspary — Universidade Federal do Rio Grande do Sul, Brazil

Treasurers

Sofoklis Kyriazakos — Converge, Greece
Brendan Jennings — Waterford Institute of Technology, Ireland

Website and Registration Chair

Sven van der Meer — Waterford Institute of Technology, Ireland

Submission Chair

Lisandro Granville — Universidade Federal do Rio Grande do Sul, Brazil

Sponsoring Co-chairs

E. Pallis   Centre for Technological Research of Crete,
                                    Greece
I. Venieris   National Technical University of Athens,
                                    Greece

Manweek 2008 Chair

George Kormentzas   University of the Aegean, Greece

Manweek 2008 Vice Chair

Francisco Guirao   European Commission

Manweek 2008 Advisors

Raouf Boutaba   University of Waterloo, Canada
Brendan Jennings   Waterford Institute of Technology, Ireland
Sven van der Meer   Waterford Institute of Technology, Ireland

IPOM 2008 Technical Program Committee

Sasitharan Balasubramaniam   Waterford Institute of Technology, Ireland
Stefano Bregni   Politecnico di Milano, Italy
Marcus Brunner   NEC Europe Ltd., Germany
Hakima Chaouchi   National Institute of Telecommunication,
                                    France
Tom Chen   Southern Methodist University, USA
Baek-Young Choi   University of Missouri-Kansas City, USA
Ken Christensen   University of South Florida, USA
Alexander Clemm   Cisco Systems, USA
Mike Devetsikiotis   North Carolina State University, USA
Petre Dini   Cisco Systems, USA
Nelson Fonseca   State University of Campinas, Brazil
Luciano Paschoal Gaspary   Federal University Rio Grande Sul, Brazil
Anastasius Gavras   Eurescom GmbH, Germany
Timothy Gonsalves   Indian Institute of Technology Madras, India
Fabrizio Granelli   University of Trento, Italy
Abdelhakim Hafid   University of Montreal, Canada
Andrzej Jajszczyk   AGH University of Science and Technology,
                                    Poland
Abbas Jamalipour   University of Sydney, Australia
Pascal Lorenz   Université de Haute Alsace, France
Edmundo Madeira   State University of Campinas, Brazil

Additional Reviewers

Table of Contents

Network Anomaly Detection

Traffic Engineering, Protection, and Recovery

Network Measurements and Applications

Network Management and Security

Towards Anomaly Detection in One-Way Delay Measurements for 3G Mobile Networks: A Preliminary Study

Peter Romirer-Maierhofer[1] and Fabio Ricciato[1,2]

[1] Telecommunications Research Center Vienna (ftw.), 1220 Vienna, Austria
romirer@ftw.at
[2] University of Salento, 73100 Lecce, Italy
ricciato@ftw.at

Abstract. In this paper we investigate the dynamics of one-way delays in an operational mobile core network. Our ultimate motivation is to develop anomaly detection schemes for the packet delay process in order to reveal network and equipment problems. This requires an online measurement system capable of collecting and processing delay statistics in real-time. We present an experimental deployment of such a measurement system in an operational General Packet Radio System (GPRS)/Universal Mobile Telecommunications System (UMTS) network and elaborate on some practical implementation issues. We present some measurement results for the Serving GPRS Support Nodes (SGSN) of UMTS and GPRS. We find that the delay at a UMTS-SGSN is moderately influenced by user mobility, while flow control and user mobility are considerably impacting the delay process at a GPRS-SGSN. We show that simple summary indicators can be extracted from the delay statistics, as a combination of percentiles and threshold-crossing probabilities. Such indicators can be used for the purpose of detecting abnormal delay deviations, pointing to problems in the network equipments.

1 Introduction

Third-generation (3G) mobile networks play an increasingly important role in the telecommunication market. Operators of a 3G infrastructure must cope with a usage environment that is rapidly evolving, as new applications emerge and terminal capabilities increase continuously. In such a scenario, it is highly desirable to automatically detect network problems such as equipment malfunctioning, point of congestion, misconfiguration and alike. One natural approach to the problem is to measure some key performance parameters on the data plane, e.g. one-way delays, and to raise an alarm whenever a significant deviation occurs from the "typical" behavior observed in the past. This approach underlies two fundamental assumptions: i) that the behavior of the process under normal conditions is highly predictable, and ii) that anomalous phenomena

N. Akar, M. Pioro, and C. Skianis (Eds.): IPOM 2008, LNCS 5275, pp. 1–14, 2008.

Table 1. List of acronyms

3G	3rd Generation
3GPP	3rd Generation Partnership Project
BSC	Base Station Controller
BSS	Base Station System
BSSGP	Base Station System GPRS Protocol
DA	Delay Aggregator
DC	Delay Client
DNS	Domain Name System
EDGE	Enhanced Data Rates for GSM Evolution
ER	Edge Routers
GGSN	Gateway GPRS Support Node
GPRS	General Packet Radio System
GPS	Global Positioning System
GSM	Global System for Mobile Communications
GTP	GPRS Tunnelling Protocol
HSPA	High Speed Packet Access
ISP	Internet Service Provider
MS	Mobile Station
PDP	Packet Data Protocol
RAN	Radio Access Network
RNC	Radio Network Controller
RRC	Radio Ressource Control
RTT	Round Trip Time
SGSN	Serving GPRS Support Node
SRNC	Serving Radio Network Controller
UMTS	Universal Mobile Telecommunications System
URA	UTRAN Registration Area
UTRAN	UMTS Terrestrial Radio Access Network
WAP	Wireless Application Protocol

(e.g., misfunctioning) generate appreciable deviations on the observed process. Therefore, the practical implementation of this approach requires a preliminary understanding of the "normal" patterns.

In [1] we presented the analysis of one-way delays at short-time scales at the Gi interface. The single-hop delay of a GPRS-SGSN (refer to Table 1 for a list of acronyms used in this paper) was dissected in [2]. In these earlier works, we showed that one-way delay measurements are a promising means to support the process of troubleshooting an operational mobile 3G networks. In this work, we extend our analysis of one-way delays to the single-hop delay process at a UMTS-SGSN and compare it in detail with that at a GPRS-SGSN. At both SGSN types queuing is the main source of delay. However, at the UMTS-SGSN the delay is moderately influenced by user mobility, while the delay at the GPRS-SGSN is considerably impacted by user mobility and flow control. Grounded on preliminary long-term observations, we present an empirical-based method to detect abnormal delays by setting thresholds on the vertical and horizontal distances in the delay distribution. We propose the AND-combination of these thresholds as a simple detection method, which is mainly invariant to time of day effects, while minimizing the risk of false positives.

2 Related Works

The initial study on single-hop one-way delays in an operational IP network was performed by Papagiannaki et al. in [3]. There the methodology based on IP header hashing and matching was presented for the first time. The analysis was then extended to the end-to-end delays across a geographical network in [4]. Those studies were performed on the Sprint backbone, while our study focuses on the core section of a cellular network, where the delay process is not only shaped by queuing, but also by user mobility and flow control procedures. Some previous works have studied the delay process in 3G mobile networks based on passive traces, e.g., [5,6,7]. They all focused on the analysis of Round-Trip-Times (RTT), estimated from TCP DATA/ACK or SYN/SYNACK pairs captured at a single monitoring point on Gi. Other works have resorted to active measurements to evaluate one-way end-to-end delays, e.g., [8,9,10]. In general, it is not possible to exploit the RTTs or the end-to-end delays to infer the internal dynamics of the Core Network. This is because the delay on the radio link is the dominant component in the total delay budget, and it exhibits a high degree of variability due to the changing radio conditions. Therefore, the fine-grain dynamics taking place within the wired section can not be observed with those approaches.

The implementation of a client-server based system for collecting one-way delays from measurement points distributed in an IP network was presented in [11]. While the high-level architecture of our implementation is similar, we move a step forward and present long-term results from an operational network.

3 Measurement Setting

3.1 Network Overview

The reference network structure and the monitoring setting is sketched in Fig. 1. In the network under study four different access schemes are available depending on the geographical location of the Mobile Station (MS) and its terminal capabilities: GPRS, EDGE, UMTS and HSPA [12]. The MSs are connected via radio link to the antennas. A set of geographically neighboring antennas is connected to the Base Station Controller (BSC) in GPRS/EDGE and the Radio Network Controller (RNC) in UMTS/HSPA. These are then connected to a set of SGSNs via the Gb (for GPRS BSC) and IuPS (for UMTS RNC) interface. The overall set of antennas, BSC/RNC and the links to the SGSNs constitute the Radio Access Network (RAN). The primary role of the SGSN is to perform mobility management, which involves frequent signaling exchanges with the MSs. The data plane traffic collected by the SGSN is concentrated within a small set of so-called Gateway GPRS Support Nodes (GGSN), which act as

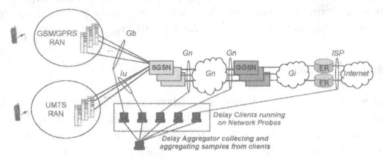

Fig. 1. Network structure and monitoring setting

IP gateways for the user traffic. The SGSNs and GGSNs are interconnected by a wide-area IP network that will be referred to as the "Gn network" following the terminology of 3GPP specifications ("Gn interface"). After the GGSN, the user packets enter into the "Gi network" (ref. Fig. 1) that is functionally similar to the Point-of-Presence network of an Internet Service Provider (ISP). The Gi section is deliminated by one or more Edge Routers (ER) and includes a number of IP-based elements: servers, WAP gateway, proxies, DNS servers, firewalls, etc. The ERs are connected to the public Internet via the ISP interface (ref. Fig. 1).

3.2 Monitoring System

The present work is based on the on-line monitoring of packet-level traces captured in the operational network of a mobile provider in Austria. The monitoring system was developed in a past project [13]. For privacy reasons, we store only the packet headers up to the transport layer, i.e., payload is stripped away. All packets are captured and no sampling is implemented. On the Gn interface, the system is capable of parsing the GPRS Tunnelling Protocol (GTP) layer and tracking the establishment and release of each "PDP-context", and to uniquely identify the MS sending or receiving each packet. Similarly to timestamps, a unique MS identifier is stored as an additional information label for each frame. To protect the user privacy, the MS identifiers are chosen as arbitrary strings, decoupled from the real user identity. The monitoring setup used for this work is depicted by the red network probes in Fig. 1. The network probes monitoring the Gb, IuPS and Gn interfaces of a SGSN (Gn-SGSN) and a GGSN (Gn-GGSN) as well as the ISP interface to the public Internet are used for the computation of one-way packet delays. Each network probe is equipped with at least one Endace DAG [14] capture card. These capture cards allow GPS-synchronized packet capturing, offering a timestamp accuracy of ± 100 ns or better [15, p.97-98]. The single network probes are inter-connected via a separate IP network. This network is used for measurement tasks requiring information from more than one interface (e.g., one-way delay computation) and for maintaining the monitoring system itself.

3.3 Delay Computation

The one-way delay was extracted online with a similar methodology as in [3]. We implemented a proprietary Delay Client (DC) program, which is running on-line at the network probes of our monitoring system. Every DC hashes each IP packet, excluding some selected header fields (e.g., Time-To-Live) into a string of length $N = 128$ via the MD5 function [16] (instead CRC-32 was used in [3]). This guarantees a negligible collision probability. For each packet the DC sends a record containing the hashed string, the arrival timestamp, and the packet direction to a server called Delay Aggregator (DA) via TCP connection. In order to extract delay samples from A to B, the DA searches the received packet records for hash-string matches and take the difference of the respective timestamps. The obtained delay samples are then aggregated into $N = 300$ exponentially spaced bins between 0 and 60 seconds in order to summarize their distribution. The bin boundary is given by the formula $b(n) = e^{(n-\delta)\cdot\alpha}$ $n = 0..N-1$, with the parameter setting $\alpha = 0.07$ and $\delta = 240$. We can combine delay computation and packet sampling - denote by $0 < r_s \leq 1$ the sampling rate - or alternatively compute the delay for *all* packets. We will elaborate on the tuning of this sampling rate r_s below. Within the implementation of the presented delay measurement architecture, several practical issues must be taken into account.

Configuration complexity. Configuring the Delay Aggregator and the distributed clients is not trivial. Each client is identified by a unique link ID. Upon start-up the DCs initiate a multicast-based control handshake to automatically discover and register at the DA by using their unique link IDs. Next, the server sends a response containing the timestamp when all clients should synchronously start the delay measurement, and establishes one TCP connection per client to receive the forthcoming packet records. During the delay measurement the respective link IDs are used to autonomously detect measurement pairs, in case of string matches from two different interfaces. If packet sampling is activated, i.e. $r_s < 1$, the sampling rate must be synchronized among all involved DCs.

Tuning the sampling rate. The DA summarizes the distribution of the delay samples into $N = 300$ exponentially spaced bins. Let denote N_S the number of samples and N_B the number of bins containing at least one delay sample. For an accurate estimation of the actual delay distribution, the sampling rate r_s should be chosen such that $N_S \gg N_B$. N_S increases with a growing IP packet rate if r_s is set to a fixed value. Hence, N_S is high during intervals of high traffic load and low during hours of less traffic activity. In our measurement setup, the bandwidth available for transmitting samples from the DCs to the DA is sufficient also for very high values of N_S. Hence, we selected a fixed rate r_s tailored to hours of low traffic load. The adaption of r_s according to varying traffic load - which requires coordination among all DCs - is left for future work.

Multiple matches. In some cases, a single hashed value observed at A has multiple matches at B. This may happen due to a retransmission of IP packets at lower protocol layers. However, only the first observation holds a meaningful delay sample, hence any duplicated samples must be filtered out. Also routing loops may cause multiple matches (a concrete example was reported in [1]).

Missing matching. A hashed value observed at the, e.g., ISP interface might have no match at the Gn-GGSN interface. This might indicate that the packet was lost on its way from the ISP interface to the GGSN, or that the packet arrives at a path that does not include the ISP interface. The latter case includes all traffic generated by a source internal to the Gi network, e.g. a DNS reply, or a WAP connection. In the network under study part of the WEB traffic is handled by a transparent proxy that modifies the TCP/IP headers, hence the related hash value. In this case no match can be found and no delay sample is produced. This reduces the actual rate of valid delay samples.

Packet Fragmentation. In [2], we showed that the arrival timestamp of the *last* fragment of an IP packet has to be chosen for the delay computation whenever fragmentation occurs at lower layers. In this way the delay components due to upstream fragmentation, which are typically dominated by a remote cause (e.g. radio link conditions for uplink packets) are excluded from the measurements.

3.4   Input Dataset

The presented work is based on online measurements performed at three consecutive days in May 2008. A set of SGSNs, a single GGSN and the ERs co-located at a single physical site were monitored, corresponding to a fraction x of the total network traffic (undisclosed [1]). For the detailed comparison of the delay process at a GPRS-SGSN and at a UMTS-SGSN, we resort to an eight-hour measurement period from 8 am to 4 pm. That means we are not focusing on the peak hour (8-9 pm in this network) but on a period of medium traffic load. Since our aim is to investigate the "normal" delay process in a well-dimensioned SGSN, choosing an off-peak observation period eliminates the risk of bias due to overload conditions. After this comparison we present long-term delay measurements about the three full consecutive days recorded in May 2008.

4   SGSN Delay in GPRS and UMTS

We start presenting the single-hop delay of a GPRS-SGSN and a UMTS-SGSN in uplink. In Fig. 2 we plot the Empirical Cumulative Distribution Function (ECCDF) along with an empirical delay histogram for the interval from 8 am to 4 pm, representing a period of medium load. Since queuing is the only source of delay for packets transmitted in uplink, at both SGSNs the majority of the samples take very low values, below 2 ms (ref. Fig. 2a). However, the UMTS-SGSN

---

[1] Several quantitative values are considered business-sensitive by the operator and subject to non-disclosure, e.g. absolute traffic volumes, number of active MS, number and capacity of monitoring links. For this reason the following graphs reporting absolute values have been rescaled by an arbitrary undisclosed factor.

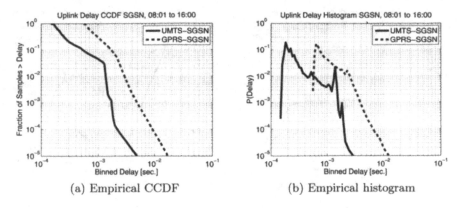

(a) Empirical CCDF   (b) Empirical histogram

Fig. 2. Uplink delay at different SGSNs

is showing lower delays than the GPRS-SGSN. At the UMTS-SGSN only 4% of the delay values are above 1 ms, while at the GPRS-SGSN 30% of the samples suffer from delays higher than 1 ms (ref. Fig. 2a). Moreover, the empirical histogram at the UMTS-SGSN in Fig. 2b shows a clear spike at around 1.5 ms. At this point we speculate that this peak is caused by the internal buffer handling of this SGSN. In [2] we presented the one-way delay process of a GPRS-SGSN from 8 am to 4 pm during a day in November 2007. The uplink delay distribution of this GPRS-SGSN was very similar to the GPRS-specific delay distribution sketched in Fig. 2a.

In Fig. 3, we plot the downlink delay distribution of the two SGSNs. At the GPRS-SGSN 20% of the samples experience a delay higher than 2 ms, while at the UMTS-SGSN only 0.5% of the values are above 2 ms (ref. Fig. 3a). The empirical histogram at the GPRS-SGSN shows a clear bump for delays higher than 20 ms (ref. Fig. 3b). Also at the UMTS-SGSN, we observe a histogram bump for higher delays. However, the relative share of this bump is lower than at the GPRS-SGSN. As reported in [2], we believe that the delay induced by flow control and mobility is the main cause of the observed histogram bumps. Their different relative shares are due to the differently designed flow control and mobility mechanisms of GPRS and UMTS.

Flow Control. As noted in [17], the wireless downlink rate in the Radio Access Network is time varying. To avoid overflow and/or underflow of the downlink buffers at the GPRS-specific BSS, the downlink transmission rate from the GPRS-SGSN to the BSS is regulated for each data connection by the flow control mechanism of the BSSGP protocol. Downlink packets may be buffered inside the SGSN if the downlink buffer at the BSS is exhausted [18]. At the IuPS interface of a UMTS-SGSN, user IP packets are tunneled via the GTP protocol, which is encapsulated into the UDP protocol [19]. The adaption of the downlink traffic rate according to the current radio conditions in the RAN is regulated between

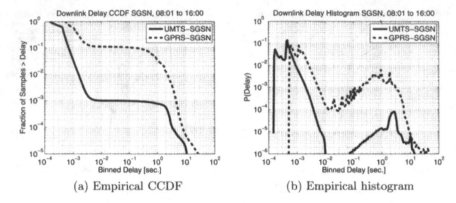

(a) Empirical CCDF   (b) Empirical histogram

Fig. 3. Downlink delay at different SGSNs

the RNC and Node b, not at the SGSN as in the case of GPRS [20, 21, 22]. Hence, this flow control does not impact the delay process at a UMTS-SGSN.

Handover. In GPRS, a handover procedure occurs when an active user is changing to another cell and/or routing area. In this case, the SGSN may temporarily store the corresponding packets until the location change is completed and the packets can be forwarded to the new location. A UMTS-SGSN tracks active users at routing area granularity. In case an active user is changing cell, the handover is performed at the RNC serving the user (SRNC) [23]. Until the cell update is complete packets may temporarily be stored inside the SRNC, not at the SGSN. Only if an active user is changing to a routing area of another RNC than the SRNC, downlink packets may be temporarily stored inside the UMTS-SGSN until the RNC-handover is completed. Due to this location management strategy, routing area-handovers at UMTS-SGSNs occur less frequent than cell-handovers at GPRS-SGSNs. Hence, the impact of handovers onto the delay process is much higher at GPRS-SGSNs than at UMTS-SGSNs.

Paging. As reported in [1] the GPRS-SGSN directly forwards downlink packets to the MSs that are in READY state, since the location of those MSs is known to the SGSN at cell granularity. After some time of inactivity the MS falls back into STANDBY state, where location changes are announced to the SGSN only at routing area level. If a downlink packet destined to a MS in STANDBY arrives at the SGSN, the latter has to perform a paging procedure to reveal the actual MS location prior to forwarding the packet to it. User packets arriving during this paging procedure are stored inside the GPRS-SGSN until the paging is completed and all packets are then forwarded. By means of active measurements (reported in a separate work, see [10]) we verified that packets forwarded after a successful GPRS paging experience a delay of around 2 sec. This explains the spike observed in Fig. 3b, which is caused by packets being delayed due to GPRS paging. Note however that these active measurements involved a different

GPRS-SGSN than that analyzed in this work. In Fig. 3b we see a second spike at around 1 sec, which is arguably due also to paging procedures.

Also in UMTS a paging is required at the SGSN, if a downlink packet destined to a MS in Radio Resource Control (RRC) idle mode arrives. After a successful paging, the SRNC of the destined MS is known at the UMTS-SGSN and the MS enters the so-called RRC cell-connected mode [23]. In this state packets can be transferred from the SGSN to the MS. After some time of inactivity a MS enters the so-called RRC URA connected mode. In this state the SRNC tracks the MS location at cell granularity [23]. Hence, at the UMTS-SGSN no paging is required if downlink packets arrive for a MS in RRC URA connected mode. Only after a longer time of traffic inactivity the RRC mode of a MS is switched back to RRC idle mode. In this mode again paging is required if downlink packets arrive at the SGSN, in order to reveal the RNC serving the MS. From our active measurements (see [10]) we found that paging in UMTS SGSN introduces an additional delay between 2-4 sec. This explains the local mode between 2-4 seconds in the empirical delay histogram (ref. Fig. 3b). Moreover, we observe that the relative share of delays samples hitting a paging procedure is much lower in the UMTS section than GPRS in the network under study. This may be explained by the two different paging strategies at the respective SGSNs.

The lesson to be learned from the presented comparison of the downlink delays is, that the impact of mobility on to the delay process is much lower at the UMTS-SGSN. Moreover, the effect of flow control onto the downlink delay process is present only in GPRS, not in UMTS. In [2], we analyzed in detail the delay process at a GPRS-SGSN different from that considered here. Comparing the delay of these two GPRS-SGSNs, we observe that the qualitative process is the same, while only details have changed.

5　Seeking for Stable Summary Statistics

Having explored the various components of the delay process at two different SGSNs, we now seek for summary indicators that can be used as input signals for the detection of abnormal delay deviations. These indicators must be stable over time, i.e. should not present wide variations due to small fluctuations in the underlying delay distributions. The simplest candidate indicators are *percentiles* and *threshold-crossing probabilities*. Given a continuous random variable x, the generic p-th percentile $d_x(p)$ denotes the value that is exceeded with probability p ($p < 1$), i.e. $d_x(p) : P(x \geq d_x(p)) = p$. Therefore, we fix the value of p and obtain from the measurements an empirical estimation of the $d_x(p)$. Conversely, we can define a fixed threshold h in the domain of the random variable x, and denote by $q_x(h)$ the relative fraction of samples that exceed this value, i.e. $q_x(h) : P(x \geq h) = q_x(h)$. Such quantity will be denoted to as *threshold-crossing delay share* (or simply "crossing share"). By plotting the empirical CCDF of x, it is immediately clear that the value of $d_x(p)$ relates to the *horizontal* distance of the CCDF from the vertical axis at the pre-defined height p, while the crossing share $q_x(h)$ refers to the *vertical* distance of the CCDF from the horizontal axis at point h.

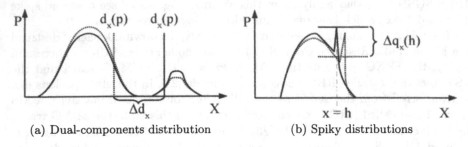

(a) Dual-components distribution   (b) Spiky distributions

Fig. 4. Possible offsets of indicators based on probability density functions

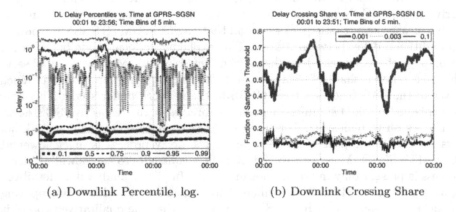

(a) Downlink Percentile, log.   (b) Downlink Crossing Share

Fig. 5. Downlink delay indicators vs. time at GPRS-SGSN, 3 days

It is natural to consider percentiles and crossing-shares as simple candidates to serve as key summary indicators for the entire delay process. The underlying assumption is that "small" fluctuations of the underlying distribution cause only small variations of such indicators. However, in some cases such assumption is challenged. Consider for example the bi-modal Probability Density Functions (PDF) given in Fig. 4a, consisting of two separate components of mass $1 - p$ and p respectively. In this case, small random fluctuations may cause large shifts of the $p-$percentile from the upper tail of the left-hand bell to the lower tail of the right-hand bell. If the distance between the two bells is large, the $p-$percentile will amplify the random fluctuations, which is undesirable effect for our purposes. In some other case, exactly the opposite is true. Consider the distribution of Fig. 4b, where a large concentration of probability mass (spike) is present around the value $x = h$. Small shifts in the location of the spike would cause large fluctuations in the value of the crossing share $q_x(h)$.

In summary, the presence of discontinuities in the distribution (i.e. "straight" segments in the CCDF) might cause the percentiles and/or crossing shares to vary widely following relatively small random fluctuations that can be considered

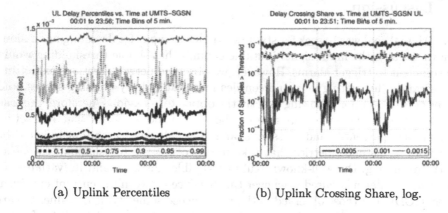

(a) Uplink Percentiles   (b) Uplink Crossing Share, log.

Fig. 6. Uplink delay indicators vs. time at UMTS-SGSN, 3 days

physiological to the process (i.e., "normal"). Curiously, in our measurements we found occurrences of both the "pathological" scenarios depicted in Fig. 4.

To further investigate, we plot the downlink delay percentiles along with different crossing shares for three days at time bins of 5 minutes in Fig. 5. As shown in Fig. 5a, the 0.9 percentile is heavily fluctuating between two orders of magnitude. This is because the empirical histogram in Fig. 3b has exactly the shape as sketched in Fig. 4a. Small variations in the distribution modes may cause significant fluctuations in some key percentiles, such that they hardly can be used for the detection of abnormal delays. The crossing share exceeding some fixed delay thresholds h should be preferred in this case. In Fig. 5b, we plot these shares for different threshold values. We observe that the shares are very stable over time, showing small variations during night hours, where the traffic load is low. The share for $h = 1$ ms is shaped by the Time-of-Day (ToD) profile. This is expected, as such value falls within the mass of the queuing delay which correlates with the global traffic load.

In Fig. 6, we plot some key percentiles along with delay crossing shares of the uplink delay distribution at the UMTS-SGSN, again for three days and at time bins of 5 minutes. The percentiles in Fig. 6a take very low values and are much more stable than in the case of downlink GPRS traffic. Again, we observe small percentile variations during the night hours. In Fig. 6b, we observe that the delay crossing share for $h = 1.5$ ms is very unstable, with fluctuations over two orders of magnitude. This is because the delay distribution in Fig. 2b has a shape similar to the distribution sketched in Fig. 4b. Small vertical shifts of the spike observed at ≈ 1.5 ms (ref. Fig. 2b) may result in a large horizontal distance of the delay crossing share. In this case the delay percentiles are the preferred input signals for an anomaly detection scheme detecting abnormal delay deviations. From our preliminary long-term investigations of the delay process at two different SGSNs we learned that we cannot blindly rely on some key percentiles and/or the relative fraction of samples exceeding some fixed threshold.

6   Discussion

Our original goal was to seek for stable statistics as input for detecting anomalous delays. Ideally, the input signal is stable enough that simple thresholding would be sufficient to trigger alarms. However, we observed network sections exhibiting significantly fluctuating delay percentiles and stable delay crossing shares, and other network sections showing exactly the opposite behavior. Therefore, the task of identifying simple indicators seems to be slightly more difficult than extraction of standard percentile and crossing shares. One alternative approach would be to resort to distance metrics that take into account the full shape of the delay distribution, e.g. the well-known Kullback-Leibler distance and its variants. In this way, an alarm is raised whenever the distance between the current empirical delay CCDF and those observed in the past exceed some "typical" value. We are investigating this approach in a separate parallel work, and we leave it for further study. Our preliminary findings point to a number of practical complications, for example the lack of absolute reference values - which complicates the task of interpreting the alarm by the network staff - and the Time-of-Day dependence of the inter-distributions distances.

Instead, here we are interested in pursuing a simpler approach that still relies on standard indicators, i.e. percentiles and/or crossing shares. The above findings suggest that a combination of *both* indicator types might be a viable strategy for implementing anomaly detection schemes for the one-way delay process. The idea is to continuously measure a set of percentiles (horizontal CCDF distance at pre-defined probability values) *and* a set of crossing shares (vertical CCDF distances at pre-defined delay values), and to set static individual thresholds on each individual indicator. Then, an alarm is raised whenever a minimum set of indicators exceeds their respective thresholds, e.g. a percentile *AND* a crossing share. This would be a general strategy applicable to both the observed distribution types (GPRS and UMTS SGSN). We are now implementing this strategy in the online system as an additional feature to the DA module.

7   Conclusions and Outlook

In this work we have explored the single-hop delay distribution at some key elements of a 3G Core Network, namely GPRS and UMTS SGSN. We showed that it is possible to implement and run a distributed client-server based delay measurement system online in an operational mobile core network. Detecting anomalous delays inside SGSNs is not trivial. Besides packet queuing due to shared link, also user mobility and flow control contribute to shape the delay process at the SGSNs. We found that the particular characteristics of the first-order delay distributions (spikes, multimodality) in the real network make it tricky to rely on standard indicators (e.g. percentiles) to mark anomalies. Based on such findings, we are now working towards a slightly more sophisticated approach, where a combination of percentiles and crossing shares are considered as the basis for anomaly detection.

Having presented preliminary investigations about these indicators during a 3 day measurement period, the next step is to extend our analysis to other network sections and to investigate the proposed indicators during longer measurement periods. We hope in this way to early detect future occurrences of congestion events and equipment misfunctioning. One critical point that remains to be assessed deals with the *sensitivity* of such approach, e.g. how severe the congestion must be such that our module is able to detect it. We plan to investigate this issue further by means of trace-driven simulations, which enable quantitative assessment. However, we believe that only the practical experience provided by actual implementation of the system in a real operational network can provide insight into the actual delay process, and clarify the concrete possibility of achieving fully automated anomaly detection and alarming in practice.

Acknowledgments

The Telecommunications Research Center Vienna (ftw.) is supported by the Austrian Government and the City of Vienna within the competence center program COMET. This work is part of the DARWIN project [13].

References

1. Ricciato, F., Hasenleithner, E., Romirer-Maierhofer, P.: Traffic analysis at short time-scales: an empirical case study from a 3G cellular network. IEEE Trans. Network and Service Management (to appear, 2008)
2. Romirer-Maierhofer, P., Ricciato, F., Coluccia, A.: Explorative Analysis of One-way Delays in a Mobile 3G Network. In: IEEE LANMAN 2008 (to appear, September 2008)
3. Papagiannaki, K., et al.: Measurement and Analysis of Single-Hop Delay on an IP Backbone Network. IEEE JSAC 21(6) (August 2003)
4. Choi, B., et al.: Analysis of Point-To-Point Packet Delay in an Operational Network. In: IEEE INFOCOM 2004, Hong Kong (March 2004)
5. Benko, P., Malicsko, G., Veres, A.: A Large-scale Passive Analysis of End-to-End TCP Performance over GPRS. In: IEEE INFOCOM 2004, Hong Kong (March 2004)
6. Vacirca, F., Ricciato, F., Pilz, R.: Large-Scale RTT Measurements from an Operational UMTS/GPRS Network. In: IEEE WICON 2005, Budapest (July 2005)
7. Kilpi, J., Lassila, P.: Micro- and macroscopic analysis of RTT variability in GPRS and UMTS network. In: Boavida, F., Plagemann, T., Stiller, B., Westphal, C., Monteiro, E. (eds.) NETWORKING 2006. LNCS, vol. 3976. Springer, Heidelberg (2006)
8. Lee, Y.: Measured TCP Performance in CDMA 1x EV-DO Network. In: Proc. of 7th Passive and Active Measurement conference (PAM 2006), Adelaide (March 2006)
9. Cano-Garcia, J.M., Gonzalez-Parada, E., Casilari, E.: Experimental Analysis and Characterization of Packet Delay in UMTS Networks. In: Koucheryavy, Y., Harju, J., Iversen, V.B. (eds.) NEW2AN 2006. LNCS, vol. 4003. Springer, Heidelberg (2006)

10. Barbuzzi, A., Ricciato, F., Boggia, G.: Discovering parameter setting in 3G networks via active measurements (in preparation)
11. Niccolini, S., Molina, M., Raspall, F., Tartarelli, S.: Design and implementation of a One Way Delay passive measurement system. In: IEEE NOMS 2004, Seoul (April 2004)
12. Bannister, J., Mather, P., Coope, S.: Convergence Technologies for 3G Networks. Wiley, Chichester (2004)
13. METAWIN and DARWIN projects, http://userver.ftw.at/~ricciato/darwin
14. Endace Measurememt Systems, http://www.endace.com
15. Donnelly, S.F.: High Precision Timing in Passive Measurements of Data Networks, Ph.D. Dissertation, CS Dept., Waikato Univ., New Zealand (June 2002)
16. The MD5 Message-Digest Algorithm, RFC 1321 (April 1992)
17. Bedekar, A.S., Agrawal, R., Ranjan, R.: A lossless algorithm for BSSGP flow control in GPRS and EDGE. In: IEEE GLOBECOM 2003, San Francisco (December 2003)
18. Digital cellular telecommunications system (Phase 2+); General Packet Radio Service (GPRS); Base Station System (BSS) - Serving GPRS Support Node (SGSN); BSS GPRS protocol (BSSGP), 3GPP TS 48.018, Version 7.12.0 (2008)
19. Digital cellular telecommunications system (Phase 2+); Universal Mobile Telecommunications System (UMTS); General Packet Radio Service (GPRS); GPRS Tunnelling Protocol (GTP) across the Gn and Gp interface, 3GPP TS 129.060, Version 7.9.0 (2008)
20. Yerima, S.Y., Al-Begain, K.: An Enhanced Buffer Management Scheme for Multimedia Traffic in HSDPA. In: IEEE NGMAST 2007, Cardiff (September 2007)
21. Legg, P.J.: Optimised Iub flow control for UMTS HSDPA. In: 61st Vehicular Technology Conference, Stockholm (May 2005)
22. Universal Mobile Telecommunications System (UMTS); Radio Link Control (RLC) protocol specification, 3GPP TS 125.322, Version 7.6.0 (April 2008)
23. Shun-Ren, Y., Yi-Bing, L.: Performance evaluation of location management in UMTS. IEEE Trans. Vehicular Technology 52(6) (November 2003)

Anomaly Characterization
in Flow-Based Traffic Time Series

Anna Sperotto, Ramin Sadre, and Aiko Pras

University of Twente
Centre for Telematics and Information Technology
Faculty of Electrical Engineering, Mathematics and Computer Science
P.O. Box 217, 7500 AE Enschede, The Netherlands
{a.sperotto, r.sadre, a.pras}@utwente.nl

Abstract. The increasing number of network attacks causes growing problems
for network operators and users. Not only do these attacks pose direct security
threats to our infrastructure, but they may also lead to service degradation, due to
the massive traffic volume variations that are possible during such attacks. The
recent spread of Gbps network technology made the problem of detecting these
attacks harder, since existing packet-based monitoring and intrusion detection
systems do not scale well to Gigabit speeds. Therefore the attention of the scientific community is shifting towards the possible use of aggregated traffic metrics.
The goal of this paper is to investigate how malicious traffic can be characterized on the basis of such aggregated metrics, in particular by using flow, packet
and byte frequency variations over time. The contribution of this paper is that it
shows, based on a number of real case studies on high-speed networks, that all
three metrics may be necessary for proper time series anomaly characterization.

1 Introduction

Attacks on our networks and server infrastructures are a growing source of concerns
for network operators and users. They may be generated by both inexperienced script-
kiddies and professional hackers, but in any case, attacks create unwanted traffic that
can affect the performance and dependability of existing services. Therefore operators
employ intrusion detection systems to identify and possibly filter suspicious traffic.

The constant increase in network traffic and the fast introduction of high speed
(tens of Gbps) network equipment [16] make it hard to still employ traditional packet-
based intrusion detection systems. Such systems rely on deep packet payload inspection, which does not scale well. In high speed environments, approaches that rely on
aggregated traffic metrics, such as *flow-based* approaches, show a better scalability and
therefore seem more promising. The advantage of *flow-based* approaches is that only a
fraction of the total amount of data needs to be analysed. For the University of Twente,
for example, we have estimated that the amount of flow data represents less than 1% of
the amount of normal packet data.

A flow is defined as an unidirectional stream of packets that share common characteristics, such as source and destination addresses, ports and protocol type. In addition,
a flow includes aggregated information about the number of packets and bytes belonging to the stream, as well as its duration. Flows are often used for network monitoring,

N. Akar, M. Pioro, and C. Skianis (Eds.): IPOM 2008, LNCS 5275, pp. 15–27, 2008.

permitting to obtain a real time overview of the network status; common tools for this purpose are Nfsen [5] and Flowscan [15], while the *de facto* standard technology in this field is Cisco Netflow, particularly its versions 5 and 9 [1,13]. The IETF IPFIX working group [14] is currently working on a standard for IP flow exporting, based on Netflow version 9.

Large networks, when creating flows, often apply *packet sampling* in order to make the approach even more scalable. In this case, only a percentage of the total number of packets passing through the monitoring point is considered in the flows. Statistical studies have been performed about correctness and precision of sampling strategies for Internet traffic [6] and high speed environments [7], as well as estimation of traffic flow characteristics from real sampled data [11]. These studies show that, despite the reduced amount of information, it is still possible to offer a correct statistical overview of the network status [6]. Packet sampling in flow creation is vastly deployed [12,17]. In particular, NetFlow relies on *systematic* sampling, where only 1 out of every n packets is considered for the accounting ($1:n$).

In the last years there has been an increasing interest in the application of flow-based techniques for anomaly and intrusion detection. The works of [8,9,10], which applies principal component analysis to traffic time series, and [19], which proposes a framework for network anomography, are examples of contributions in this field. Another example is provided by [2], which aims to detect worm spread in high speed network on a connection basis. In a similar environment, [3] addresses the problem of detecting DoS attacks and scans. In this case, the authors particularly focus on aggregated header information, as they can be exported by NetFlow (TCP flags). In addition, the presented approach is interesting because it explicitly addresses the problem of measure variation over time (with the use of value forecasting). In [4], the role of timely analysis of flow data is central. The author proposes a general purpose platform for parallel time-based analysis of flow information for attack detection, focusing in particular on DoS attacks (SYN-flood and web server overloading). From a network monitoring point of view, time series on flows, packets, and bytes are considered to be a useful tool: they permit to have a *dynamic* and *real time* overview of the network on the basis of the stream of information coming from the exporter [12,15].

In this paper, we investigate the use of traffic time series for identifying anomalies and detecting intrusions. In particular, we are interested in *whether it is necessary to consider 1) flows, 2) packets as well as 3) bytes time series, or whether it is sufficient to consider only one or two of these*. In addition, we want to know if the conclusion *also holds in the presence of sampling*. The novelty of our approach is that we rely on real case studies, performed in high-speed networks with links of 10 Gbps. Our measurements have been performed simultaneously on two different networks, the University of Twente (UT) and SURFnet, the Dutch research network, [18]. SURFnet applies 1:100 packet sampling during the flow creation.

The paper is organized as follow. Section 2 presents the measurement environment in which our analysis has been conducted. Sections 3 and 4 analyze anomalies in flow traces, focusing in particular on two real examples. Finally, Section 5 presents our conclusions.

2   Measurement Setup

The analysis presented in this paper has been conducted on flow traces collected at the University of Twente and on the SURFnet infrastructure [18]. In particular, the analyzed traces cover a period of time of two working days, namely between Wednesday August 1st 2007, 00:00 and Thursday August 2nd 2007, 23:59. The two networks have different sizes and coverage. The UT one is a /16 network providing connectivity to the employees and the students on the university buildings and the campus. SURFnet has national coverage and connects via optical path the most important research institutions in the Netherlands. Since SURFnet is also the UT network service provider, the majority of the incoming and outgoing UT traffic is routed through SURFnet. UT and SURFnet traces rely on a different measurement setup. Indeed, while UT processes all the packets passing through the measuring point, SURFnet applies a systematic sampling with ratio 1:100. In this paper, the real amount of traffic is estimated scaling all the measurements by a factor of 100.

Figure 1 shows the bytes traffic time series in the considered time frame. In this paper, all the time series have been created considering a time interval of 600 seconds, a good compromise between accuracy and number of samples. As expected, both networks show a clear night-day pattern, with peak of activity between 8:00 and 18:00 and with a minimum around 4:00. Around 16:00, on August 1st 2008, the amount of traffic on SURFnet drops abruptly. Since no error has been detected in our measuring setup, we suspect the down-peak to be caused by a flow creation and exporting failure in the SURFnet infrastructure, or, less likely, to a network hardware failure. Nevertheless, this event is not affecting our analysis. Table 1 presents the average, minimum and maximum traffic loads and the total data volume measured on the two networks during the observation period, together with the number of collected flows.

Table 1. Average, maximum and minimum traffic loads, data volume and number of flows during the period of observation on UT and SURFnet

	Avg Load	Max Load	Min Load	Volume	Flows
UT	652Mbps	1.01Gbps	259Mbps	21.65TB	982.7M
SURFnet	7.73Gbps	10.5Gbps	4Gbps	162.3TB	523.7M

During our monitoring time, UT seemed to be object of repeated and diverse attacks, even if apparently without real damage. Due to space constraints, we decide to concentrate our analysis on the following examples: ssh and dns traffic traces. The choice of these two specific sub-traces is due to the fact that, quite surprisingly, the ssh service resulted to be one of the major attack targets, both in intensity and in number of attacks. Similarly, by experience we noticed that dns tends to produce a quite regular traffic volume. This characteristic made quite easy to detect suspicious variation in traffic intensity. To properly evaluate if the observation in both networks are consistent, the ssh and dns traffic in SURFnet have been filtered in order to keep into account only the incoming-outgoing traffic from the UT network.

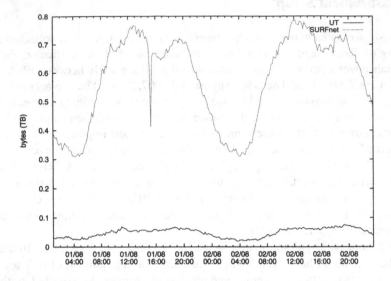

Fig. 1. Bytes time series, showing UT and SURFnet (estimated values) traffic

3   SSH Traffic

Ssh is one of the most common protocols to connect with remote machines. In general, it corresponds to the 1% of packets and the 1.2% of bytes of the total incoming-outgoing UT traffic.

3.1   Traffic Analysis

Figure 2 shows the byte traffic time series in the observation time frame. In the same graph, both UT and SURFnet (estimated) traffic volume are shown. It is possible to notice that the two measurements show the same trends, and only occasionally SURFnet strongly differs from UT. In general, the bytes trend in the observation period is quite irregular with sharp peaks and down-peaks. This situation is understandable because ssh can be used for both remote communications and file transfers. As a consequence, in the byte time series there is no clear evidence of attacks.

On the other side, looking at the packet time series (Figure 3), it is possible to notice that during the two days of observations, the UT network saw a massive increase of its ssh traffic. The time series is indeed characterized by sudden peaks during which the number of packets per time interval can raise of several millions. In some cases, we observe a difference of up to almost 8 millions packets. If we consider the flow time series, as in Figure 4, we can observe how the trend is also in this case characterized by peaks during which the number of flows per time interval raises form few thousand to half million. Again, the number of flows per time interval in SURFnet increases following the same behavior of the UT trace, despite the use of sampling. This phenomenon is particularly visible during the massive peaks, namely in the early morning of August 1st and in the late morning of August 2nd.

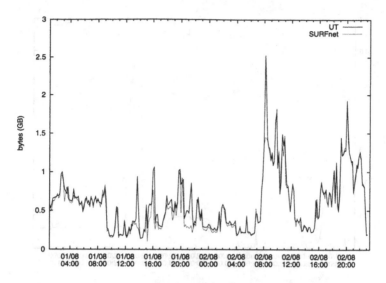

Fig. 2. Bytes time series, showing UT and SURFnet (estimated values) ssh traffic

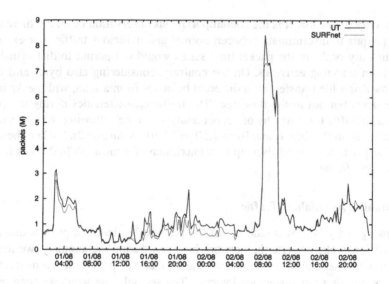

Fig. 3. Packets time series, showing UT and SURFnet (estimated values) ssh traffic

Summarizing, in the moments of major ssh activity, we observe a suspiciously high number of flows, matched by a very high number of packets, but with almost negligible amount of sent and received bytes. This suggest that the hosts involved are sending/receiving relatively small packets to many different hosts, scenario that suggests the possibility of a scan. A more detailed inspection of the trace shows indeed that few source hosts made the UT network object of massive ssh scans, during which the attackers were performing user-guessing on almost all the hosts in the UT network. It is

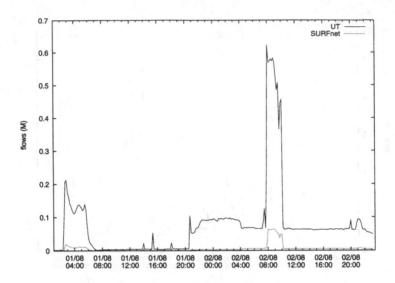

Fig. 4. Flows time series, showing UT and SURFnet ssh traffic

important to underline that it is the contemporaneous observation of all the three measure that permits to discriminate between normal and malicious traffic. For example, considering only peaks in the packet time series would not permit to distinguish file transfers from scanning activities. On the contrary, considering also bytes and flows would show that a file transfer has a different behavior from a scan, with peaks in the byte time series but not in the flow one. The traffic characteristics during the peaks made the ssh traffic trace worthy of deeper analysis. In the following, we concentrate only on the peak in the time frame from 7:50 to 10:10 on August 2nd, when the number of flows per time interval rises up to a maximum of almost 600000 flows (*(ssh)* *anomalous time frame*).

3.2   Normal vs Anomalous Traffic

The following analysis proves indeed that the previously identified peak is due to an attack. In order to characterize the network behavior during the anomaly, we need to compare it with a second observation time frame, that will provide us an overview of the network during a not suspicious interval. The second time windows span over a period of 2 hours, between 8:00 and 10:00 of August 1st. During this time frame, we are not observing any fast variation of the flow frequency. Since we are interested in scans and we are assuming that ssh scans produce variation in the flow frequency, we also assume the second time frame to be an example of *normal* network behavior (*normal time frame*).

   Looking at the number of active hosts in the anomalous and normal time frames, Table 2 shows that the normal time frame is characterized by a balanced number of sources and destinations, both in UT and SURFnet. On the contrary, in the anomalous time frame, we can observe an increased number of destinations, several times bigger

Table 2. Number of distinct source and destination addresses during the anomalous and normal time frames in the UT and SURFnet traces

	Anomalous time frame		Normal time frame	
	Sources	Destinations	Sources	Destinations
UT	2763	65342	629	647
SURFnet	597	3020	192	192

than the number of sources. The number of destination hosts in the UT trace suggests that the scan covers the entire UT network (that is, as reported in Section 2, a /16 network), while the increased number of source hosts is an effect of the scanning activity (some of the destination hosts react to the probes). A similar trend is visible in SURFnet.

The study of the top active sources w.r.t. the number of originated flows shows that the anomalous time frame is dominated by the presence of three major senders, that caused the attack. Table 3 shows how the traffic, expressed in flows, packets and bytes, is distributed with respect to the sources during the anomalous time frame. Together, the three most active sources are responsible for the 98 - 99% of the total amount of flows in both UT and SURFnet. All the three hosts were scanning the UT network. As already suspected during the time series analysis, also the packet repartition is unbalanced towards the major senders (responsible of $\sim$ 70% of the packets in both UT and SURFnet). Finally, it is important to notice that the scan *does not* deeply affect the bytes distribution: the 75% and the 69% of the bytes volumes respectively in UT and SURFnet is still due to normal traffic.

In order to give a visual representation of the network behavior during the anomalous and normal time frame, the scatter-plot in Figure 5 is presented. A time interval is characterized by a number of packets, bytes and flows. Let us suppose to assign to each measure an axis in a 3D space and plot each time interval as a point in this space. Figure 5 shows a representation of the anomalous and normal time frame. In the case of the anomalous time frame, also the projections on the planes are plotted. The graph permits to see that points belonging to the normal time frame tend to group together in a part of the space characterized by relatively small number of packets and bytes. Moreover, the time intervals in this group show a very low number of flows. On the contrary, the spatial disposition of the anomalous time frame describe a totally different behavior. Also in this case, the time intervals during the anomaly tend to be spatially close. This is an

Table 3. Percentage of flows, packets and bytes for the attackers and the not suspicious hosts during the ssh anomalous time frame

	Flow Percentage		Packets Percentage		Bytes Percentage	
	UT	SURFnet	UT	SURFnet	UT	SURFnet
SSH TOP 1	82.6%	89.5%	65.7%	71.2%	22.3%	28.1%
SSH TOP 2	13.5%	9.2%	6.7%	7.3%	2.3%	2.8%
SSH TOP 3	2.1%	0.3%	0.4%	0.3%	0.1%	0.1%
SSH OTHERS	1.8%	1%	27.2%	21.2%	75.3%	69.0%

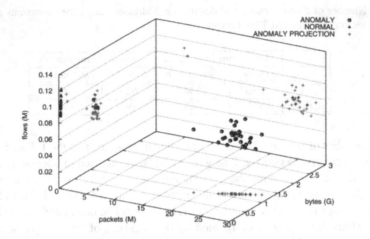

Fig. 5. ssh anomalous and normal time frame space disposition (UT trace)

indication of the fact that they share common features. In addition, as emphasized by the projections, points in this group present high values of the coordinates x (packets) and z (flows), while only few cases show a massive byte volume (y axis). Most importantly, the two groups are spatially distant to each other, confirming that anomalous and normal time intervals show clearly detectable differences.

4   DNS Traffic

Dns is the second trace we analyze in this paper. Commonly, dns is responsible of the less than 1% of the incoming-outgoing data volume at the UT network.

4.1   Traffic Analysis

In Section 3, ssh traffic seems to suggest that the flow frequency analysis can easily enlighten the presence of anomalies. Unfortunately, this hypothesis does not hold for dns traffic. As it is possible to see in Figure 6, the number of flows per time interval is almost constant during the entire observation period and nothing would suggest the presence of an anomaly.

The situation appears to be different if we are interested not in the flow time series but in the packet and byte ones. Figures 7 and 8, indeed, show that in the time windows between 1:40 and 7:00 am on August 1st, the UT network saw a massive increase in the volume of dns traffic, both in packets and in bytes. In particular, both measures raise abruptly from few thousands to millions (between 10 to 28 millions in a time interval). The SURFnet trace shows the same behavior, even in presence of sampling.

The just described anomaly is unnoticeable if only the flow time series is taken into account. This observation is particularly relevant because it witness how flow frequency variation is not expressive enough to characterize anomalies. By definition,

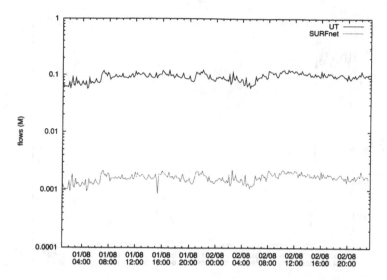

Fig. 6. Flows time series, showing UT and SURFnet dns traffic (in logarithmic scale)

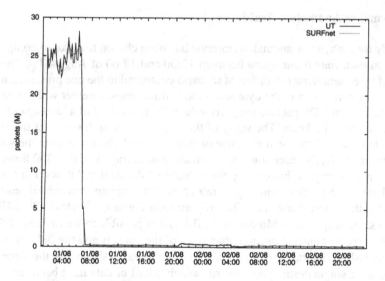

Fig. 7. Packets time series, showing UT and SURFnet (estimated values) dns traffic

dnstraffic produces quite small UDP packets during the query process and it relies on TCP only in case of databases updates. Since the analysis of the protocol repartition during the anomaly shows that the 99.7% of the flows are UDP and they are responsible of the 99.9% of the bytes volume, we can exclude that the anomalies is caused by a database update. Under this consideration, we proceed for a more detailed analysis of the anomaly.

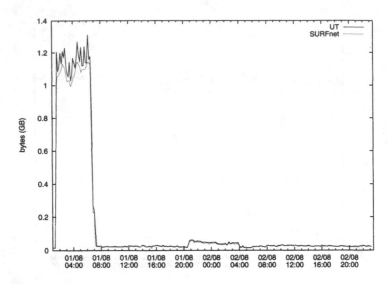

Fig. 8. Bytes time series, showing UT and SURFnet (estimated values) dns traffic

4.2 Normal vs Anomalous Traffic

As already for ssh, a not-anomalous interval has been chosen for sake of comparison. The *dns normal time frame* spans between 12:00 and 17:00 of August 1st. The large amount of bytes sent depicts a different scenario compared to the one presented in Section 3: the sharp variation in the byte and packets time series, together with the use of a large percentage of UDP packets suggests indeed the possibility of a DoS against a few number of destination hosts. The study of the anomalous time frame w.r.t the volume of byte sent clearly show the prevalence of three sources. Far away from the scenario of the ssh anomaly, the three sources are creating in average less that 300 flows each, being in this way responsible of only the 0.003% of the total UT flows. On the other side, each one of the major sources generates a packets volume almost 50 times bigger than all the other sources together. The proportion in the case of bytes is 20. SURFnet shows the same proportions. More generically, as it is possible to see in Table 4 the top senders host are responsible of more than 99% of the packets and the 98% of bytes in both UT and SURFnet traces. A deeper analysis of the traces shows that the three major sources share a single destination, towards which 33GB of data have been sent during the entire anomalous time frame (with packets of constantly exactly 46B in size). This configuration support the thesis that the destination host has been victim of a Distributed DoS targeting the dns service.

As previously in Section 3, a 3D representation of the anomalous and normal time frames is presented in Figure 9. Also in this case, the spatial disposition of the points in the two groups confirms the diversity between anomalous and normal time intervals. Points in the normal time frame show a relative variability in the number of flows, but almost no changes in the number of packets and bytes. On the contrary, the points in the anomalous group are characterized by large x and y coordinates (packets and bytes).

Table 4. Percentage of flows, packets and bytes for the attackers and the not suspicious hosts during the dns anomalous time frame

	Flow Percentage		Packets Percentage		Bytes Percentage	
	UT	SURFnet	UT	SURFnet	UT	SURFnet
DNS TOP 1	0.01%	0.14%	35.3%	35.3%	34.9%	34.8%
DNS TOP 2	0.01%	0.15%	32.6%	32.6%	32.3%	32.5%
DNS TOP 3	0.01%	0.14%	31.4%	31.4%	31%	31%
DNS OTHERS	99.97%	99.56%	0.7%	0.7%	1.8%	1.7%

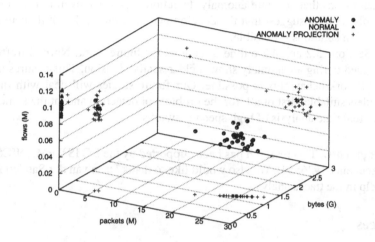

Fig. 9. dns anomalous and normal time frame space disposition (UT trace)

Only two time intervals during the anomalies are distant from the majority: they show indeed a relatively small number of packets and bytes. Nevertheless, the xy-projection of the anomaly confirms that this points are in any case anomalies. All the points in the anomalous time frame, with no exception of the two just described, belong to the same straight line. This is a consequence of the fact that the attackers were flooding the victim with fixed size packets. As final observation, in the graph it is possible to see that the number of flows during the anomalous and normal time frames does not differ enough to detect the ongoing attack, confirming the observation about the flow time series.

5 Conclusions

An important contribution of this paper is that our conclusions are based on extensive measurements on real, high speed networks, with line speeds of 10 Gbps. Our analysis confirm previous findings, that indicate that flows contain sufficient information to detect network intrusions. In particular, our study investigated whether flow, packet and byte time series are all needed to identify intrusions, or whether it is sufficient to consider only one or two of these metrics. Detailed analysis of two anomalies brought us to the conclusion that, to correctly identify suspicious traffic in general, all three metrics should be taken into consideration.

Our analysis also showed that, for certain classes of attacks, the choice to monitor only a single metric may still be sufficient. This is for example the case in our flow time series for ssh traffic. On the other hand, such choice entails the risk of hiding other attacks. This is, for example, the case for the dns DoS attack, which does not appear in the flow time series. Therefore it is important to observe flow, packet as well as byte time series variation, to properly characterize anomalies.

Our study proves that this conclusion also holds in the presence of sampling. Sections 3 and 4 showed that the sampled traces closely approximate the non-sampled traces, which means that accurate anomaly detection is possible even in case of sampling. This observation suggest that the development of scalable, but still accurate intrusion detection solutions is possible.

Finally, Sections 3.2 and 4.2 ouline directions for future work. Normal traffic and traffic generated during an anomaly show a clear spatial division. This ensures us that modelling network behaviours is possible. Our future studies will deal with the creation of models suitable, first of all, for the problem of detection and, at the same time, effective for real time analysis of high speed networks.

Acknowledgments. This research has been supported by the EC IST-EMANICS Network of Excellence (#26854). We also would like to thank Daan van der Sanden for his valuable help in the traces analysis.

References

1. Claise, B.: Cisco Systems NetFlow Services Export Version 9. Request for Comments: 3954, IETF (October 2004)
2. Dubendorfer, T., Plattner, B.: Host behaviour based early detection of worm outbreaks in internet backbones. In: WETICE 2005: Proc. of the 14th IEEE International Workshops on Enabling Technologies: Infrastructure for Collaborative Enterprise, pp. 166–171. IEEE Computer Society, Washington (2005)
3. Gao, Y., Li, Z., Chen, Y.: A dos resilient flow-level intrusion detection approach for high-speed networks. In: ICDCS 2006: 26th IEEE International Conference on Distributed Computing Systems, pp. 39–39 (2006)
4. Munz, G., Carle, G.: Real-time analysis of flow data for network attack detection. In: IM 2007: 10th IFIP/IEEE International Symposium on Integrated Network Management, 2007, pp. 100–108 (2007)
5. Haag, P.: Nfsen: Netflow sensor (April 2008), nfsen.sourceforge.net
6. He, G., Hou, J.C.: An in-depth, analytical study of sampling techniques for self-similar internet traffic. In: ICDCS 2005: Proc. of the 25th IEEE International Conference on Distributed Computing Systems, pp. 404–413. IEEE Computer Society, Los Alamitos (2005)
7. Izkue, E., Magaña, E.: Sampling time-dependent parameters in high-speed network monitoring. In: PM2HW2N 2006: Proc. of the ACM international workshop on Performance monitoring, measurement, and evaluation of heterogeneous wireless and wired networks, pp. 13–17. ACM, New York (2006)
8. Lakhina, A., Crovella, M., Diot, C.: Characterization of network-wide anomalies in traffic flows. In: IMC 2004: Proc. of the 4th ACM SIGCOMM conference on Internet measurement, pp. 201–206. ACM, New York (2004)

9. Lakhina, A., Crovella, M., Diot, C.: Diagnosing network-wide traffic anomalies. In: SIG-COMM 2004: Proc. of the Conference on Applications, technologies, architectures, and protocols for computer comm., pp. 219–230. ACM, New York (2004)
10. Lakhina, A., Papagiannaki, K., Crovella, M., Diot, C., Kolaczyk, E.D., Taft, N.: Structural analysis of network traffic flows. SIGMETRICS Perform. Eval. Rev. 32(1), 61–72 (2004)
11. Yang, L., Michailidis, G.: Sampled based estimation of network traffic flow characteristics. In: INFOCOM 2007. 26th IEEE International Conference on Computer Communications, pp. 1775–1783. IEEE, Los Alamitos (2007)
12. Cisco IOS NetFlow (April 2008), http://www.cisco.com/go/netflow
13. Cisco IOS NetFlow Configuration Guide (April 2008), http://www.cisco.com
14. IP Flow Information Export Working Group (April 2008), http://www.ietf.org/html.charters/ipfix-charter.html
15. Plonka, D.: Flowscan (April 2008), http://www.caida.org/tools/utilities/flowscan/
16. Internet2 NetFlow: Weekly Reports. netflow.internet2.edu/weekly (April 2008)
17. sFlow (April 2008), http://www.sflow.org
18. SURFnet (April 2008), http://www.surfnet.nl
19. Zhang, Y., Ge, Z., Greenberg, A., Roughan, M.: Network anomography. In: Proceedings of the Internet Measurement Conference 2005 on Internet Measurement Conference, pp. 317–330. USENIX Association (2005)

Diagnosis of IP-Service Anomalies Based on BGP-Update Temporal Analysis

Osamu Akashi and Atsushi Terauchi

NTT Network Innovation Laboratories,
3-9-11 Midori-cho, Musashino, Tokyo 180-8585, Japan
{akashi,terauchi}@core.ntt.co.jp

Abstract. Diagnosing IP-service anomalies requires network operators to analyze routing and service-application behavior at the protocol level from multiple viewpoints. For analyzing anomalies whose effects can be observed as static inconsistency among BGP routing tables, the multi-agent-based diagnostic system called ENCORE has been developed and successfully applied to actual autonomous systems (ASes). This system can integrate BGP routing information observed at multiple ASes and verify whether the routing information is being correctly distributed throughout the Internet. However, actual IP-service failures sometimes require temporal analysis of routing updates to identify specific causes and, moreover, comprehensive analysis from the viewpoint of interaction with other protocols than BGP. Thus, we have integrated such functions in the ENCORE architecture and developed a comprehensive diagnostic system called IP-MIND. It can consider historical BGP routing updates and the behavior of other protocols in conjunction with BGP-information reachability analysis in order to identify specific causes. It also enables diagnosis of a class of anomalies that cause reachability failures while not creating any inconsistency among the current BGP routing tables at multiple ASes.

1 Introduction

The Internet consists of more than 28000 autonomous systems (ASes). An AS is the basic unit of inter-domain routing, and control of routers in an AS is based on a policy provided by a single administrative authority. The routing of inter-connected ASes is controlled by using BGP-4 [1], which is the de facto standard. However, inter-AS routing is not stable [2]. Analyses of this routing behavior and causes of routing instability have been reported [3,4,5,6,7,8,9,10]. Reachability failures are easily caused by various reasons, such as hardware failure, routing protocol failure, and router configuration error. An essential problem is the difficulty of understanding the spread of routing information advertised by an AS [11]. Unlike intra-AS anomalies, the causes of inter-AS anomalies typically exist outside a network operator's domain, while the effects of the anomalies are sometimes observed only in the advertising AS.

N. Akar, M. Pioro, and C. Skianis (Eds.): IPOM 2008, LNCS 5275, pp. 28–40, 2008.

For analyzing anomalies whose effects can be observed as static inconsistency among BGP routing tables, the multi-agent-based diagnostic system called EN-CORE [11] has been developed and successfully applied to actual ASes. This system can integrate BGP routing information observed at multiple ASes and analyze whether the routing information originating from an AS is being correctly distributed throughout the Internet.

However, actual IP-service failures sometimes require temporal analysis of routing information to identify detailed causes, and moreover, comprehensive analysis from the viewpoint of interaction with protocols other than BGP is also desirable. Thus, we have integrated such functions in the ENCORE architecture and developed a comprehensive diagnostic system called IP-MIND. It can consider historical BGP routing updates and behavior of other protocols in conjunction with analyzing BGP reachability. It enables diagnosis of a class of anomalies that cause reachability failures while not creating any inconsistency among the current BGP routing tables at multiple ASes. This paper focuses on these diagnostic functions of IP-MIND.

This paper is organized as follows. First, section 2 briefly explains the background of our application domain and the ENCORE architecture, whose diagnosis uses integrated BGP routing information observed at multiple ASes. Then section 3 discusses improvement requirements that enable more detailed analysis: functions for more comprehensive analysis considering temporal routing behavior and interaction with other protocols. Section 4 focuses on the IP-MIND system and how it manages stochastic factors. Section 5 then discusses the effectiveness of the basic design of the IP-MIND system using diagnostic scenarios where historical BGP routing updates are used for detailed analysis.

2 Background

2.1 Difficulties in Inter-AS Routing Management

Difficulties in inter-AS routing management arise from the architecture, where more than several thousand independent ASes exchange BGP information in a hop-by-hop manner according to each policy. We are currently unclear about their detailed dynamics.

Spatial changes easily lead to inconsistent routing states among several ASes, even though each AS is working consistently with respect to neighbor ASes. Moreover, the ASes experiencing anomalies may be different from those causing the anomalies. Therefore, we need to obtain a global view of routing information to verify whether advertised routing information is spreading as the originating AS intends. The temporal changes make advance analysis invalid. Overcoming this problem requires verification at multiple observation points on an on-demand basis. Operators can use tools such as `ping`, `traceroute`, and `looking glass` [12], but they have to use these tools repeatedly over a long period to confirm their own AS's advertised information and find anomalies as soon as possible.

A method using cooperative distributed problem solving (CDPS) coincides with this control structure and supplements these other analytical tools. In addition to handling the autonomy of each AS, CDPS has several advantages over the centralized system approach. From the viewpoint of diagnostic systems, CDPS can be efficient and scalable because 1) statistical calculation to extract local trends in traffic or routing information is performed at the observation points; and 2) the distributed entities, *agents*, exchange only abstracted, analyzed results, rather than raw data. A simple repeated query-and-reply scheme produces a lot of traffic. From the viewpoint of diagnostic functions, CDPS offers higher availability because an agent can act even under conditions where some paths on certain IP networks are unreachable. Agents can try to communicate with each other by relaying messages through a number of cooperative agents. Moreover, a CDPS can effectively perform analysis because an agent can request other agents to invoke various sensing tools, such as `traceroute` or `ping`, to obtain the remote data and accurately isolate causes of problems. Centralized approaches are, however, incapable of performing these actions at remote points.

There are several diagnostic tools for analyzing inter-AS routing anomalies. WWW-based systems such as looking glass [12], RIS tools [13], RouteViews [14], and various visualization tools are widely used by network operators to monitor routing information. These systems, however, are designed to be used by humans and cannot be straightforwardly applied to the CDPS framework. Although analyses of temporal and topological behavior of BGP path changes [3,4,5] and diagnosis methods of these anomalies using temporal analyses [6,7] and configuration analyses [8,9] have been reported, they emphasize path instability identification or clustering rather than reachability diagnosis in conjunction with the behavior of other protocols. Although the inherent problem in BGP and its modification was also reported [10], it cannot cover all cases. For real-time anomaly detection by analyzing BGP updates, the signature-based method and the statistics-based method have been proposed [15]. These methods can effectively identify anomalous BGP events, but they also emphasize anomalous BGP routing dynamics. The hybrid system of human and statistically analyzed results described in [16] is unique and effective. Although it is a kind of visualization tool and cannot be directly applied, it could work in complement if some patterns were extracted as interpretable rules. Listen and Whisper [17] can eliminate a large number of problems due to misconfiguration by considering network topology. However, Listen only verifies routes in the data plane and Whisper focuses on verifying routes in the control plane.

2.2   ENCORE Architecture

A global view of the current routing information that has spread among different administrative domains is essential for diagnosing inter-AS routing anomalies. Since complete understanding of this view is impossible, we adopt the use of routing information observed almost simultaneously at multiple ASes. By integrating these observed results, we can infer a part of the global view for the purpose of diagnosis.

The basic idea of this system is the reflector model illustrated in Fig. 1. The essence of this model is to provide a function by which an agent can request

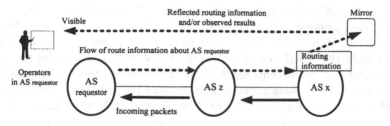

Fig. 1. Reflector model: basic idea for observing spread of information

remote agents to observe routing information about a specific AS, which is usually the AS of the requesting agent. The routing information observed and analyzed by the remote agents is sent to the requesting agent. Thus, we can say that this architecture is based on the verification of BGP-information reachability.

Agents' roles in the basic cooperative strategy in ENCORE are *investigation*, *relay*, and *friend*. ENCORE dynamically searches agents suitable for these three roles based on their functional capability and topological conditions. Location information about agents on the BGP topology map and agents' capabilities are managed by an agent group management system called ARTISTE [18], which is a system independent of ENCORE. When cooperative diagnosis is performed, an agent sends a query to ARTISTE, which then responds with a list of active agents that can perform the requested role and satisfy a given topological requirement on the BGP map. For example, ARTISTE can search agents that match a given requirement, such as "Find agents that can relay messages and are located within 2 AS-hops from ASx".

An investigation agent is used to send back requested information observed in its environment. This role is typically assigned to agents located in major transit ASes as it is in ENCORE, because they can observe the large amount of routing information exchanged there. From the viewpoint of connectivity at the AS level on the BGP topology map, it was also reported that the agent in an AS that has higher connectivity has higher capability for detecting and preventing hijacked routes than agents in ASes with lower connectivity [19]. Investigation agents in transit ASes are also used at an early stage of each diagnostic action and are considered as first contact points. A friend agent is used to continuously observe the state from outside the AS. Candidates for friend agents can be selected using topological requirements, such as being agents in a neighbor AS, a transit AS, or an AS on the other side of central ASes of the Internet. A relay agent is used to control the routing of exchanged messages at the application level. If an agent cannot obtain results within a predefined time, the agent selects relay agents and requests them to relay messages to the destination agent.

3   Requirements for Comprehensive Analysis

The ENCORE architecture, which uses confirmation of BGP entries at multiple ASes, is designed to diagnose stable-state anomalies. These anomalies occupy the major part of trouble management actions in our AS according to analysis in [11]. ENCORE has demonstrated its effectiveness in the actual operation of deployed ASes. However, it has also shown that some cases remain where the system cannot identify the specific cause or has difficulty finding anomalies themselves even if the current state seems stable. The IP-MIND system is designed to try to diagnose a part of these remaining anomalies that require integration with temporal analysis and consideration of other protocols. In the remainder of this section, we explain these kinds of anomalies and the diagnostic requirements for coping with them.

3.1   Integration with Temporal Analysis

The problems that arise from the lack of temporal routing aspects of anomalous states are described as follows. These situations require the system to monitor, save, then analyze the BGP update sequence. The first and second denote the extensional direction of the function that is achieved easily by the architecture based on the verification of BGP-information reachability. The third points out a requirement for an effective search strategy among distributed agents.

- Although the existence of a BGP entry indicates routing legality concerning the entry at that time from the viewpoint of that router, it does not necessarily guarantee routing legality just before that time. In more detail, this existence does not also necessarily guarantee legal routing of the entire path to the final destination at that time, because the propagation of a BGP entry can take a long time especially by MRAI timers [1].
- The lack of a BGP entry means the routing concerning that entry is impossible. However, the reason for this route disappearance cannot be identified specifically. It could be a filter setting error, temporal disappearance caused by route damping [20], or an intended operation due to a change in management policy.

These points mean that the architecture based on verification of BGP-information reachability, which is used in ENCORE, should be extended to analyze for how long before and how often the target prefix was advertised previously as well as to check that the prefix exists in the current BGP table.

For example, an agent in AS_x recognizes that AS_x advertised its BGP entry concerning an IP prefix, denoted as IP-prefix-1, to AS_i, as shown in Fig. 2. When all agents in other ASes (i.e., AS_y and AS_z) find a static anomalous state where no BGP entry concerning IP-prefix-1 exists in their routing tables, there are various possible causes. If none of the agents in AS_y or AS_z have observed update messages concerning IP-prefix-1 in the past, there should be some management policy to filter IP-prefix-1 in AS_i or neighboring ASes. If some agents have seen only the preceding part of the update message sequence, updates concerning IP-prefix-1 should be temporarily damped in AS_i or other intermediate ASes.

On the contrary, when all agents in other ASes find no static anomalous state, which means BGP entries concerning IP-prefix-1 exist in their routing

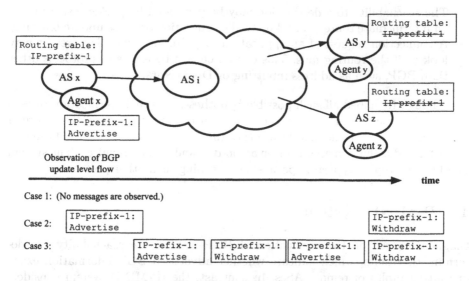

Observation of BGP
update level flow

Case 1: (No messages are observed.)

Fig. 2. Observation of temporal aspect

tables, recent update messages also should be checked. If a recently advertised
withdrawal message was observed, it could affect the reachability between the
advertising AS and recently received AS. Therefore, a detailed diagnosis requires
the system to check the temporal sequence concerning BGP updates. It should
be integrated with diagnosis results based on the verification of BGP-information
reachability.

- If a route was hijacked, the BGP AS path information of a previously advertised BGP entry should be considered to determine the previous and current
  state.

The AS path information in the previously advertised BGP entry could contain the path along which the entry traversed from the legal origin. This information should be used for identifying the legal origin and for effectively searching
contaminated areas. It can also be used as a hint for finding agents that can relay
messages between the agent in the legal origin AS and the agent that detected
the hijack.

3.2   Consideration of Other Protocols and Environmental Status

Even if the existence of a BGP entry and the analysis of previously observed
BGP updates indicate routing legality at that time, packets may not reach their
destinations. This means that factors other than the BGP routing should be
considered and integrated with the acquired diagnostic results. These factors
include the interaction with protocols other than BGP and also other environ-
mental statuses, such as traffic congestion. The problems that arise from the
lack of consideration for factors other than BGP are described as follows.

- The reachability to a destination may be prevented by packet discarding in an intermediate router caused by traffic congestion or route update bursting.
- A connection request of an application may fail, and what is worse, it may look as if the routing fails. This can be caused by errors in protocols other than BGP, such as address inputting or DNS errors.

Although to embed all such possible hypotheses and their verification rules is ideal, to assume and prepare all these cases in practice is difficult. Therefore, a system in which heuristic modifications to the acquired diagnostic results should be performed by human operators on an on-demand basis is required. The system should also prepare typical hypotheses concerning such other protocols.

4   IP-MIND System

Diagnoses based on the verification of BGP-information reachability use deterministic results, which indicate whether advertised BGP information exists in routing tables of remote ASes. In contrast, the IP-MIND system considers stochastic factors, which may cause anomalous network phenomena. This function cannot easily be integrated with a diagnostic framework that consists of hypotheses and their verification rules because the stochastic factors have indeterministic states and differ depending on where and when they are observed. Therefore, they have a huge number of possible states. All these cases are difficult to clearly arrange and describe in advance. In the IP-MIND approach, we try to resolve this situation by actively prompting operators to verify and/or modify current diagnostic statuses and reflect the results in diagnostic knowledge on an on-demand basis. In other words, operators supplement this ambiguity by using heuristics based on local trends and their own experience. This means that the system accepts modification requests from operators and changes its diagnostic behavior as a result.

4.1   System Structure

The IP-MIND system is built on a network agent platform that was used for implementing ENCORE and provides basic action primitives on distributed environments. The structure of the IP-MIND system is similar to that of the EN-CORE system, as shown in Fig. 3, and is implemented using Allegro Common Lisp (ACL)/CLOS.

The extended part of the system is the user-defined macro controller, which can overwrite acquired diagnostic results temporally and interrupt the inference engine if needed. As a result, it can modify the behavior of the inference engine indirectly according to operators' heuristic requests. The BGP controller can receive BGP update level information via an iBGP session with border routers and maintain the BGP update. The controller sends back BGP-related information in a required fashion based on requests from the inference engine.

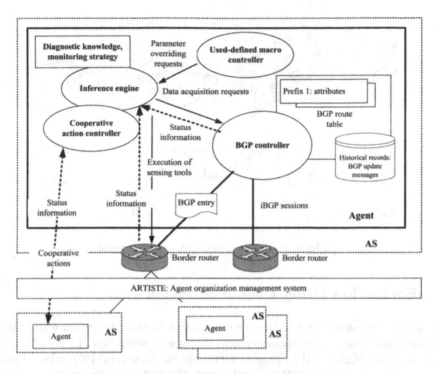

Fig. 3. IP-MIND system structure

4.2 Management of Stochastic Factors

When the system finds stochastic factors, such as bursting route-update messages, some packets might be discarded in that period even if concerned BGP prefixes exist in other ASes in that period. Therefore, the result of the diagnostic rule that verifies reachability might have to be "false" during that period, even if the system successfully receives ICMP reply messages. This means that ICMP messages could be sent by the destination and be successfully received by the IP-MIND system in some cases. Therefore, the system should consider such uncertain states.

In such a case, operators can try to diagnose the situation again as if the rule that verifies the reachability was false. To cope with this situation, the IP-MIND system provides an interactive diagnosis mode in which operators can mask acquired diagnostic results. Operators who mask the results can restart diagnosis and obtain other results that are derived under masked conditions.

If this kind of heuristic setting is sometimes required, this modification by operators should be stored as a named user macro and hence can be restored. This function can be used for representing heuristic rules that are repeatedly observable in a deployed local environment.

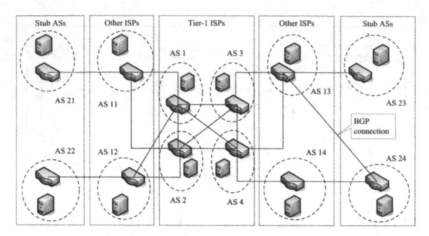

Fig. 4. Example of emulation environment

5 Evaluation Using Diagnosis Scenarios

We have constructed an emulation environment in order to evaluate the validity of our basic design using some typical diagnostic scenarios. This environment uses VMware Server [21] to provide virtual hosts on several PCs, where Quagga router software [22], IP-MIND agents, and ARTISTE agents are running. Each Quagga router establishes BGP connections, and a typical constructed BGP topology is shown in Fig. 4. In this routing topology, four ASes that correspond to Tier-1 ASes have full-meshed connections. Four second-level ISPs have one or two connections to Tier-1 ASes. Similarly, stub ASes have one or two connections to upstream ISPs.

5.1 Diagnosis of Web Server Reachability

In the first scenario, an operator checks a URL (``http://www.test.sample:80'') that is assumed to have access problems. A typical diagnosis procedure is as follows.

1. First, the IP-MIND system tries to get the DNS A-record of www.test.sample.
2. If this A-record exists, the system checks whether the IP address is reachable by using ICMP echo/reply and verifying BGP-information reachability.
3. If this check succeeds, the system checks whether the http port 80 works by sending request messages.

   When all these verification rules are satisfied, the operator can conclude that the http server now works well and that the problem appears to be fixed although the cause has not been identified. In the conventional diagnosis, which does not check stochastic factors or temporal phenomena, the system does not need to check for a more specific cause because the rule that verifies reachability to the

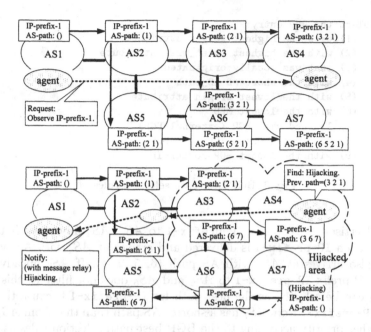

Fig. 5. Contamination by hijacked route delivery

target IP address has already been shown to be true. In the diagnosis of IP-MIND, then, stochastic factors and temporal phenomena that might affect the results of previous verification rules are checked. The checked hypotheses in this example are as follows.

– Bursty BGP update messages
– Temporal analysis of BGP update messages concerning `www.test.sample` and the IP prefixes that belong to operator's AS

If some of these hypotheses are true, they might affect the rule that checks reachability. The bursty BGP updates might prevent ICMP messages from being delivered during that anomalous state, and the temporal analysis might show a transient disappearance of a concerned prefix. Therefore, operators using IP-MIND can mask the result of ICMP echo/reply as if it failed and restart the diagnosis to check whether this modification satisfies the situation.

5.2   Diagnosis of Hijacked Routes

In this scenario, a simpler topology (Fig. 5) is used for simplifying the explanation of how temporal update information is used in hijack related diagnoses. An agent R_1 requests a friend agent R_4 to observe BGP entries advertised from AS_1. An example of a detailed request is "Notify R_1 if the origin AS number, which should be AS_1, in any BGP entries concerning target IP prefixes is changed or if any of these BGP entries disappear."

```
Select the BGP entry:
    (1) with the highest weight attribute
    (2) with the highest local_pref attribute
    (3) that was locally originated
    (4) with the shortest AS_path
    (5) with the lowest origin attribute
    (6) with the lowest MED
    (7) learned via eBGP (external BGP)
    (8) with the closest IGP neighbor
    (9) with the lowest BGP router-ID
```

Fig. 6. BGP best-path-selection rules

AS_1 advertises its IP prefix IP-prefix-1 to AS_2. AS_2 advertises it to AS_3 and AS_5. Then IP-prefix-1 is delivered and arrives at AS_4 with AS path (3, 2, 1). It also arrives at AS_7 with AS path (6, 5, 2, 1). If AS_7 misadvertises the same IP prefix IP-prefix-1 to AS_6 and AS_6 does not filter it, this prefix from AS_7 can be selected as the best path for IP-prefix-1 because the BGP entry of IP-prefix-1 from AS_7 has a shorter AS path than that from AS_1. This means higher priority according to the BGP best-path selection rules as shown in Fig. 6 [1]. Note this assumes that AS_6 does not have a special management policy concerning IP-prefix-1, which means AS_6 does not set any local_pref values on BGP entries concerning IP-prefix-1, or local_pref values of BGP entries concerning IP-prefix-1 from AS_5 and AS_7 are the same. Although the weight attribute has the highest priority, it is not defined as the standard [1] and cannot be distributed outside Cisco routers.

In a similar way, hijacked routes diffuse and contaminate routing tables in some other ASes. In these contaminated ASes, packets destined for IP-prefix-1 are forwarded to AS_7 without the intention of the operator. This misadvertised prefix also reaches AS_3 and AS_5. If the misadvertised route is selected in AS_3, AS_4 is also contaminated. The contaminated routing table prevents direct communication between AS_1 and AS_4 since packets in AS_3 destined for AS_1 are forwarded to AS_7.

Therefore, R_4 extracts the previous BGP entry for AS_1 and finds the previous AS path (3, 2, 1) while the current is (3, 6, 7). Then, R_4 tries to find a relay agent in AS_2 because AS_2 only appears in the previous path and seems to have a correct route to AS_1. If R_4 cannot find suitable agents, it tries to find other candidate agents that reside around AS_1 or AS_2. In this scenario, R_4 can find a relay agent in AS_2 and communicates indirectly with R_1. Thus, R_1 can be notified that the origin AS number, which should be AS_1, was changed to AS_7 in AS_4.

As shown in Fig. 7, suspicious ASes are searched based on the information that is acquired by comparing the AS paths of these two BGP entries, namely (3, 6, 7) and (3, 2, 1). The separation point of these two paths is AS_3. Therefore, R_1 first checks AS_3 and its neighbor, AS_2. Then along with the current path, AS_6 and its neighbor, AS_5, are checked. Therefore, R_1 can discover the contaminated area

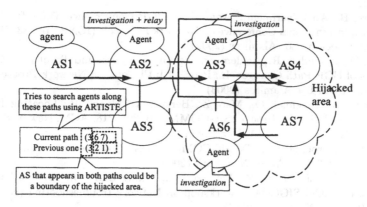

Fig. 7. Cooperative analysis of hijacked route

by repeatedly sending queries to these agents. The hijacked AS without these cooperative actions can only know that some remote ASes such as AS_4 or AS_7 are not accessible while some neighboring or nearby ASes are accessible. Centralized systems such as MyASN cannot notify the hijacked AS of this situation because notify messages are prevented by this anomalous state itself.

Although fatal accidents or attacks such as the 1997 failure that disturbed the entire Internet through the unintentional advertisement of full routes might not occur because of the careful filtering conducted by several major ISPs, cases of small-scale or partial-area misadvertising have been observed several times in the past few years. Thus, continuous observation and diagnosis by adequately deployed agents are still needed. Detailed analysis of the agent deployment strategy for detecting and preventing hijacked routes from the viewpoint of the AS adjacency topology of an actual Internet structure is described in [19].

6   Conclusion

We have developed the IP-MIND system for diagnosing IP-service anomalies. The system can analyze anomalies from the viewpoint of temporal aspects of BGP update messages and the behavior of other protocols in conjunction with BGP-information reachability analysis. It can diagnose specific anomalies by considering stochastic factors that may cause anomalous network phenomena. It also enables diagnosis of a class of anomalies that cause reachability failures while not creating any inconsistency in the current BGP routing tables at multiple ASes. We have started experimentally using the IP-MIND system on an actual network and have been evaluating its diagnostic coverage.

References

1. Rekhter, Y., Li, T.: A Border Gateway Protocol 4 (BGP-4), RFC1771 (1995)
2. The North American Network Operators' Group: NANOG mailing list, http://www.nanog.org

3. Premore, B.: An Experimental Analysis of BGP Convergence Time. In: Proc. of the Ninth International Conference on Network Protocols (ICNP), pp. 53–61. IEEE Computer Society, Los Alamitos (2001)
4. Chang, D., Govindan, R., Heidemann, J.: The Temporal and Topological Characteristics of BGP Path Changes. In: Proc. of Int'l Conf. on Network Protocols, pp. 190–199. IEEE, Los Alamitos (2003)
5. Feldmann, A., Maennel, O., Mao, Z., Berger, A., Maggs, B.: Locating Internet Routing Instability. In: Proc. of SIGCOMM, pp. 205–218. ACM, New York (2004)
6. Teixeira, R., Rexford, J.: A Measurement Framework for Pin-pointing Routing Changes. In: Proc. of the ACM SIGCOMM workshop on Network troubleshooting (NetT), pp. 313–318. ACM, New York (2004)
7. Chandrashekar, J., Zhang, Z., Peterson, H.: Fixing BGP, One as at a Time. In: Proc. of the ACM SIGCOMM workshop on Network troubleshooting (NetT), pp. 295–300. ACM, New York (2004)
8. Feamster, N., Balakrishnan, H.: Detecting BGP Configuration Faults with Static Analysis. In: Proc. of NSDI, pp. 43–56. USENIX/ACM (2005)
9. Mahajan, R., Wetherall, D., Anderson, T.: Understanding BGP Misconfiguration. In: Proc. of SIGCOMM, pp. 3–16. ACM, New York (2002)
10. Afek, Y., Bremler-Barr, A., Schwarz, S.: Improved BGP Convergence via Ghost Flushing. In: Proc. of 22nd INFOCOM, pp. 927–937. IEEE Computer Society, Los Alamitos (2003)
11. Akashi, O., Terauchi, A., Fukuda, K., Hirotsu, T., Maruyama, M., Sugawara, T.: Detection and Diagnosis of Inter-AS Routing Anomalies by Cooperative Intelligent Agents. In: Schönwälder, J., Serrat, J. (eds.) DSOM 2005. LNCS, vol. 3775. Springer, Heidelberg (2005)
12. Kern, E.: http://nitrous.digex.net
13. RIPE: http://www.ripe.net/
14. Meyer D.: http://www.routeviews.org
15. Zhang, K., Yen, A., Zhao, X., Massey, D., Wu, S., Zhnag, L.: On Detection of Anomalous Routing Dynamics in BGP. In: Proc. of Networking, IFIP, pp. 259–270 (2004)
16. Teoh, S., Ma, K., Wu, S., Massey, D., Zhao, X., Pei, D., Wang, L., Zhang, L., Bush, R.: Visual-Based Anomaly Detection for BGP Origin AS Change (OASC) Events. In: Brunner, M., Keller, A. (eds.) DSOM 2003. LNCS, vol. 2867, pp. 155–168. Springer, Heidelberg (2003)
17. Subramanian, L., Roth, V., Stoica, I., Shenker, S., Katz, R.: Listen and Whisper: Security Mechanisms for BGP. In: Proc. of Networked Systems Design and Implementation. USENIX, pp. 127–140 (November 2004)
18. Terauchi, A., Akashi, O., Maruyama, M., Fukuda, K., Sugawara, T., Hirotsu, T., Kurihara, S.: ARTISTE: An Agent Organization Management System for Multi-agent Systems. In: 8th Pacific Rim Int'l Workshop on Multi-Agents (PRIMA), IFMAS, pp. 245–259 (September 2005)
19. Akashi, O., Fukuda, K., Hirotsu, T., Sugawara, T.: Analysis of Diagnostic Capability for Hijacked Route Problem. In: Medhi, D., Nogueira, J.M., Pfeifer, T., Wu, S.F. (eds.) IPOM 2007. LNCS, vol. 4786. Springer, Heidelberg (2007)
20. Villamizar, C., Chandra, R., Govindan, R.: BGP Route Flap Damping, RFC2439 (1998)
21. VMware: http://www.vmware.com
22. The quagga routing suite, http://www.quagga.net

Achieving Fast BGP Reroute with Traffic Engineering Using Multiple Routing Planes

Yu Guo[1], Ning Wang[1], Kin-Hon Ho[1], Michael Howarth[1], and George Pavlou[2]

[1] Centre for Communication Systems Research, University of Surrey,
United Kingdom, GU2 7XH
{Y.Guo,N.Wang,K.Ho,M.Howarth}@surrey.ac.uk
[2] Networks and Services Research Lab, University College London (UCL),
United Kingdom, WC1E 7JB
G.Pavlou@ee.ucl.ac.uk

Abstract. In today's BGP routing architecture, traffic delivery is in general based on single path selection paradigms. The lack of path diversity hinders the support for resilience, traffic engineering and QoS provisioning across the Internet. Some recently proposed multi-plane extensions to BGP offer a promising mechanism to enable diverse inter-domain routes towards destination prefixes. Based on these enhanced BGP protocols, we propose in this paper a novel technique to enable controlled fast egress router switching for handling network failures. In order to minimize the disruptions to real-time services caused by the failures, backup egress routers can be immediately activated through locally remarking affected traffic towards alternative routing planes without waiting for IGP routing re-convergence. According to our evaluation results, the proposed multi-plane based egress router selection algorithm is able to provide both high path diversity and balanced load distribution across inter-domain links with a small number of planes.

1 Introduction

The current Internet topology offers high path richness between domains [21], mainly due to the increasing use of multi-homing. However, the standard BGP protocol only allows single path selection, which does not take full advantage of this inter-domain path richness. Although the rationale behind this is to achieve high scalability in BGP routing, the lack of diverse paths significantly hinders support for Quality of Services (QoS) and resilience against network failures, both of which are vital for real-time multimedia services. On the other hand, Internet Traffic Engineering (TE) [1] is often used for optimizing network resources (e.g. load balancing) and sometimes also for supporting end-to-end QoS with high assurance guarantees. Without path diversity enabled by the inter-domain routing paradigms, the effectiveness of this TE could be significantly limited. This problem is especially significant for inter-domain peering links which often become the bottleneck of the end-to-end path in the Internet due to their scarce bandwidth resources [2].

It has been observed that handling intra-domain network failures is a daily occurrence in today's Internet [22]. As far as real-time multimedia services are concerned,

N. Akar, M. Pioro, and C. Skianis (Eds.): IPOM 2008, LNCS 5275, pp. 41–52, 2008.

network failures may lead to significant disruptions to end users. First of all, in order to minimize or even eliminate perceived service disruption by end users due to QoS degradation, the overall loss-of-connectivity duration should be no more than 50 milliseconds [3]. Given the relatively slow re-convergence behavior of the current IGP/BGP protocols, it is not possible to achieve this goal without introducing additional complications. Secondly, another important issue to be considered for QoS assurance is how to avoid network congestion in both the normal state and the post-failure state. To tackle the first challenge, Fast Reroute (FRR) techniques can be applied for rapidly diverting affected traffic from failed network components to repairing paths. It should be noted that most of the existing FRR techniques only deal with intra-domain routing [4, 5, 6], while very few consider the simple scenario of inter-domain link failures [3]. One important observation is that inter-domain routing can be also disrupted by intra-domain link failures, typically due to the Hot Potato Routing effect [7]. For instance, the breakdown of an intra-domain link may lead to a change of egress points for the affected transit traffic. In general, FRR techniques, which have only the single aim of minimizing the duration of loss-of-connectivity, do not tackle such routing disruption. Instead, inter-domain traffic engineering mechanisms [2, 8, 9] are responsible for routing optimization in both normal and post-failure states. In the literature, FRR and TE are two separate research topics being investigated independently, while a holistic solution for eliminating service disruptions is still yet to be obtained.

Recently, the concept of network virtualization has been developed, with the basic idea being to partition network resources for different service/engineering requirements, not only including the physical bandwidth, but also "soft" resources such as routing/forwarding tables. Related multi-plane techniques have been proposed both for intra- and inter-domain routing, such as Multi-topology OSPF/IS-IS [10, 11], QoS-enhanced BGP [12] and BGP path splicing [13, 14]. As far as inter-domain routing is concerned, the main idea is to provision coexisting diverse BGP routes towards each destination prefix. In the literature, proposals have typically been made to use these multi-plane routing mechanisms for *one* of the following purposes: service differentiation [12], traffic engineering [15] and fast failure recovery [4, 16]. In this paper, we consider how existing multi-plane techniques can be used as the underlying routing platform for achieving both FRR and bandwidth resource optimization, both of which are vital for supporting QoS assurance. More specifically, we consider how to enable *controlled* fast egress router switching for handling intra-domain link failures through multi-plane aware BGP protocols. The main idea is that additional egress routers can be pre-provisioned in backup routing planes, so that the affected transit traffic can be immediately switched to backup egress points without waiting for IGP re-convergence. A fundamental issue to be considered in the management plane is how the primary and backup egress points for each destination prefix are selected in multiple planes in order to maximize intra-domain path diversity for high failure coverage. Based on this multi-plane routing platform, existing egress point selection algorithms based on conventional BGP routing are extended for achieving improved load balancing across inter-domain links.

2 Multi-plane BGP Fast Reroute Overview

In our proposed scheme, multi-plane routing is used to enable fast reroute for customer traffic when intra-domain links fail without waiting for IGP re-convergence. In addition, we also investigate intelligent egress router selection is also addressed for achieving improved load balancing on inter-domain links. We first consider the scenario where conventional BGP is used as the underlying routing protocol without any fast reroute support. Once an intra-domain link fails, the IGP routing protocol needs to re-converge before the updated routing table is populated. In addition, the new IGP path may force BGP to switch egress points for some affected traffic due to the hot potato routing effect, as some ingress points may find that other border routers become closer (in terms of IGP distance) than the original primary egress points after the intra-domain link fails. Such egress point switching might not be always anticipated by the network administrator, and as a result post-failure network congestion may happen due to uncontrolled traffic shifting across inter-domain links.

In our proposed scheme, if multiple border routers have received BGP advertisements towards a specific destination prefix, instead of only installing one single route a dedicated egress point can be enforced within each BGP routing plane. In the normal state, only the egress router in the *primary* routing plane is used for delivering traffic. Once an intra-domain link fails, its head node, which is also called repairing router, immediately switches to use alternative egress point(s) installed in other routing planes by changing the tag (also known as remarking) of the IP packets, which indicates which plane should be used for carrying the affected traffic. Take the BGP path splicing [13, 14] as an example, $log_2 (k)$ bits are used in the splicing header for indicating the active routing plane out of k planes. This value can be remarked at the repairing routers for achieving path switching. As far as BGP FRR is concerned, a basic requirement is that *the failed link should not be included in the shortest IGP path from the repairing router to the backup egress point*. In order to enable fast recovery, careful egress point selection needs to be performed in order to achieve maximum intra-domain path diversity across multiple routing planes. To be compliant with the current BGP route enforcement, the rule of Single Egress Selection (SES) [2] is followed within each specific plane, which means that all the customer traffic assigned to that plane to a certain prefix should exit through one single egress router. This is effectively enforced by assigning the highest BGP *local preference* value to the selected egress point in each plane. Let's take the simple network shown in Fig. 1 as an example where individual routers have full-mesh i-BGP sessions. Assume ingress routers i_1 and i_2 have transit traffic to be delivered towards a specific remote prefix P, which can be reached via border routers j_1, j_2 and j_3. As Fig. 1(a) shows, the IGP link weights of all intra-domain links are assumed to be 1 except the one between i_1 and c which is 3. If the network operator decides to use three BGP routing planes, then each of these three border routers can be selected as the primary egress point for prefix P in one of these planes. As shown in the Fig. 1(b), if egress router j_1 is selected in the first plane, customer traffic injected from individual ingress routers will follow the solid paths towards the destination prefix. Similarly, the paths with dot and dash links represent respectively the shortest IGP paths from ingress routers to the selected egress points j_2 and j_3 towards prefix P in the second and third planes.

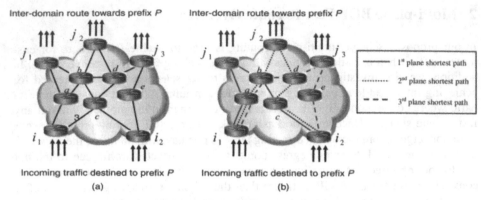

Fig. 1. IGP paths in different routing planes

The first plane is used as the default one for traffic delivery in the normal state, which means j_1 is the actual primary egress router for carrying customer traffic to destination prefix P in the absence of link failures. In this case the actual shortest IGP paths from individual ingress routers to j_1 are $i_1 \rightarrow a \rightarrow j_1$ and $i_2 \rightarrow c \rightarrow b \rightarrow j_1$ respectively. If the head router c of link $c \rightarrow b$ has detected the failure of the link, it immediately remarks the traffic toward prefix P to switch the customer traffic from the default plane to an alternative plane where the failed link is not involved in the corresponding IGP paths. For example, the affected traffic can be remarked to use the second plane where j_2 is selected as the primary egress for P after the failure has been detected. In this case the backup IGP path $c \rightarrow d \rightarrow j_2$ is activated to deliver the affected traffic out of the local domain without waiting for the underlying IGP to re-converge. A more general case is to activate more than one backup plane so that the affected traffic can be delivered out of the local domain via multiple alternative egress points. The proportion of the shifted traffic across these backup planes can be determined according to the current available bandwidth associated with these alternative egress routers.

A key issue to be considered in the management plane is how to optimize the egress router selection in individual planes in order to maximize protection coverage against intra-domain link failures. It can be easily inferred that if an intra-domain link is involved in the IGP paths in all planes for a specific destination prefix, the affected traffic cannot avoid using it no matter which plane is used (e.g. link $i1 \rightarrow a$ in Fig. 1(b)). To avoid this situation, the egress point selection should aim to obtain high path diversity inside the local network across individual planes. As a result there is a high chance of having alternative feasible egress points that do not involve the failed intra-domain link. As far as traffic engineering is concerned, we consider how transit traffic can be balanced across individual inter-domain links based on multi-plane BGP routing. In the literature, optimized egress point selection for inter-domain TE based on conventional BGP routing has been widely investigated. In this paper we address the issue of achieving both BGP fast reroute and inter-domain traffic engineering in order to provide a holistic solution for resilience against link failures. More specifically, an optimization problem is formulated and solved with a heuristic for maximizing link failure protection as well as load balancing across multiple inter-domain links. Finally it should be noted that, we only propose in this paper a generic optimization problem in the management plane rather than going into details on how the idea is actually implemented using any specific routing mechanism. On the other hand, although we use multi-plane BGP protocols where packets can be tagged to indicate the active planes for traffic delivery, other advanced BGP protocols are also applicable, e.g. the MIRO scheme [17]. In this case packets need to be encapsulated in order to be tunnelled to alternative egress points, rather than changing the tag of the packets to be rerouted. Finally, it can be easily inferred that the proposed scheme can be also used for inter-domain link failures, as any primary egress router can also re-mark the affected traffic to use backup ones in other routing planes when it detects the failure of the directly attached inter-domain link.

3 Egress Router Selection for Path Diversity and Load Balancing

3.1 Network Modeling and Problem Formulation

As previously mentioned, the problem we are considering is to perform intelligent egress point selection across multiple planes for achieving (1) maximum intra-domain path diversity in order to maximize the chance for controlled fast BGP reroute in case of intra-domain link failures, and (2) load balancing on inter-domain links in the normal state. As far as network modeling is concerned, each Autonomous System (AS) has a set of edge routers which can be further classified into an ingress router set I and an egress router set J, through which transit traffic is injected into and delivered out from this domain respectively. In addition an AS may contain some core routers that are not directly connected to customers or other ASes. In BGP routing, egress routers receive reachability advertisements for remote destination prefixes through e-BGP sessions from neighboring domains. Let K denote the set of prefix advertisements received across all edge routers. For each prefix k ($k \in K$), let $Out(k)$ denote the set of egress routers at which an advertisement for prefix k has been received. On the other hand, the overall customer flows entering the domain through individual ingress routers with destination prefix k need to be estimated *a priori* before being assigned to individual egress routers. We use $t(i,k)$ to denote the aggregate traffic demand with destination prefix k ($k \in K$) that is injected into the domain through ingress router i ($i \in I$).

Regarding multi-plane extensions to BGP, we consider M logical planes to be pre-provisioned by the local AS so that a dedicated egress router can be selected for each destination prefix k within each plan $m \in M$. To enforce egress router selection for customer traffic, specific local preference (Local-Pref) values can be configured independently within each plane m. It is also worth mentioning that the intra-domain routing protocol running within the local domain is standard IGP which is not multi-plane aware. In this case the IGP distance between each ingress/egress pair is the same across all routing planes.

Considering our purpose to maximize path diversity, a fundamental issue is how to "represent" path diversity appropriately. Recall from the example shown in Fig. 1, it is important to avoid the situation that for one ingress router, no matter which egress router is to be used for carrying the incoming traffic in individual plane, the traffic cannot avoid traversing a certain link (for instance, link $i1 \rightarrow a$ in Fig. 1, which is fully shared by the IGP paths from i across all three planes). This would mean that all the possible IGP paths from that ingress router have to go through this critical link, which we call it *fully-shared link*. It can be easily inferred that if a fully-shared link fails, there are no alternative IGP paths in any plane for the affected traffic to perform fast reroute, and most probably IGP needs to re-converge before the traffic delivery service is restored. In this case, egress router selection with minimum number of fully-shared links is desirable. Towards this end, we design a variable $Q^l_{(i,k)}$ to indicate whether the intra-domain link l is the fully-shared link with regard to each aggregate customer flow injected from ingress router i and destined to prefix k. More specifically

$$Q^l_{(i,k)} = \begin{cases} 1 & if \ \sum_{m \in M} Y^{l,m}_{(i,k)} = M \\ 0 & otherwise \end{cases}$$

where

$$Y^{l,m}_{(i,k)} = \begin{cases} 1 & if \ l \ constitutes \ the \ IGP \ path \ in \ plane \ m \ for \ the \ injected \ traffic \\ & from \ ingress \ i \ and \ destined \ to \ prefix \ k \\ 0 & otherwise \end{cases}$$

We also define another binary variable $X^{j,m}_k$ to indicate the actual egress point selection for prefix k in each plane m. As previously mentioned, Single Egress point Selection (SES) is adopted in our scheme, which means one single egress is selected for each prefix across *all* ingress routers within each plane. That is

$$X^{j,m}_k = \begin{cases} 1 & if \ j \ is \ selected \ for \ prefix \ k \ as \ the \ egress \ router \ in \ plane \ m \\ 0 & otherwise \end{cases}$$

In summary, the overall objective is to determine the value of a set of $X^{j,m}_k$ for each considered prefix k in each routing plane m in order to:

$$\text{Minimize} \sum_{i \in I} \sum_{k \in K} \sum_{l \in E} Q^l_{(i,k)}$$

subject to the following constraints:

$$\text{if } X^{j,m}_k = 1, \text{ then } j \in Out(k) \quad \forall j \in J, \ m \in M, \ k \in K \tag{1}$$

$$X^{j,m}_k \in \{0,1\}, Y^{l,m}_{(i,k)} \in \{0,1\} \quad \forall j \in J, \ m \in M, \ k \in K \tag{2}$$

$$\sum_{m \in M} \sum_{i \in I} \sum_{k \in K} X^{j,m}_k \times t(i,k) \le C^j_{inter} \quad \forall j \in J \tag{3}$$

Constraint (1) means the selected egress router j must be able to reach the destination prefix k. Constraint (2) makes sure that both variables X and Y are binary. Constraint (3) indicates the inter-domain link capacity constraint, meaning that all the customer traffic going through the selected egress router j should not exceed its inter-domain link capacity (C_{inter}^j).

3.2 Proposed Heuristic Algorithm

We proposed a simple heuristic algorithm to solve the problem. First of all, we adopt single plane traffic assignment in the normal state, that is, customer traffic is always assigned to the single egress router selected for the default plane. Other backup planes are only used when they are needed for fast BGP reroute in case of link failures. Entries for these additional egress routers selected for other planes are maintained in the router memory.

Step 1. Sort all the destination prefixes in the descending order according to their overall customer traffic demand, which is represented as $\sum_{i \in I} t(i, k)$. This strategy aims to put higher priority in the egress point assignment for the prefixes with higher traffic volume. Following that all the egress routers that satisfy the reachability constraint $j \in Out(k)$ are taken into consideration which ensures that by selecting egress router j, each destination prefix k can be reached. Any other egress routers that cannot satisfy this constraint are not considered any further.

Step 2. This step can be viewed as a pre-selection phase regarding bandwidth availability on candidate egress routers. In each plane, the problem is based on the Single egress selection problem, so all the customer traffic assigned to that plane to the same prefix from different ingresses should exit through a single selected egress router. Before the selection algorithm proceeds, the feasibility in terms of bandwidth constraint is checked. More specifically, any candidate egress router that does not have sufficient bandwidth resources to accommodate the traffic demand associated with the current destination prefix is excluded.

Step 3. For the first (default) plane, the egress router with the currently lowest bandwidth utilization is selected. This utilization is represented as the ratio of bandwidth used up by previously assigned traffic to the capacity of the inter-domain link. If there are equally lowest utilized links, one is selected randomly. Once the egress router in the default plane is selected for the prefix, we map the overall traffic demand onto the corresponding inter-domain link and update its bandwidth utilization.

Step 4. Now we consider the backup egress point selection in other planes. A key problem is how to perform the selection that can achieve the highest path diversity as we defined. For each backup plane, we consider the IGP paths the customer traffic will follow if we choose a certain egress router, and compare them with the paths already fixed in the previous step. We first count and sum up the total number of shared links between the two trees (the egress routers being considered as the root, and individual ingress routers as leaves). This summation value is inverse proportional to the degree of path diversity as we explained in Section 3.1. So the egress router associated with the smallest summation value can provide the highest path diversity. If there are several egress routers with equal path diversity, the selection will tie-break on the minimum bandwidth utilization of the inter-domain link associated with the egress router. If there are still equal candidates, one will be selected randomly. We then consider the next plane and follow the above selection process until all the planes have been considered. Until now, the selection process for one prefix is completed and the customer traffic for this prefix will all be assigned to the egress router selected for the default plane.

Step 5. We then consider the next prefix in the sorted order and repeat the procedure from steps 2 to 4. The heuristic finishes when all the prefixes have been considered.

4   Performance Evaluation

4.1   Experiment Setup

In order to evaluate the performance of our proposed algorithm, we used the topologies of two operational networks, namely the Abilene network [18] and the GÉANT network [19]. The Abilene network contains 11 Point-of-Presence (PoP) nodes and 28 unidirectional links. The GÉANT network contains 23 PoP nodes and 74 unidirectional links. In our experiments we use the actual IGP link weights configured in both operational networks. According to [20], only a small fraction of IP address prefixes are responsible for a large fraction of the Internet traffic. Based on this, we consider 100 popular routing prefixes in our experiments. As these routing prefixes are usually popular destinations, we assume that each egress router can reach all of them. For simplicity we assume that all inter-domain links have the same bandwidth capacity for both network topologies, and the traffic demand associated with each destination prefix is randomly generated. To produce more accurate results, each of the data points is an average of 10 independent trials.

4.2   Experiment Results

We first examine the overall path diversity performance by comparing the percentage of links that are fully shared by all M planes over the total number of links used by these planes (M is the number of planes used in the network). We assume 4 and 9 egress routers associated with the Abilene and the GÉANT network respectively. It should be noted that the total number of egress routers can be used as the upper bound for the number of routing planes to be used, as any additional routing plane will not help to increase path diversity any further. Consequently we only consider up to 4 routing planes in the Abilene network and 9 routing planes in the GÉANT network. What we are interested in is the proportion of those links that are fully shared or nearly fully shared by all routing planes as far as each ingress-prefix pair (i, k) is concerned. The reason for this is as follows. In order to maximize the chance of BGP fast reroute in case of intra-domain link failures, minimum number of fully shared links is desired. In addition, for those links that are not fully shared but are nearly fully shared by all routing planes, although it is still possible to perform fast reroute, as the number of feasible alternative egress routers is low, chances might be that these egress routers could suffer from congestion as the head node of the failed link has no alternative but to switch to them after the failure. Instead, if each head node has ample alternative egress routers in backup planes, it is able to perform intelligent egress

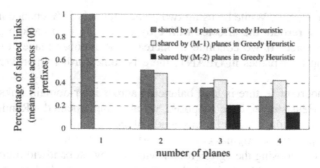

Fig. 2. Percentage of links shared by *M, (M-1)* and *(M-2)* planes separately in the Abilene network

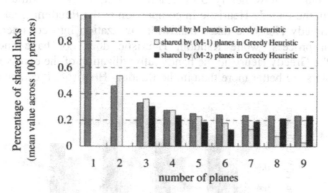

Fig. 3. Percentage of links shared by *M, (M-1)* and *(M-2)* planes separately in the GÉANT network

router switching in order to avoid post-failure congestion at backup egress routers. This feature will be investigated in our future work. Figures 2 and 3 present the percentage of links shared by *M, (M-1)* and *(M-2)* planes in the Abilene and GÉANT topologies respectively.

Both figures show that by increasing the total number of planes used in the network, the percentage of links shared by all *M* planes decrease. This can be explained as follows. When the number of planes increases, the total number of diverse paths that can be used to deliver customer traffic also increases; this can be reflected by the dramatic decreased number of shared links across individual topologies. For instance, if only one single topology is used (i.e. the conventional BGP routing), there is only one single intra-domain path from each of the ingress routers towards the selected egress point and apparently fast BGP reroute cannot happen in case of intra-domain link failures. If two routing topologies are used (*M=2*), the overall proportion of fully shared link drops significantly down to 52% and 46% in the Abilene and GÉANT networks respectively. As far as BGP fast reroute is concerned, let us assume one particular link fails in the current IGP path in the default plane from an ingress router to an egress router. If we use only one single plane, the traffic delivery will be disrupted because the traffic is unable to use the path until IGP re-converges. While by using two planes, there is 54% chance in GÉANT to successfully fast reroute the affected traffic by remarking it to backup planes which are already in place. If we continue to increase the number planes to 4 planes in Abilene and up to 9 planes in GÉANT, there is some further improvement but not significant.

Another important feature is load balancing across inter-domain links. In addition to the Greedy Heuristic we have proposed, we also implemented a Random Heuristic where no consideration is taken for any load-balancing purpose. More specifically, in Step 3 and Step 4 in the original Greedy Heuristic (shown in section 3.2), we ignore the procedure of choosing the egress router with the lowest bandwidth utilization, and instead we perform a purely random selection procedure. Figures 4 and 5 illustrate the maximum bandwidth utilization of each inter-domain link after network configuration using the Greedy Heuristic and Random Heuristic separately.

Figures 4 and 5 show nearly 30% improvement in the maximum bandwidth utilization from the Greedy Heuristic in comparison to the Random Heuristic. This is because the Greedy Heuristic takes bandwidth utilization into consideration in the path selection process, while Random Heuristic does not have such concern. Therefore in the Greedy Heuristic the bandwidth utilization of the egress links among the egress routers are better more than in the Random Heuristic. It can be also noticed

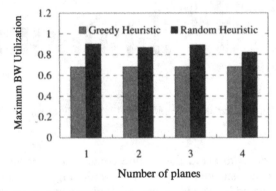

Fig. 4. Bandwidth utilization of each egress in the Abilene network

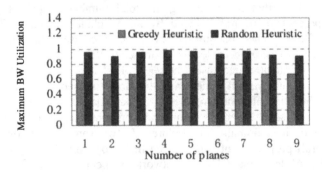

Fig. 5. Bandwidth utilization of each egress in the GÉANT network

that the maximum bandwidth utilization does not decrease with the increase in the number of routing planes. This is because we adopt the strategy that only one default plane is used for traffic delivery in the normal state with additional planes only activated in case of intra-domain link failures for fast reroute purposes. Of course further load balancing can be achieved *in the normal state* by optimally splitting the traffic across multiple active routing planes, therefore they can follow different IGP paths and use more than one egress router to be delivered out of the local domain. We will continue our investigation with this feature in our future research work.

5 Summary

Multi-plane aware routing protocols have been designed for providing diverse paths in traffic delivery. Based on the existing techniques, we have proposed a simple but efficient paradigm that enables multiple egress router selection for fast BGP reroute purposes in case of intra-domain link failures. More specifically, dedicated backup routing planes are provisioned a priori so that the repairing router is able to immediately remark the affected customer traffic to use additional egress points to be delivered out of the local domain without waiting for IGP to re-converge. In order to enable maximum chance for fast reroute, we developed a heuristic algorithm that aims to obtain maximum intra-domain path diversity across individual planes with the consideration of load balancing across egress routers. Our experiment results based on existing operational networks show that our proposed algorithm is able to produce significant diverse IGP paths with improved traffic engineering performance in comparison to random selection based solutions.

Our future work will focus on the improvement of the intra-domain path diversity, and we envisage that by intelligently manipulating IGP link weights will help improving such performance even without necessarily introducing multi-plane IGPs. In addition we will also investigate the scenario of using co-existing routing planes in the normal state (instead of using always one as described in this paper) in order to achieve adaptive load balancing against unpredicted traffic dynamics.

References

1. Awduche, D., et al.: Overview and Principles Of Internet Traffic Engineering, Request for Comments 3272, Network Working Group (May 2002)
2. Bressoud, T.C., et al.: Optimal Configuration for BGP Route Selection. In: IEEE INFOCOM (2003)
3. Bonaventure, O.: Achieving Sub-50 Milliseconds Recovery upon BGP Peering Link Failures. IEEE/ACM Transactions on Networking 15(5) (October 2007)
4. Kvalbein, A., et al.: Fast IP Network Recovery using Multiple Routing Configurations. In: Proc. IEEE INFOCOM 2006 (2006)
5. Shand, M., et al.: IP Fast Reroute with Notvia Addresses, IETF Internet draft, work in progress (February 2008)
6. Atlas, A.: Basic Specification for IP Fast-Reroute: Loop-free Alternates., IETF Internet draft, work in progress (2008)

7. Teixeira, R., et al.: Network Sensitivity to Hot-Potato Disruptions. In: Proc. ACM SIGCOMM, pp. 231–244 (2004)
8. Quoitin, B., et al.: Interdomain traffic engineering with BGP. IEEE Communications Magazine 41(5), 122–128 (2003)
9. Amin, M., et al.: Making Outbound Route Selection Robust to Egress Point Failure. In: Proc. IFIP Networking (May 2006)
10. Psenak, P., et al.: Multi-Topology (MT) Routing in OSPF, RFC 4915 (June 2007)
11. Przygienda, T., et al.: M-ISIS: Multi Topology (MT) Routing in IS-IS. RFC 5120 (February 2008)
12. Grffin, D., et al.: Inter-domain Routing through Quality of Service Class Planes. IEEE Communications 45(2), 88–95 (2007)
13. Feamster, N., et al.: Path Splicing with Network Slicing. In: Proc. ACM SIGCOMM Hot-Nets (2007)
14. Motiwala, M., et al.: Path Splicing. In: Proc. ACM SIGCOMM (2008)
15. Wang, J., et al.: Edge Based Traffic Engineering for OSPF Networks. Computer Networks 48(4), 605–625 (2005)
16. Menth, M., et al.: Network Resilience through Multi-Topology Routing. In: Proc. IEEE DRCN 2005 (2005)
17. Xu, W., et al.: MIRO: Multi-path Inter-domain Routing. In: Proc. ACM SIGCOMM (2006)
18. The Abilene Network,
    http://www.stanford.edu/services/internet2/abilene.html
19. The GÉANT Network, http://www.geant.net
20. Feamster, N., et al.: Guidelines for inter-domain traffic engineering. ACM SIGCOMM Computer Communications Review (fall 2003)
21. Han, J., et al.: An Experimental Study of Internet Path Diversity. IEEE Transactions on Dependable and Secure Computing 3(4) (October 2006)
22. Iannaccone, G., et al.: Analysis of Link Failures in a Large IP Backbone. In: Proc. ACM Internet Measurement Workshop (IMW) (2002)

Load-Balanced IP Fast Failure Recovery

Mingui Zhang[1], Bin Liu[1], and Beichuan Zhang[2]

[1] Computer Science and Technology Dept., Tsinghua University, Beijing, 100084, P.R. China
[2] Computer Science Dept., University of Arizona, Tucson, Arizona 85721, USA
zmg06@mails.tsinghua.edu.cn, bzhang@cs.Arizona.edu

Abstract. As a promising approach to improve network reliability, Proactive Failure Recovery (PFR) re-routes data traffic to backup paths without waiting for the completion of routing convergence after a local link failure. However, the diverted traffic may cause congestion on the backup paths if it is not carefully split over multiple paths according to their available capacity. Existing approach assigns new link weights based on links' load and re-calculates the routing paths, which incurs significant computation overhead and is susceptible to route oscillations. In this paper, we propose an efficient scheme for load balancing in PFR. We choose an adequate number of different types of loop-free backup paths for potential failures, and once a failure happens, the affected traffic is diverted to multiple paths in a well balanced manner. We formulate the traffic allocation problem as a tractable linear programming optimization problem, which can be solved iteratively and incrementally. As a result, only the flows affected by the failures are re-allocated to backup paths incrementally without disturbing flows not directly affected by the failures. Simulation results show that our scheme is computationally efficient, can effectively balance link utilization in the network, and can avoid route oscillations.

Keywords: OSPF; failure recovery; load balance; Linear Programming.

1 Introduction

One of the primary design goals of the Internet was to continue to function despite of the component failures [1]. At the IP level, when routers or links fail, the network should still be able to deliver the packets as long as alternative paths exist. In current routing protocols, such as OSPF (Open Shortest Path First) and IS-IS (Intermediate System to Intermediate System), routers are informed about network topology changes by update messages, and then re-calculate their routing paths accordingly. However, this approach incurs convergence delay, as it takes considerable long time for the update messages to propagate throughout the network and for the routers to re-calculate routing paths [2]. During the convergence period, packets may be delayed, dropped, or fall in temporary routing loops, which will definitely lead to significant performance degradation of on-serving applications.

A different approach for handling physical failures is Proactive Failure Recovery (PFR) ([3]), in which routers compute and store backup paths for potential failures beforehand, and once a *local* link failure is detected, a router will redirect traffic to backup paths right away instead of waiting for the completion of network-wide routing

N. Akar, M. Pioro, and C. Skianis (Eds.): IPOM 2008, LNCS 5275, pp. 53–65, 2008.

convergence. PFR has short failure recovery time and reduces the overhead of both update propagation and path re-calculation. Given that a large portion of failures in IP networks is short, transient failures [4], PFR should be able to improve the quality of packet delivery significantly.

In both the conventional routing convergence approach and the early work on PFR, routers redirect traffic affected by failures to alternative paths without load balancing considerations. The diverted traffic will easily cause uneven traffic reassignments, which either congests on already heavily loaded links, or under-utilizes lightly loaded links. Especially if other links are congested due to the diverted traffic, it defeats the goal of minimizing the impacts of failures to the application performance. Therefore, to be robust against failures, post-failure load balancing is particularly important.

Recently, "weight-setting" method [5] was used for load balancing in PFR [6]. Given that the demands have been projected from previous measurements, in order to find the weight set that can avoid congestions, the weights of links are re-assigned according to the load they carry: large weights for heavily loaded links and small weights for lightly loaded links, and then the routing paths are re-calculated based on the new link weights. In this way, part of the traffic will be shed from heavily loaded links to lightly loaded ones. The results in [5] show that changing weights for just a small percentage of links can significantly re-balance traffic load over the entire network.

However, re-calculating routing paths (e.g., running Dijkstra's algorithm) network-wide is expensive and time-consuming, and it may easily lead to routing oscillations as well. Weight-setting is often formalized as an optimization problem of Integer Linear Programming (ILP), which is NP-hard. Existing work has to resort to heuristics such as Tabu search [4] and local search [5]. The result does not guarantee convergence in that new weight assignment redistributes traffic, which will in turn affect weight assignment in the next round, and so forth. In some network settings, route oscillations can easily happen [7]. More recent work ([4], [6]) has put much efforts to try to refine the weight-setting method but no substantial improvements have been achieved.

Thinking in a different way, in this paper, instead of working on the "weight-seting", we turn to propose another light-weight yet efficient and stable scheme for post-failure load balancing with PFR. Each router prepares multiple backup paths for potential failures based on the best-path routing tables when the network is stable. Once a failure happens, the router will distribute the affected traffic over multiple backup paths through solving a Linear Programming (LP) problem incrementally, which is tractable and requires much less computation than ILP. The diverted traffic will be allocated on the multiple backup paths and the allocation will be further refined with the subsequent LP iterations. With this scheme, link weights keep unchanged and routers do not need to re-calculate their routing paths, but the load-balancing goal is perfectly achieved.

Two design challenges are addressed here in PFR and its post-failure load balancing: 1) how to select multiple loop-free backup paths with small overhead, and 2) how to decide the amount of affected traffic to be shed on each backup path in a well balanced manner. By proposing a unique solution, we make the following four contributions. 1) We explore and identify another two additional types of loop-free alternative paths locally besides the Equal-Cost-Multiple-Path [8] [9], which gives more path diversity for post-failure delivery; 2) In deciding traffic distribution over multiple paths, we formulate it as a LP problem minimizing the sum of link utilization. By solving the problem iteratively and assigning penalty factors to heavily loaded links, we actually achieve the goal of minimizing the maximum link utilization in the network; 3) We introduce a bias factor into the LP iteration to damp the oscillations; 4) Once a failure happens, the LP problem can be solved *incrementally* since only the traffic affected by the failures is taken into consideration by the LP objective function. Simulation results show that our scheme can effectively balance the load over multiple paths, has small computation overhead and converges fast.

The rest of the paper is organized as follows. Section 2 presents how we choose loop-free backup paths for failure recovery. Section 3 formulates the traffic allocation as a LP problem and describes how we solve it iteratively and incrementally. Section 4 evaluates the scheme's performance. Section 5 concludes the paper.

2   Alternative Paths Setup

In PFR, routers try to detect and recover failures locally rather than relying on network-wide routing convergence. Generally, a link failure will trigger the physical detection, which reports the event to the IP layer immediately. A router can locally find multiple paths forwarding the affected traffic on the failed link(s) via its neighbors. Figure 1(a) illustrates this by a simple example. Node u's next hop on its shortest path towards d is f. Node u also maintains alternative paths to reach d through other neighbors such as $a_1, a_2, \ldots, a_n$. When a local link $u \rightarrow f$ fails, u will shift its affected traffic to alternative paths, e.g., via a_1, without waiting for the completion of routing convergence. The diverted packets are marked (e.g., using the Type Of Service (TOS) field in the packet), so that the downstream routers will know that the packet is diverted and can make appropriate forwarding decisions.

PFR works mainly in intra-domain routing, or IGP, such as OSPF and IS-IS. It can handle single-link failures and multiple-link failures that do not affect each other. In other words, as long as the multiple failures do not disable all the alternative paths and the packets diverted to the alternative paths do not encounter another failure again, PFR works fine. Our work is within the same intra-domain routing scope and inheres the same limitation regarding multiple link failures. Our contribution is to set up and utilize multiple alternative paths (e.g., paths via $a_1, a_2, \ldots, a_n$ in Figure 1(a)) efficiently

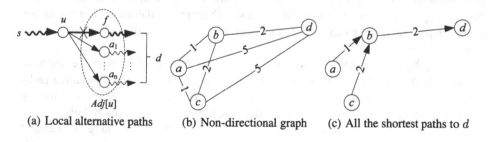

(a) Local alternative paths   (b) Non-directional graph   (c) All the shortest paths to d

Fig. 1. Demo graphs

to spread the adjusted traffic load to avoid potential post-failure congestions. This section describes how we choose multiple paths, and the next section describes how we distribute traffic over the multiple paths.

On one hand, given a destination, there can be a huge number of alternative paths from a router to reach the destination. It is not only impractical but also unnecessary to find all the possible alternative paths and store them. On the other hand, the number of alternative paths cannot be too small, otherwise they will not be able to serve the purpose of failure recovery and load balancing. Therefore, we need to find *adequate* number of *loop-free* alternative paths without significant computation overhead.

One way of doing multi-path routing is to split traffic among paths with the same IGP costs [8]. Those ECMPs should be able to be used for post-failure load balancing without introducing routing loops. We extend the Dijkstra's algorithm to calculate ECMP from a router to all destinations. We use ECMP for load balancing, but they do not have the adequate path diversity yet. At this point, we need other types of loop-free alternative paths.

We represent the network by a positive weighted bi-directional graph $G = (\mathcal{V}, \mathcal{A})$, where $\mathcal{V}$ is the set of vertexes and $\mathcal{A}$ is the set of arcs. Running Dijkstra's algorithm on G will generate shortest paths that form a tree rooted at the source vertex s. This tree is known as Shortest Paths Tree (SPT) [10]. We call the shortest paths generated by Dijkstra's algorithm the type-0 paths. Running the extended Dijkstra's algorithm will generate ECMP, which are called the type-1 paths. Type-0 paths are the primary forwarding paths, and type-1 paths are alternative paths. Further, we will calculate another two types of paths and prove that they can be used as alternative paths too.

We reverse the direction of each arc in the graph G, and then run Dijkstra's algorithm to get SPT regarding vertex d as the "root". Finally, by reversing back the directions of the arcs, we get a subgraph that gives every vertex's shortest path to the given destination d. Let G_π be the subgraph we get. Figure 1(c) is an example of G_π for the graph given in Figure 1(b). In the following discussion, we focus on the paths to a single given destination, i.e., G_π. It is difficult and unnecessary for u to get all the information of G_π locally. However, we can get a part of the information from u and its neighbors locally, as depicted in Figure 1(a). This part of information is enough for u to set up the other two types of alternative paths, as described in the following. We define the shortest path from s to d on G_π by $s \rightsquigarrow d$. $s \rightsquigarrow u \rightsquigarrow d$ is the shortest path from s to d going through u, $s \rightsquigarrow u \rightarrow f \rightsquigarrow d$ is the shortest path from s to d via arc $u \rightarrow f$, and $s \rightsquigarrow d/u \nrightarrow f$ represents the shortest path from s to d not via arc $u \rightarrow f$. Suppose there is a shortest path $p \rightsquigarrow q$. $s \rightsquigarrow d/p \nrightarrow q$ denotes the shortest path from s to d does not use any vertex or arc on $p \rightsquigarrow q$. When p can not reach q due to failures, s can still reach d safely using $s \rightsquigarrow d/p \nrightarrow q$.

On G_π, there is a single successor for each vertex. Assume f is the successor of u. We disable the connection of arc $u \rightarrow f$ proactively to prepare the alternative paths for u, which is $u \rightsquigarrow d/u \nrightarrow f$. In our work, we resolve $u \rightsquigarrow d/u \nrightarrow f$ locally instead of fixing up $s \rightsquigarrow d/u \nrightarrow f$ directly. When the arc $u \rightarrow f$ really fails, we use $s \rightsquigarrow u \rightsquigarrow d/u \nrightarrow f$ to replace $s \rightsquigarrow d/u \nrightarrow f$. u must go through its neighbors except f to bypass the failure: $u \rightsquigarrow d/u \nrightarrow f = u \rightarrow a \rightsquigarrow d/u \nrightarrow f$, here $a \in Adj[u] - \{f\}$.

Let $\mathbb{A}(u) = Adj[u] - \{f\}$. Since a's shortest path to d may or may not be affected by the failure, $\mathbb{A}(u)$ can be divided into 2 disjoint sets: $\mathbb{A}_1(u) = \{a|a \in \mathbb{A}(u)$ and $a \rightsquigarrow d = a \rightsquigarrow d/u \nrightarrow f\}$ and $\mathbb{A}_2(u) = \{a|a \in \mathbb{A}(u)$ and $a \rightsquigarrow d \neq a \rightsquigarrow d/u \nrightarrow f$ (i.e. $a \rightsquigarrow d = a \rightsquigarrow u \rightarrow f \rightsquigarrow d)\}$.

Theorem 1. *If $a \in \mathbb{A}_1(u)$ then $a \rightsquigarrow d = a \rightsquigarrow d/s \nrightarrow u$, i.e., $a \rightsquigarrow d$ does not use any vertex or arc on $s \rightsquigarrow u$.*

Proof. Assume $a \rightsquigarrow d$ uses any vertex v on $s \rightsquigarrow u$, v will go through $u \rightarrow f$ to d, then $a \rightsquigarrow d$ must be affected by the failed arc $u \rightarrow f$, namely $a \rightsquigarrow d \neq a \rightsquigarrow d/u \nrightarrow f$, i.e., $a \notin \mathbb{A}_1(u)$. We obtain a contradiction here. $\qquad\square$

Theorem 1 tells us that when $u \rightarrow f$ is failed, the shortest path of the neighbors in set $\mathbb{A}_1(u)$ is safe to be used by u without any risk of incurring a loop. Thus, we safely replace $u \rightsquigarrow d/u \nrightarrow f$ with $u \rightarrow a \rightsquigarrow d$.

The failure of arc $u \rightarrow f$ on the shortest path from s to d can be recovered by u locally. These alternative paths are stored *proactively* in router u, and we call them the type-2 paths.

All neighbors in set $\mathbb{A}_2(u)$ are not safe to be used, but we still have a method to obtain the alternative paths via part of them. Assume $u' \in \mathbb{A}_2(u)$. u' has its own type-2 alternative paths to bypass their shortest path failure of arc $u' \rightarrow f'$. Let $a' \in \mathbb{A}_1(u')$. If the type-2 alternative path $u' \rightarrow a' \rightsquigarrow d$ luckily does not go through the failed arc $u \rightarrow f$, i.e. $u' \rightarrow a' \rightsquigarrow d = u' \rightarrow a' \rightsquigarrow d/u' \nrightarrow f' = u' \rightarrow a' \rightsquigarrow d/(u' \nrightarrow f', u \nrightarrow f)$, u may use this path to establish its own alternative path as well. The paths established in this way are also safe for u, which can be insured by the following theorem.

Theorem 2. *If $u' \in \mathbb{A}_2(u)$, and $a' \in \mathbb{A}_1(u')$, assume $a' \rightsquigarrow d = a' \rightsquigarrow d/u \nrightarrow f$, then $a' \rightsquigarrow d = a' \rightsquigarrow d/s \nrightarrow u$.*

Proof. There are two possibilities for u': a) $u' \in \mathcal{V}[s \rightsquigarrow u]$ and b) $u' \notin \mathcal{V}[s \rightsquigarrow u]$. Here, $\mathcal{V}[s \rightsquigarrow u]$ denotes the set of all the vertexes on the shortest path from s to u. We get the contradictions respectively as following to prove the theorem.

a) $u' \in \mathcal{V}[s \rightsquigarrow u]$. Because f' is the successor of u' on G_π, u' is on the path $s \rightsquigarrow u$ and $u' \neq u$, f' must be on the path $s \rightsquigarrow u$ too. Then, $u' \rightarrow f' \in \mathcal{A}[s \rightsquigarrow u]$. $\mathcal{A}[s \rightsquigarrow u]$ denotes the set of all the arcs on the shortest path $s \rightsquigarrow u$. Here, f' may happen to be u. For the purpose of contradiction, we suppose $a' \rightsquigarrow d \neq a' \rightsquigarrow d/s \nrightarrow u$. That is to say the type-2 alternative path of u', $u' \rightarrow a' \rightsquigarrow d$ must go through a vertex v on the shortest path $s \rightsquigarrow u$, i.e. $v \in \mathcal{V}[s \rightsquigarrow u]$. If u uses this path, a loop will occur. According to theorem 1, $v \notin \mathcal{V}[s \rightsquigarrow u']$, thus $v \in \mathcal{V}[f' \rightsquigarrow u]$. $v \rightsquigarrow d$ must go through arc $u \rightarrow f$ as well. Consequently, $a' \rightsquigarrow d \neq a' \rightsquigarrow d/u \nrightarrow f$, which contradicts our assumption.

b) $u' \notin \mathcal{V}[s \rightsquigarrow u]$.
Obviously, $u' \rightarrow f' \notin \mathcal{A}[s \rightsquigarrow u]$, the failure of $u' \rightarrow f'$ will not break the connectivity of $s \rightsquigarrow u$. If the type-2 alternative path of u' goes through the vertex on $s \rightsquigarrow u$, it must go through the arc $u \rightarrow f$ as well. The contradiction is easy to get. $\qquad\square$

Therefore, according to Theorem 2, if u' meets the assumption in the theorem, we can safely replace $u \rightsquigarrow d/u \nrightarrow f$ with $u \rightarrow u' \rightarrow a' \rightsquigarrow d$. We call this kind of alternative

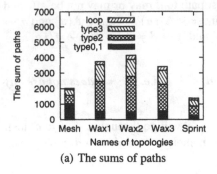
(a) The sums of paths

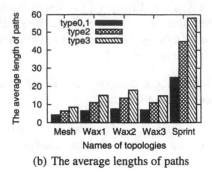
(b) The average lengths of paths

Fig. 2. The statistics of different kinds of paths

paths type-3 paths. u's remaining neighbors whose type-2 paths are affected by the failure of arc $u \rightarrow f$ can not be used or else loops will occur.

Always, the alternative paths can be configured explicitly using MPLS (Multiprotocol Label Switching) [11]. Nevertheless, MPLS does not appeal to ISPs due to its configuration overhead and vulnerability to human errors [9]. Mechanisms that can be employed in pure IP networks appear to be more potential in the near future [12]. When a failure occurs, the upstream router adjacent to the failure takes charge of the failure before the finish of the time-consuming routing convergence. It uses the alternative paths to bypass the failure, and mark whether the packets should be detoured or normally delivered by its downstream. The downstream router will determine locally which kind of paths should be used. The TOS field is a natural choice for us to do the marking, and there is similar work in IETF that deals with Multi-Topology routing [13]. However, our scheme need only one bit while Multi-Topology routing has to exploit several bits.

Figure 2 shows the statistics of different topologies including the Mesh-16-4 topology[1], three topologies with 20 nodes produced by the Waxman model [14] and the PoP-level North American Sprint IP backbone topology got from [4]. We use "Mesh", "Waxman" or "Wax" and "Sprint" for short respectively in this paper. Figure 2(a) shows that the alternative paths are plentiful and Figure 2(b) shows that the length of them are not very long despite of the bypass.

So far, the first design question has been solved efficiently and sufficiently. We move on to the next question: divert and balance the affected traffic onto the alternative paths.

3   Post-failure Load Balancing

After choosing the extra loop-free backup paths (type-2, type-3) besides ECMPs (type-1), we use them to balance the load in case of link failures. This section describes how to divert traffic onto backup paths so that the risk of causing congestions is minimized.

---

[1] There are 16 nodes and every node connects to 4 neighbors. The weight of each link is 1.

Table 1. ODL matrix

	ODL$(:,:,1)$				ODL$(:,:,4)$				ODL$(:,:,5)$			
	a	b	c	d	a	b	c	d	a	b	c	d
a	0	0	0	4	0	0	0	0	0	0	0	4
b	0	0	0	0	0	0	3	0	0	0	0	0
c	0	0	0	0	0	0	0	10	0	0	0	10
d	0	0	0	0	0	0	0	0	0	0	0	0

3.1 ODL Matrix

The traffic matrix of an IP network can be represented by the Origination-Destination matrix, i.e., the **OD** matrix [7]. $\mathbf{OD}(j,k)(j,k = 1, 2, ..., N; j \neq k)$ denotes the traffic volume originated from node j and destined to node k. Here N is the total number of nodes in the network.

Based on **OD** matrix an $N \times N \times L$ matrix, called **ODL** (Origin-Destination-Link) matrix, is devised in our work to record the details of the load distributed onto network links. Here, L is the total number of the links in the network. On the network in Figure 1(b), for example, router a wants to send 4 units of traffic to router d, router b wants to send 3 units of traffic to router c, and router c wants to send 10 units of traffic to router d. Given that only type-0 paths are used. The **ODL** matrix is given in Table 1.

All the elements of $\mathbf{ODL}(:,:,2)$, $\mathbf{ODL}(:,:,3)$ and $\mathbf{ODL}(:,:,6)$ are zeros which are not exhibited in Table 1.

The load of every link can be calculated conveniently from the data structure **ODL** through the manipulation of summarizing specific matrix's elements. We use vector **LLV** to denote the load on every link. For **ODL** given in Table 1, $\mathbf{LLV} = [4, 0, 0, 13, 14, 0]$.

3.2 The Formulation of Linear Programming

Previous work of the weight-setting approach formulates the traffic allocation problem as an ILP problem, which is NP-hard. We formulate it to a different LP problem instead, which is more tractable. With the multiple alternative paths established and the details encoded by the data structure **ODL**, the LP problem can be formulated as follows.

Suppose $\mathcal{P}_{jk}$ is the set of the paths from j to k. x_{jkp} is the share of traffic originated from j and destined to k through the pth path of $\mathcal{P}_{jk}$. Let **X** be the vector $[-x_{jkp}-](j,k = 1, 2, ..., N; j \neq k; p = 1, 2, ..., |\mathcal{P}_{jk}|)$. Denote the links' capacities as $\mathbf{c} = [c_1, c_2, ..., c_L]$ and link utilization as $\mathbf{u}=[u_1, u_2, ..., u_L] = \mathbf{LLV}./\mathbf{c}$, where the operator "./" denotes the element-by-element division of two vectors, i.e., $u_l = \mathbf{LLV}(l)/c_l$.

We simply sum up every link's utilization to get the objective function $f(\mathbf{X})$. An optimization problem of Linear Programming can be depicted as follows. By solving this problem, we get the optimal share of the traffic demand $\mathbf{X_{OPT}}$.

$$\min \; f(\mathbf{X}) = \sum_{l=1}^{L} u_l \tag{1}$$

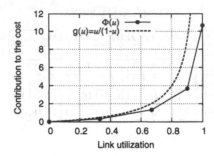

Fig. 3. The comparison between two cost functions. The curve of $\Phi(u)$ is similar to that of $g(u)$.

$$\text{subject to} \sum_{p=1}^{|\mathcal{P}_{jk}|} x_{jkp} = 1 \tag{2}$$

$$x_{jk(p-1)} \geq x_{jkp} \quad p = 2, \ldots, |\mathcal{P}_{jk}| \tag{3}$$

$$0 \leq x_{jkp} \leq 1 \tag{4}$$

Intuitively, longer paths should get less traffic. The paths in $\mathcal{P}_{jk}$ are indexed in an increasing order of the paths' lengths.

Weight-setting method has to resort to heuristic search to solve the ILP which is NP-hard [5]. We know that LP is always simpler than ILP. Therefore, our method should be simpler than weight-setting method.

When LP is finished, the backup paths already get their proportion of traffic according to their available capability. But we are not content with this and try to further refine the result in the next subsection.

3.3   LP Iteration

We use $f(\mathbf{X}) = \sum_{l=1}^{L} u_l$ in the last subsection as the objective function of LP, which treats the contribution of every link utilization to the overall cost equally. But $f(\mathbf{X})$ is not the true objective function of optimization. We introduce the *LP iteration* to do the refinement in the following.

First of all, the contribution of each link utilization u_l to the overall cost function can be estimated by

$$\mathbf{Ctb}(u_l) = \begin{cases} u_l/(1 - u_l), & 0 \leq u_l < 0.9 \\ 9, & u_l \geq 0.9 \end{cases} \tag{5}$$

This is based on the following analysis. Assume the IP network is a Jackson queuing network. A frequently used formula from [7] is:

$$D_{ij}(F_{ij}) = \frac{F_{ij}}{C_{ij} - F_{ij}} + d_{ij}F_{ij} \tag{6}$$

where F_{ij} is the traffic load on link (i, j) expressed in bit/s, C_{ij} is the transmission capacity of link (i, j) measured in the same units as F_{ij} and d_{ij} is the processing and propagation delay.

Suppose the utilization of link (i, j) is $u_{ij} = F_{ij}/C_{ij}$, and $d_{ij} = 0$, then

$$\sum_{(i,j)} D_{ij}(F_{ij}) = \sum_{(i,j)} \frac{u_{ij}}{1 - u_{ij}} \tag{7}$$

Let u be the utilization of a specific link, then this link's contribution to the cost function is

$$g(u) = u/(1 - u), u \in [0, 1] \tag{8}$$

The curve of $g(u)$ is depicted in Figure 3.

Previous work in [5] and [6] uses a piece-wise cost function:

$$\Phi(l(a)) = \begin{cases} l(a) & , 0 \le u(a) < 1/3 \\ 3l(a) - 2c(a)/3 & , 1/3 \le u(a) < 2/3 \\ 10l(a) - 16c(a)/3 & , 2/3 \le u(a) < 9/10 \\ 70l(a) - 178c(a)/3 & , 9/10 \le u(a) < 1 \\ 500l(a) - 1468c(a)/3 & , 11/10 \le u(a) < \infty \end{cases} \tag{9}$$

Here, $l(a)$ is the load carried by link a, $c(a)$ is the capacity of a and $u(a)$ is the utilization of a. Suppose $c(a) = 1$, then $l(a) = u(a)$. Depict the curve of $\Phi(u)$ in the same figure as $g(u)$. We find that the two curves are similar to each other. However, the objective function in Equation (9) is used arbitrarily without any analysis in [5] and [6]. It is still too complex to be used in the n-objective function, as it is a piece-wise linear function rather a linear function. Based on our analysis of a simplified network model, we use cost function (5) to estimate the contribution of a link to the overall cost.

With $\mathbf{Ctb}$, we define a penalty vector $\mathbf{p}$ as follows:

$$\mathbf{p} = (\mathbf{Ctb}/\max(\mathbf{Ctb}) + bias)/(1 + bias) \tag{10}$$

At each iteration, $f(\mathbf{X})$ is substitute with $\mathbf{p}.*f(\mathbf{X})$ and the LP is solved over and again. The operator ".*" denotes the element-by-element multiplication of two vectors. $bias$ is a substantial bias factor used to damp potential route oscillations. $bias \in [0, \infty)$ and $\mathbf{p} \in [0, 1]$. In [7], $bias$ has been mentioned as a measure for damp oscillations. Here, we use the $bias$ in a simple way in order not to introduce much computation cost. In our experiments, oscillations can happen too if the $\mathbf{Ctb}$ is used directly without $bias$. By comparison, weight-setting method mentioned in [4], [6] and [5] even does not address the issue of potential route oscillations.

3.4 Incremental LP Iteration

The traffic of the working paths affected by the failures should be shed on the alternative paths locally. If there is no alternative path for recovering the failures, the upstream router can send an ICMP (Internet Control Message Protocol) redirection message to the source, and then the source redirects its traffic to its own alternative paths. However, the traffic unaffected by the failures should remain undisturbed. That is to say, the shifting of the diverted traffic should be done *incrementally*. With the help of **ODL** matrix, the detail of the affected traffic can be easily gotten. We re-allocate affected traffic based on the current traffic distribution state with LP once. When LP is finished, the failure is recovered and the affected traffic is shifted onto the backup paths wisely. Then we further refine the traffic allocation with *incremental LP iteration*.

What incremental LP iteration regards as variables is the share of the failed traffic among alternative paths which can be denoted as $\mathbf{X}' = [-x_{jkp}-]$ ($\mathbf{OD}$ pairs (j, k) are the pairs whose type-0 paths are broken by the failures, $p = 2, 3, \ldots, |\mathcal{P}_{jk}|$). The sum of the variables here is smaller than that in the vector $\mathbf{X}$.

Incremental LP iteration does its best to avoid congestions and not to disturb the failure-unaffected traffic being carried by the network simultaneously. Weight-setting method usually decreases the lightly loaded links' weights to attract traffic while increasing the heavily loaded links' weights to reduce traffic. However, changing links' weights may affect a wide range of traffic, including those not directly affected by the failures. In certain network settings, this can easily cause route oscillations or performance degradation.

The speed-up of our work compared with the weight-setting method is three-fold: It replaces ILP with light-weighted LP; It damps oscillations so that the iteration converges quickly; Finally, it balances the diverted load locally without resorting to the time-consuming re-calculation of the routing paths in the whole network.

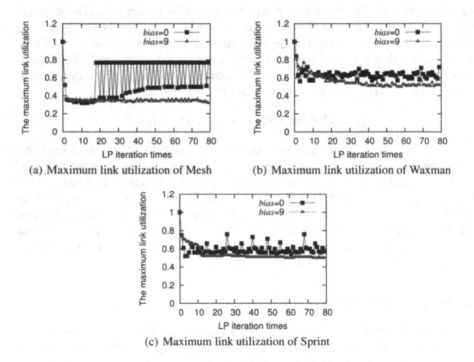

(a) Maximum link utilization of Mesh   (b) Maximum link utilization of Waxman

(c) Maximum link utilization of Sprint

Fig. 4. The comparison between LP iteration with and without *bias*. The *bias* damps the oscillations of LP iteration and makes it converge quickly.

4   Performance Evaluation

In our experiments, we use three kinds of different topologies mentioned in Section 2: Mesh, Waxman and Sprint. We generate the OD matrices synthetically according to the Gravity Model ([4], [15]) to conduct simulations to evaluate our scheme's performance.

We first evaluate the convergence of the LP iteration. Figure 4 compares the maximum link load resulted from using different *bias* values. It clearly shows that without the *bias* factor, oscillations can easily happen. The punishment from the penalty vector **p** is too harsh. The max link load varies greatly with iteration times and the algorithm does not converge. In the Mesh topology, the objective function even begins to get no feasible solution after a few iterations. With the *bias* factor, LP iteration is able to avoid route oscillations and converges fast. The value of *bias* can be tuned for particular IP networks as the operator usually has the full knowledge of the network. As to the topologies used in our simulation, the *bias* 9 is enough to damp the oscillations. Too large *bias* slows down the convergence of the LP interation. The stop condition can be easily got by setting an upper threshold for the maximum link utilization, e.g., 80%.

We fail each link independently in the networks of three kinds of topologies separately to evaluate the performance of incremental LP iteration. Figure 5 shows its results in comparison with what are achieved by Dijkstra's algorithm used in the "routing

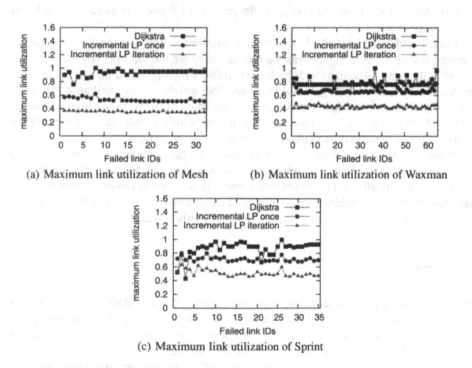

(a) Maximum link utilization of Mesh   (b) Maximum link utilization of Waxman

(c) Maximum link utilization of Sprint

Fig. 5. The maximum link utilization when incremental LP iteration and routing convergence happen respectively after each link's failure

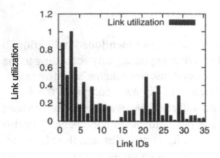

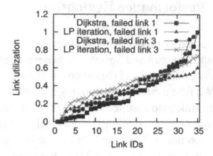

(a) Link utilization of Sprint before failures.

(b) Link utilization after routing convergence.

Fig. 6. Link 1 and link 3 are the most loaded links

convergence" after the failure. For most links (except link 1 and link 3 in Sprint topology), the "Incremental LP iteration" achieves much smaller maximum link load than Dijkstra's algorithm. It clearly demonstrates the effectiveness of using incremental LP iteration for post-failure load balancing. The lines with dots show the maximum link utilization when the incremental LP iteration is run one round immediately after the failure. Most of the time, the results of "Incremental LP once" is already much better than that of Dijkstra's.

Link 1 and link 3 are the links with the smallest weights in the Sprint topology derived from [4]. From Figure 6(a), we find that they are the most heavily loaded links. When either one fails, there will be lots of traffic which needs to be shed onto other paths. Conventional routing convergence and the weight-setting method re-calculate all routing paths, resulting in a widespread re-shuffling of traffic and smaller maximum link load. Incremental LP iteration keeps the impact within a small range of the network instead, and in these two particular cases, results in slightly higher link load.

If we let LP iteration take into consideration all traffic regardless of whether they are affected by the failures, our scheme can achieves better load balancing. Figure6(b) shows the results after the failure of link 1 and link 3 in Sprint topology. This time, LP iteration takes into consideration all the traffic carried on the network. Clearly it is able to shed more traffic from heavily loaded links to lightly loaded ones.

5   Conclusion

In this paper, we propose an efficient scheme to achieve load balancing with Proactive Failure Recovery (PFR). The algorithms are devised to set up loop-free alternative paths proactively. The redundancy of Internet offers us enough margin to set up alternative paths to re-allocate the traffic affected by the link failures.

Through Incremental Linear Programming, traffic demands are split among multiple paths optimally for the objective function and hence potential congestions are avoided. After the failed working routes shed their load and the diverted traffic is absorbed by the multiple alternative paths, the load can be further balanced with the help of incremental LP iteration. Our simulation results show that the proposed scheme is effective in reducing the maximum link load in the network after failures.

Acknowlegements

We would like to thank the anonymous reviewers for their feedback. This work was partly supported by NSFC (60573121, 60625201), China 973 program (2007CB310701), the Cultivation Fund of the Key Scientific and Technical Innovation Project, MoE, China (705003), the Specialized Research Fund for the Doctoral Program of Higher Education of China (20060003058), Tsinghua Basic Research Foundation(JCpy2005054), 863 high-tech(2007AA01Z216) and the China/Ireland Science and Technology Collaboration Research Fund (2006DFA11170).

References

1. Clark, D.D.: Design philosophy of the darpa internet protocols. Computer Communication Review 25(1), 102–111 (1995)
2. Francois, P., Filsfils, C., Evans, J., Bonaventure, O.: Achieving sub-second igp convergence in large ip networks. Computer Communication Review 35(3), 35–44 (2005)
3. Kvalbein, A., Hansen, A.F., Cicic, T., Gjessing, S., Lysne, O.: Fast ip network recovery using multiple routing configurations. In: Proceedings - IEEE INFOCOM, Barcelona, Spain, pp. 23–29 (2006)
4. Nucci, A., Bhattacharyya, S., Taft, N., Diot, C.: Igp link weight assignment for operational tier-1 backbones. IEEE/ACM Trans. Networks 15(4), 789–802 (2007)
5. Fortz, B., Thorup, M.: Internet traffic engineering by optimizing ospf weights. In: Proceedings - IEEE INFOCOM, Tel Aviv, Isr, vol. 2, pp. 519–528 (2000)
6. Kvalbein, A., Cicic, T., Gjessing, S.: Post-failure routing performance with multiple routing configurations. In: Proceedings - IEEE INFOCOM, Anchorage, AK, United States, pp. 98–106 (2007)
7. Bertsekas, D., Gallager, R.: Data Networks, 2nd edn. Prentice-Hall, Inc., Upper Saddle River (1992)
8. Chim, T.W., Yeung, K.L., Lui, K.S.: Traffic distribution over equal-cost-multi-paths. Computer Networks 49(4), 465–475 (2005)
9. Iselt, A., Kirstadter, A., Pardigon, A., Schwabe, T.: Resilient routing using mpls and ecmp. In: IEEE Workshop on High Performance Switching and Routing, HPSR, Phoenix, AZ, United States, pp. 345–349 (2004)
10. Cormen, T.H., Leiserson, C.E., Rivest, R.L., Stein, C.: Introduction to Algorithms, 2nd edn. MIT Press, Cambridge (2001)
11. Elwalid, A., Jin, C., Low, S., Widjaja, I.: Mate: Mpls adaptive traffic engineering. In: Proceedings - IEEE INFOCOM, Anchorage, AK, vol. 3, pp. 1300–1309 (2001)
12. Shand, M., Bryant, S.: Ip fast reroute framework. IETF Draft, Work in progress (June 2007)
13. Psenak, P., Mirtorabi, S., Roy, A.: Multi-topology (mt) routing in ospf. IETF RFC 4915 (June 2007)
14. Waxman, B.M.: Routing of multipoint connections. IEEE Journal on Selected Areas in Communications 6(9), 1617–1622 (1988)
15. Medina, A., Taft, N., Salamatian, K., Bhattacharyya, S., Diot, C.: Traffic matrix estimation: existing techniques and new directions. In: Proceedings - ACM SIGCOMM 2002, pp. 161–174. ACM, New York (2002)

A Study on Two New Protection Strategies

Alfred Bashllari and Dritan Nace

Laboratoire Heudiasyc UMR CNRS 6599
Université de Technologie de Compiègne
60205 Compiègne Cedex, France
{Alfred.Bashllari,Dritan.Nace}@hds.utc.fr

Abstract. In this paper we propose two new protection strategies based on the end-to-end survivability concept. The first one, called Shared Protection Robust Routing (SPRR) strategy can be seen as a generalized version of end-to-end rerouting with stub release. Numerical tests give encouraging performances for this scheme in comparison to the conventional end-to-end rerouting ones. However, as expected, it requires a higher (still not excessive) number of routes comparing to conventional schemes. A new, slightly different, scheme, called Elastic Robust Routing (ERR) strategy is provided next. Computational results for realistic network instances provide a comparison of both protection strategies and end-to-end rerouting with stub release in terms of overall network cost.

Keywords: Protection strategies, rerouting strategies, multi-commodity flow, linear programming, path generation, survivable networks.

1 Introduction

The recent apparition of new Internet services require additional resources. On the other hand, the Optical Transport Network (OTN) technology is replacing more and more the old transport layer technologies. Optical networks concentrate a huge amount of traffic in a single fiber, which could lead to considerables loss for telecommunication operator even in case of single link failure. Hence, it is a crucial issue for operators to find effective and fast survivable strategies in order to ensure the continuity of service in network even in failures state[1] situations. Moreover, the complexity of implementation and the cost of network configuration are very important issues to taken into account in survivable strategy choice. There exists actually several survivable strategies, each of them has its drawbacks and advantages concerning investment cost, management efforts and restoration performances. We distinguish two principal survivable strategies in telecommunication networks, *protection* and *rerouting* strategies. Protection strategies set up backup paths before failures occur and in case of failures switch the traffic verse backup paths. On the other hand, rerouting strategies reroute

---

[1] Failure state is defined as a network state where some hardware, in our case a link, has ceased to function. Conversely, nominal state is defined as the state where all network hardware is operational (without failure).

N. Akar, M. Pioro, and C. Skianis (Eds.): IPOM 2008, LNCS 5275, pp. 66–77, 2008.

the traffic over new precomputed backup paths after a failure occurred, see for instance two key references [3] and [4]. In this paper we propose two new protection strategies. The first one is called "Shared protection Robust Routing" (SPRR) strategy and the second one, "Elastic Robust Routing" (ERR) strategy. They allow, thanks to paths diversity, a high robustness level to cope with traffic oscillations and failure sitiations. More recently a new survivability concept, called demand-wise shared protection, has been proposed (for detail see [2,5,6,7]). Finally, this work is in continuation of our earlier works on survivable networks [1,9].

The paper is organized as follows. In section 2, we focus on rerouting strategies and give an example. In Section 3, we give in detail the mathematical models for SPRR and ERR strategies and describe how to solve them. Some numerical results illustrating the behavior of these protection schemes with respect to link failures as well as comparisons with classical end-to-end rerouting schemes are reported in Section 4. Finally in Section 5, we conclude.

2 Rerouting Strategies: An Example

With respect to traffic rerouting, various strategies exist to withstand single link failure. We recall here two rerouting strategies: the partial end-to-end rerouting with stub release, and global rerouting. For the first strategy, only the interrupted traffic may be rerouted (i.e., *partial*), in contrast to global rerouting which allows the rerouting of all traffic. More precisely, the partial end-to-end rerouting with stub release corresponds to the case where network resources used for traffic routing, can be released after a failure, and reused for traffic rerouting see for instance [10,11]. The above strategies were the starting point for studying new ones, as described below. Hence, we propose two protection strategies based on path diversity and bandwidth sharing to cope with traffic oscillations and link failure situations. The main idea behind the first strategy (i.e. SPRR) is as follows: the routing associated to each demand ensures a certain level of survivability thanks to path diversity. Next, when necessary, one can use backup paths to restore some disturbed demand (essentially through bandwidth released from some nominal paths). Indeed, the non disturbed demands will eventually contribute to restore the situation through releasing helpful resources used on their nominal routing paths. This is possible since the nominal routing allows practically to satisfy more than the nominal traffic demand value. As expected, this new scheme gives interesting performances in comparison to the conventional end-to-end rerouting ones. However, it requires a higher (still not excessive) number of routes comparing to conventional schemes. On the other hand it needs several releases and booking of paths which could become a burden from the operational point of view. To remedy this we propose another variant, called Elastic Robust Rerouting (ERR) scheme. *Elastic* stands here for the option of varying the bandwidth ratio associated with nominal paths according to the failure state. The main difference with respect to SPRR, is to use the same

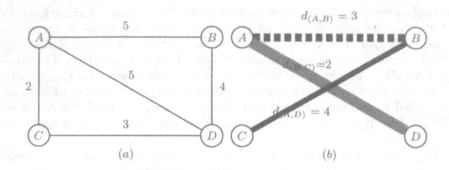

Fig. 1. Network description (a) and traffic demands (b)

set of nominal paths for both routing and rerouting. Let us now focus on the functioning of both methods through the following example.

Consider a network composed of 4 nodes A, B, C et D, 5 links (A, B), (A, C), (A, D), (B, D) and (C, D) with respectively 5, 2, 5, 4, and 3 unit capacities on them. (Figure 1(a)).

We assume three traffic demands: $(A, B), 3$ (black dashed), $(B, C), 2$ (black solid) et $(A, D), 4$ (gray), (Figure 1(b)).

Figure 2(a) shows the nominal routing, which satisfies the traffic demands beyond the nominal level. Figure 2(b) reports the obtained rerouting in case of failure of link (C, D). For instance, notice that there are two traffic demands perturbed from this failure: the black solid and the gray one. Clearly, for the gray demand there is no need to do any rerouting since the non perturbed nominal paths ensure 100% of the traffic demand, (one just need to switch the traffic on the perturbed path on the two remaining ones). On the other hand, we need to proceed with rerouting some of the lost traffic for the black solid demand. For this, we release some bandwidth from the nominal path $[A - D - B]$ already used for the black dashed demand, which will allow to establish the path $[C - A - D - B]$ to reroute one trafic unit for the black solid demand.

Let us see now how the ERR strategy works. Figure 3(a) reports the nominal routing, while in Figure 3(b) we show what happens in case of failure of link (C, D). We remark two perturbed demands: the black solid and the gray one. Contrarily to the SPRR strategy, we are not allowed to use a new path, that is, we are only allowed to enlarge the nominal paths. For this, we use bandwidth already available in the network and some other released from nominal paths of non perturbed demands. In this way, nominal paths $[A - B]$ et $[A - D - B]$ will release some bandwidth to be used for enlarging the capacity of $[B - A - C]$ et $[B - D - A - C]$ nominal paths used for the black solid demand. This allows to achieve full satisfaction for the black solid traffic demand. Nevertheless, the amount of available bandwidth is not sufficient to satisfy the gray demand more than 87.5% of its nomimal traffic volume.

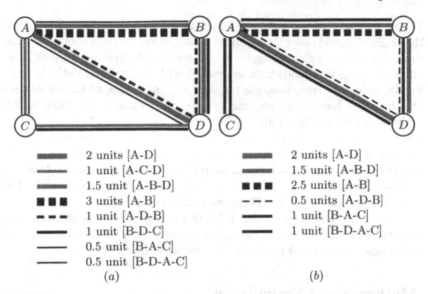

2 units [A-D]
1 unit [A-C-D]
1.5 unit [A-B-D]
3 units [A-B]
1 unit [A-D-B]
1 unit [B-D-C]
0.5 unit [B-A-C]
0.5 unit [B-D-A-C]
(a)

2 units [A-D]
1.5 unit [A-B-D]
2.5 units [A-B]
0.5 units [A-D-B]
1 unit [B-A-C]
1 unit [B-D-A-C]
(b)

Fig. 2. SPRR strategy: routing (a) and routing modifications after failure link (C, D) (b)

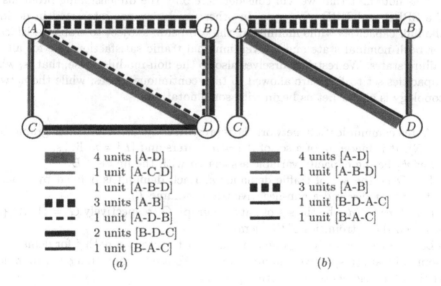

4 units [A-D]
1 unit [A-C-D]
1 unit [A-B-D]
3 units [A-B]
1 unit [A-D-B]
2 units [B-D-C]
1 unit [B-A-C]
(a)

4 units [A-D]
1 unit [A-B-D]
3 units [A-B]
1 unit [B-D-A-C]
1 unit [B-A-C]
(b)

Fig. 3. ERR strategy: routing (a) and routing modifications after failure link (C, D) (b)

For a better comprehension of the above, several points have to be emphasized:

1. There is no separation between resources devoted to routing and those devoted to restoration/protection; all the available bandwidth can be used in both situations.

2. The computed routing paths are dimensioned such that they allow satisfying the traffic demands over the nominal expected traffic (this should be possible since there is a single common pole of resources). Notice also that this will allow reducing the bandwidth associated with the routing paths in order to handle only the corresponding nominal traffic in case of failure situations. On the other hand, such routing scheme can handle peak traffic situations without any rerouting at all.

3. The restoration is realized by only enlarging the bandwidth associated with the routing paths of disturbed demands. This is made possible since some additional resources will become available by the bandwidth released from the failed routing paths as well as when reducing the bandwidth of some other routing paths of non-disturbed traffic demands[2].

4. The above method seems to be different of these known in literature as link or path restoration schemes, as well as these proposed in research literature as demand-wise shared protection for instance (see [2]).

3   Mathematical Formulation

Let us note first that we will consider here only the dimensioning problems for the SPRR and ERR strategies. In other words, we are interested in deciding the link capacities while minimizing the total sum subject to traffic satisfaction for both nominal state and a given minimal traffic satisfaction rate for all link failure states. We restrict ourselves also to the non-modular case, that is, where capacities set to links are allowed to take continuous values, while the network topology is given. Let us begin with some notation:

- A telecommunication network is represented by an undirected graph $G = (V, E)$. It is made up of a set of $|V| = n$ routers and $|E| = m$ links.
- Let ψ_e be the capacity variable associated with the link $e \in E$.
- Let D be the set of traffic demands d. Each demand is defined by a pair of extremity nodes and a non-negative traffic volume T_d.
- Let $h^0(d)$ ($h^l(d)$) be the set of paths of graph G (respectively $G^l = (V, A \setminus \{l\})$) between the extremities of the demand d.
- Let $x_{j,d}$ (respectively $z^l_{j,d}$) be the traffic part routed on path j for demand d in nominal state (respectively failure state l). We use the notation $e \in j$ to indicate that link e belongs to the routing path j.
- Let D'_l be the set of demands $d \in D$ disturbed from the link failure l: There exist a path $j \in h^0(d)$ such that $x_{j,d} \geq 0$ and $l \in j$.
- Let $y_{j,d}$ be the diminution value of nominal traffic part routed on path j of demand d, where $d \in D \setminus D'_l$.

---

[2] An option could be to have in addition to routing paths a few back-up restoration paths. This can lead to further reducing the amount of resources necessary for implementing this scheme.

The mathematical formulation for dimensioning problem of SPRR strategy is as follows:

$$Min \quad \sum_{e \in E} \psi_e$$

subject to:

$$(\pi_e^0) \qquad \psi_e \geq \sum_{\substack{j \in h^0(d), d \in D \\ e \in j}} x_{j,d} \qquad e \in E \tag{1}$$

$$(\mu_d^0) \qquad \sum_{j \in h^0(d)} x_{j,d} \geq T_d \qquad d \in D \tag{2}$$

$$(\pi_e^l) \quad \psi_e \geq \sum_{\substack{j \in h^0(d) \\ d \in D \setminus D_l', e \in j}} (x_{j,d} - y_{j,d}^l) +$$

$$\sum_{\substack{j \in h^0(d), l \notin j \\ d \in D_l', e \in j}} x_{j,d} + \sum_{\substack{j \in h^l(d) \\ d \in D_l', e \in j}} z_{j,d}^l \quad e \in E, l \in E \tag{3}$$

$$(\mu_d^l) \quad \sum_{\substack{j \in h^0(d) \\ l \notin j}} x_{j,d} + \sum_{j \in h^l(d)} z_{j,d}^l \geq \alpha T_d \quad d \in D_l', l \in E \tag{4}$$

$$(\theta_d^l) \qquad \sum_{j \in h^0(d)} (x_{j,d} - y_{j,d}^l) \geq \alpha T_d \qquad d \in D \setminus D_l', l \in E \tag{5}$$

$$x_{j,d} - y_{j,d}^l \geq 0 \qquad d \in D \setminus D_l', \forall j, l \tag{6}$$

$$x_{j,d} \geq 0, z_{j,d}^l \geq 0, y_{j,d}^l \geq 0, \psi_e \geq 0 \; \forall d, j, l, \tag{7}$$

where α gives the satisfaction demand rate in failure case, fixed from network operator.

Constraints (1) (respectively (3)) express capacity constraints in nominal (respectively failure) state. Constraints (2) ensure the satisfaction of traffic in nominal state and constraints (4) (respectively (5)) ensure that minimal traffic satisfaction rate for disturbed (respectively non-disturbed) demands in any link failure state is equal to α. Constraints (6) guarantee that diminution of traffic volume over non-disturbed demand paths is lower then correspondent nominal traffic. Finally, non negativity of variables is expressed by constraints (7).

Before considering the ERR case, let us recall that the main difference with the SPRR one consists in two points: first, with ERR we are not allowed to build a new rerouting/backup path; only these already used for nominal routing are available; second, we restrict the release of bandwidth from nominal paths to a certain level. Thus, we use a set of nominal paths with varying bandwidth (within given limits) in order to cope with failure situations. In the following, let us note with $w_{j,d}^l$ the increasing value of nominal traffic part routed on non-perturbed path j of demand d, where d is disturbed from link failure l ($d \in D_l'$). The mathematical formulation for dimensioning problem of ERR strategy is as follows:

$$Min \sum_{e \in E} \psi_e$$

subject to:

$$(\pi_e^0) \quad \psi_e \geq \sum_{\substack{j \in h^0(d), d \in D \\ e \in j}} x_{j,d} \qquad e \in E \tag{8}$$

$$(\mu_d^0) \quad \sum_{j \in h^0(d)} x_{j,d} \geq T_d \qquad d \in D \tag{9}$$

$$(\pi_e^l) \quad \psi_e \geq \sum_{\substack{j \in h^0(d) \\ d \in D \setminus D_l', e \in j}} (x_{j,d} - y_{j,d}^l) +$$

$$\sum_{\substack{j \in h^0(d), l \notin j \\ d \in D_l', e \in j}} (x_{j,d} + w_{j,d}^l) \qquad e \in E, l \in E \tag{10}$$

$$(\mu_d^l) \quad \sum_{j \in h^0(d), l \notin j} (x_{j,d} + w_{j,d}^l) \geq \alpha T_d \qquad d \in D_l', l \in E \tag{11}$$

$$(\theta_d^l) \quad \sum_{j \in h^0(d)} (x_{j,d} - y_{j,d}^l) \geq \alpha T_d \qquad d \in D \setminus D_l', l \in E \tag{12}$$

$$x_{j,d} - w_{j,d}^l \geq 0 \qquad d \in D_l', \forall j, l \tag{13}$$

$$k x_{j,d} - y_{j,d}^l \geq 0 \qquad d \in D \setminus D_l', \forall l, j \tag{14}$$

$$x_{j,d} \geq 0, w_{j,d}^l \geq 0, y_{j,d}^l \geq 0, \psi_e \geq 0 \; \forall d, j, l \tag{15}$$

where α give the satisfaction demand rate en failure case, fixed from network operator and k gives the allowed diminution bandwidth ratio associated with nominal routing paths. For example for $k = 1/2$ we limit the traffic diminution until 50% of nominal traffic in corresponding paths. Constraints (14) ensure that diminution of traffic volume over non-disturbed demand paths is lower then correspondent nominal traffic and constraints (13) guarantee that traffic increase value in non-perturbed paths of disturbed demands does not exceed traffic nominal in corresponding paths.

Complexity issues: The above problem can be solved using the column generation method where the new columns represent candidate paths. We can remark that the reduced cost associated with each column (path $j \in h^0(d)$) is given as follows:

$$-\sum_{e \in j}(\pi_e^0 + \sum_{l \notin j} \pi_e^l) + \sum_{l \notin j} \mu_d^l + \mu_d^0. \tag{16}$$

The problem of computing paths of negative reduced costs has been studied by Maurras and Vanier in [10] and Orlowski in [11]. They consider a general formulation of the above problem[3], and show its NP-completeness. However, it

---

[3] Indeed, no considerations on the relation among dual coefficients involved in (16) are taken into account and therefore no conclusions can be drawn on the complexity of the initial problem itself.

can be shown that this problem can be solved in polynomial time for the case of a fixed l link failure (see [9]).

To solve the ERR dimensioning problem we use the column generation method where once again the reduced cost associated with each column (path $j \in h^0(d)$) is given by (16). Hence, the pricing problem associated with (8)-(15) problem is NP-Complete.

4   Computational Results

We provide here some computational results with respect to the above presented dimensioning problems. The solution methods are based on the column generation method, which in our case, corresponds to the shortest path computation in the initial graph valued by dual coefficients. They are implemented in C++ using CPLEX 10.1. All tests are run on a machine with the following configuration: Windows XP, Duo processor 1,66 GHz, 1 GB of RAM.

In Table 1 we summarize the main characteristics of the network instances used in our tests.

Table 1. Networks description

Networks	NET_6	NET_11	NET_15
Nodes	6	11	15
Links	11	25	30
Demands	15	55	105

Let us note with *SumSPRR* (respectively *SumERR*, *SumWR* and *SumGR*) the optimal objective function value for the dimensioning problem related to shared protection robust routing (respectively elastic robust routing, end-to-end with stub release rerouting and global rerouting).

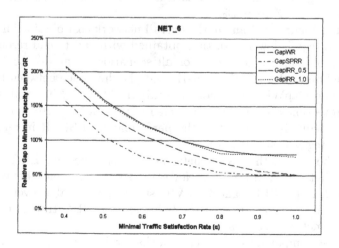

Fig. 4. Relative gaps for the 6 nodes network

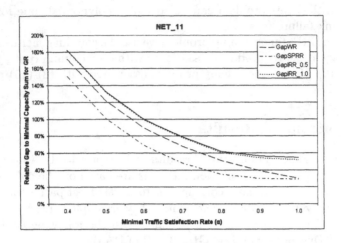

Fig. 5. Relative gaps for the 11 nodes network

GapSPRR: The relative gap between *SumSPRR* and *SumGR* calculated according to formula : 100*(SumSPRR - SumGR)/SumGR.

GapWR: The relative gap between *SumWR* and *SumGR* calculated according to formula : 100*(SumWR - SumGR)/SumGR.

GapERR: The relative gap between *SumERR* and *SumGR* calculated according to formula : 100*(SumERR - SumGR)/SumGR.

For ERR strategy we note **GapERR_0.5** (respectively **GapERR_1.0**) the relative gap corresponding to dimensioning problem for $k = 0.5$ (respectively $k = 1.0$). In Figure 4 (respectively 5 and 6) we present **GapSPRR**, **GapERR_0.5**, **GapERR_1.0** and **GapWR** as function of minimal traffic satisfaction rate for failures stats (α), for networks of 6 (respectively 11 and 15) nodes. We consider 7 scenarios varying the minimal traffic satisfaction rate for all situations (nominal and failures) from 40% to 100%.

As shown in Figures 4, 5 and 6, the overall network cost obtained implementing SPRR strategy is lower than that obtained with end-to-end rerouting with stub release, and this remains true for all scenarios (from 40% to 100%) and all considered networks. We also remark that the difference between two curves (GapSPRR and GapWR) is considerable (about 20%) and it remains constant till a high protection level (85%), to become insignifiant for protection level equal to 100%. Consequetly as expected, the performance of SPRR in relation with rerouting strategies is satisfactory.

On the other hand, the overall network cost obtained for ERR strategy is higher than that with WR strategy. Nevertheless, the difference between curves (GapERR_1.0, GapERR_0.5 and GapWR) stays in reasonable level, it varies to 10% till 20%. We also remark that the behaviour of ERR strategy for different values of parameter k is almost the same.

We have also compared the number of paths involved in respectively three different strategies discussed above (SPRR, WR and ERR) in all considered net-

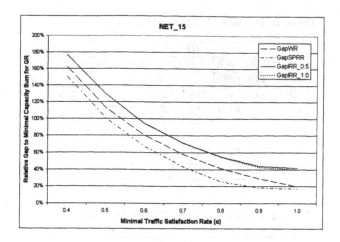

Fig. 6. Relative gaps for the 15 nodes network

works. In table 2 (respectively 3 and 4) we report the number of paths for different traffic satisfaction rate level and for three strategies implemented on network of 6 (respectively 11 and 15) nodes. We note that for WR and SPRR strategies this number includes all rerouting paths used in different link failure situations.

SPRR: Number of routing/rerouting paths for dimensioning problem of SPRR strategy.

WR: Number of routing/rerouting paths for dimensioning problem of WR strategy.

ERR: Number of routing/rerouting paths for dimensioning problem of ERR strategy.

DiSPRR: Number of diminutions in routing paths for dimensioning problem of SPRR strategy.

DiERR: Number of diminutions in routing paths for dimensioning problem of ERR strategy.

InERR: Number of increases in routing paths for dimensioning problem of ERR strategy.

Table 2. Number of paths for 6 nodes network

NET_6					
α	SPRR	WR	ERR	DiSPRR	DiERR	InERR
40%	39	97	14	50	11	1
50%	40	88	34	54	31	16
60%	55	91	14	82	10	2
70%	65	97	10	77	11	9
80%	82	107	43	94	80	65
90%	78	108	44	94	87	71
100%	61	89	48	52	82	80

Table 3. Number of paths for the 11 nodes network

NET_11						
α	SPRR	WR	ERR	DiSPRR	DiERR	InERR
40%	140	395	52	195	108	7
50%	147	413	118	245	117	265
60%	188	428	114	370	228	96
70%	225	426	129	550	701	200
80%	282	454	144	1155	988	249
90%	329	460	145	1045	1041	276
100%	302	418	137	524	896	261

Table 4. Number of paths for the 15 nodes network

NET_15						
α	SPRR	WR	ERR	DiSPRR	DiERR	InERR
40%	269	798	158	305	413	108
50%	267	838	210	339	586	106
60%	345	971	217	541	822	207
70%	371	1040	259	616	699	361
80%	425	1048	261	1593	937	420
90%	589	1091	270	2507	1198	530
100%	614	898	273	1045	1155	536

From Tables 2, 3 and 4 we remark first that the number of paths obtained for ERR strategy is about three times less than this for WR strategy, and this holds for all scenarios and all considered networks. This property could probably facilitate the implementation of this strategy. Hence, we can say that in spite of less performance of ERR in relation to the WR from the cost point of view, it seems more simple and fast to implement.

We remark also that the number of routing/rerouting paths obtained for SPRR strategy is lower then this for WR strategy and for some scenarios it becomes till two times less. On the other hand, SPRR gives always better performances in comparison to WR strategy.

5   Conclusion

In this paper we propose two new protection strategies and develop a computation method with respect to the routing paths associated to these strategies. The number of obtained paths remains quite acceptable: in our experiments we have more or less three paths associated to a traffic demand. We estimate also the induced cost with respect to all above cited protection or rerouting strategies. The obtained results show that ERR gives encouraging results comparing to these with end-to-end rerouting strategies (path restoration), well-known in the literature.

We think that the proposed method has the merit of handling both peak traffic situations and failure ones by simply relying on a given predetermined set of paths. From resource performance viewpoint, this method can be placed between the global rerouting, which requires rerouting of all traffic demands (disturbed or not), and the partial end-to-end rerouting, which apply for rerouting of only disturbed traffic demands between the corresponding extremities. We also hope that from the operational point of view, its implementation can be handled in a simpler way by making use of MPLS. However, from operational/feasibility viewpoint at least two questions need to be clarified: First, what is the signaling procedure associated with. The second point is related to the potential of the MPLS in implementing such an idea; that is checking if the "re-dimensioning" of LSP paths with respect to the failure situation is possible.

References

1. Bashllari, A., Nace, D., Gourdin, E., Klopfenstein, O.: A Simple Robust Routing Scheme. In: 6th International IEEE Conference on Design of Reliable Communication Networks (DRCN 2007), La Rochelle, France,October 7-10 (2007)
2. Koster, A.M.C.A., Zymolka, A., Jager, M., Hulsermann, R., Gerlach, C.: Demand-wise Shared Protection for Meshed Optical Networks. Journal of Network and Systems Management 13(1), 35–55 (2005)
3. Grover, W.D.: Mesh-based survivable networks. Prentice Hall, Englewood Cliffs (2003)
4. Pickavet, M., Demeester, P., Vasseur, J.Ph.: Network recovery. Morgan Kaufmann, San Francisco (2004)
5. Wessaly, R., Orlowski, S., Zymolka, A., Koster, A.M.C.A., Gruber, C.: Demand-wise Shared Protection Revisited: A new Model for Survivable Network Design. In: Proc. of International Network Optimization Conference (INOC), Lisbon, pp. 100–105 (March 2005)
6. Gruber, C., Wessaly, R., Orlowski, S., Zymolka, A., Koster, A.M.C.A.: A Computational Study for Demand-wise Shared Protection. In: Proc. of International Workshop on Design of Reliable Communication Networks (DRCN), pp. 421–428 (October 2005)
7. Hulsermann, R., Jager, M., Koster, A.M.C.A., Orlowski, S., Wessaly, R., Zymolka, A.: Availability and Cost Based Evaluation of Demand-wise Shared Protection. In: Proc. ITG Workshop on Photonic Networks, pp. 161–168. VDE Verlag GmbH, Leipzig, Germany (2006)
8. Pioro, M., Medhi, D.: Routing, Flow and Capacity Design in Communication and Computer Networks. Morgan Kaufmann Publishers, San Francisco (2004)
9. Bashllari, A., Nace, D., Gourdin, E., Klopfenstein, O.: The Max-Min Fair Rerouting Computation Problem. In: International Network Optimization Conference (INOC 2007), Spa, Belgium, April 22–25 (2007)
10. Maurras, J.-F., Vanier, S.: Network Synthesis under Survivability Constraints. 4OR Quarterly Journal of Belgian, French, and Italian Operations Research Societies 2(1), 53–67 (2004)
11. Orlowski, S.: Local and global restoration of node and link failures in telecommunication networks. Diploma thesis, Konrad-Zuse-Zentrum fr Informationstechnik Berlin (ZIB), Berlin, Germany (2003)

IP Multicast Traffic Measurement Method with IPFIX/PSAMP

Atsushi Kobayashi, Yutaka Hirokawa, and Haruhiko Nishida

NTT Information Sharing Platform Laboratories
3-9-11 Midori-cho, Musashino, Tokyo 180-8585, Japan
akoba@nttv6.net, hirokawa.yutaka@lab.ntt.co.jp,
nishida.haruhiko@lab.ntt.co.jp

Abstract. This paper presents a method of measuring traffic of IP multicast streaming, such as IPTV, by using IPFIX/PSAMP. An IP multicast streaming service has recently become one of the popular network services. Yet, the method of IP multicast operation has not been established. In particular, traffic measurement of IP multicast streaming encounters two big challenges, such as monitoring a multicast path tree and QoS performance. There is no method to monitor them continuously in large-scale networks. Hence, we focus on the IPFIX/PSAMP applied in the standardization as a successor of NetFlow/sFlow, and explore the new measurement method and system architecture suitable for larger-scale networks. In addition, we demonstrate experimental results of a prototype measurement system.

Keywords: IPFIX, PSAMP, IPTV, Multicast.

1 Introduction

IP multicast is a useful service for offering video streaming, such as IPTV, to a lot of users, by consuming minimal network resources. Increasing the number of broadband users leads to heavy demand for IP multicast streaming services. On the other hand, IP multicast traffic needs to be monitored from a different perspective than that of IP unicast and managed in more complex situations.

In that case, network operators already use several tools for aiding network management, troubleshooting, and diagnosis for multicasts, but they are not enough for monitoring IP multicast streaming services. The following shows several tools and their weak points.

- Multicast ping and trace route

Network operators try to investigate failure points between sender and receivers by using multicast ping and multicast trace route when network failure occurs or customers inquire about the multicast service condition. Multicast ping can collect responses from end hosts, but that is not actual traffic, and investigating failure points is not easy. Multicast trace route can also show the multicast path, but that path is

N. Akar, M. Pioro, and C. Skianis (Eds.): IPOM 2008, LNCS 5275, pp. 78–90, 2008.

incomplete because the path indicates the reverse path of actual traffic from downstream to upstream.

- Multicast routing MIB

To ensure the reach of multicast traffic for subscribers, network operators need to manage subscribers of multicast services, and understand the multicast path tree by multicast routing entries based on the pair of source address and multicast group address using Multicast Routing MIB [1]. However, the MIB module related to only IPv4 has not become a popular solution to multicast measurement, nor has an MIB module related to IPv6 been established.

- Packet mirroring

To confirm service quality, network operators make use of packet mirroring as the last resort. Network operators need to examine carefully mirrored multicast packets, and they check if there are lost packets or disordered packets. To monitor the service quality, using mirroring packets is the only solution at this time. This solution cannot be introduced into the whole network domain. It is a costly alternative.

These existing tools work well within some network domain scale. However, existing tools cost a great deal and a lot of effort is required to introduce them to Internet Service Providers (ISPs). In addition, actual multicast traffic behavior that passes through networks cannot be monitored constantly between receiver and sender.

Regarding the traffic measurement, IP Flow Information eXport (IPFIX) [2] and Packet SAMPling (PSAMP) [3] have proposed the flow- or packet-based passive measurement methods in IETF to support several monitoring applications, such as anomaly detection and QoS monitoring. Therefore, IPFIX/PSAMP allows operators to monitor the actual IP multicast streaming services, such as multicast service quality and multicast path tree, and provide easy operation with a cost-effective method.

A QoS measurement method used with IPFIX for RTP has been proposed by several groups [4,5]. However, measurement methods for IP multicast using IPFIX/PSAMP have not yet been studied much. In the near future, if the estimation approach for Quality of Experience (QoE) by monitoring packets is developed, network operators would be able to monitor QoE by using IPFIX/PSAMP. A QoE estimation method has just started, as described in [6].

In IP multicast streaming traffic measurement, there are two big challenges, such as monitoring service quality and the multicast path tree. To overcome those challenges, we mainly propose the system architecture for IP multicast traffic measurement on large-scale networks and traffic information elements, which are notified by IPFIX protocol. In addition, we evaluate the feasibility of this approach by developing a prototype of the measurement system.

The organization of this paper is as follows. Section 2 explains the IPFIX protocol and PSAMP summary as an introduction. Section 3 summarizes the requirements for IP multicast streaming traffic measurement methods. In Section 4, we propose measurement methods based on these requirements. In Sections 5 and 6, we show the prototype version of measurement systems and its evaluation results. Finally, we conclude this paper in Section 7.

2 IPFIX/PSAMP Summary

Flow-based measurements, such as NetFlow [7] or sFlow [8], are widely used in several ISPs. The standard for flow-based measurement, which is IPFIX, has been proposed in IETF. IPFIX mainly defines the protocol that delivers flow statistics data from IPFIX exporters, such as routers or switches, to IPFIX collectors that visualize or analyze that data. A flow indicates a set of packets, which have common properties in a given time interval at an observation point. IPFIX mediators in [9], as intermediate devices, have recently been discussed in IETF. The following sections show the features of IPFIX protocol and PSAMP.

2.1 IPFIX

IPFIX protocol has been developed as extended NetFlow v9 in [7]. NetFlow v9 uses flexible and extensible template architecture, as opposed to a fixed format style, such as NetFlow v5. The template, which includes information element identifier fields and their own length fields defined in [7], indicates the data structure of a flow record. Hence, NetFlow v9 can accommodate various kinds of packets, such as IPv6 or MPLS, by changing the template data structure. Optional data, which is metadata related to the flow record, is exported by using an option template. Generally, exporting a sampling rate and a sampling algorithm is used by an option template. Other than template structure, IPFIX has the following features.

- Reliable SCTP/TCP transport session protocols can be used.
- Enterprise-specific information elements can be applied as vendor-specific extensions. Therefore, each vendor can create unique information elements except for IPFIX-specified information elements [10].
- Variable length information elements can be applied to the template. That makes a more flexible data structure. For example, packet-based data, such as IP header or Ether frame header, which means a series of octets from the start of the header that can also be included with parts of the payload, can be delivered through the IPFIX protocol.

2.2 PSAMP

PSAMP mainly defines several sampling and filtering techniques to measure the packet-based traffic behavior in [11]. The combination of these techniques provides more elaborate traffic measurement from the viewpoint of efficiency and accuracy. Extracted packet-based data are also delivered by IPFIX protocol from exporters to collectors. Basic sampling and filtering methods are listed below.

- Sampling: Systematic Sampling, Random Sampling
- Filtering: Property match Filtering, Hash-based Filtering

Random sampling performed by the sampling algorithm means that the algorithm decides whether to select or not select observed packets by generating a randomized number. Generally, this method is widely used to reduce the load of exporters in ISPs. Systematic sampling means that all packets observed are selected periodically according to a time-based selection interval or packet-count-based selection interval. The property match filtering is similar to the access list filtering widely embedded in routers. In addition, routers' status properties, such as uRPF or unreachable packet, are supported. Hash-based filtering is called Trajectory Sampling.

2.3 Multicast Flow

Regarding multicast flow, the IPFIX requirement RFC [12] mentions that IPFIX exporters should maintain incoming flow and discrete flow per different output interface. Therefore, IPFIX collectors can recognize an input interface and output interfaces by gathering all the data. However, replicated flow records are exported all at once in detecting a flow timeout. That burst IPFIX packets become a serious problem at access routers in which thousands of subscribers have joined, as described in [13]. If operators reduce a flow timer to measure more accurate traffic, the volume of IPFIX packets becomes larger and larger. And also, packet-based data reports become huge volume. It is clearly the overload for collectors. In PSAMP documents, there is no description about exporting packet-based data by using PSAMP.

3 Requirements of Measurement System

As mentioned in Section 1, the main requirement of the measurement system for network operators is to keep rough track of the behavior of IP multicast streaming traffic on large-scale networks. Measurement systems are assumed to be utilized for trouble shooting, when an incident happens or customers inquire about the service conditions. Therefore, in-depth measurement for determining service quality, zapping, and accounting management are outside the scope of this paper. We describe the requirements to keep track of IP multicast streaming traffic, as follows.

- Requirement #1: Visualizing Multicast Path Tree
Measurement system needs to visualize a multicast path tree per multicast group address in real time on the network topology to monitor the streaming path from upstream servers to downstream subscribers. Therefore, network operators can recognize if the route of a multicast path on the network topology is correct or not.
- Requirement #2: Detecting Service Quality Deterioration
IP multicast streaming service is sensitive to network performance, such as packet loss or disorder. Therefore, detecting a packet loss or disorder continuously is required, even if at a certain level accuracy is not sufficient. In large-scale networks, the observed packets in multiple IPTV channels at multiple observation points generate a large amount of traffic data. Thus, monitoring all streaming packets and estimating the precise service quality is difficult.

To build the system, we need to utilize the sampling functions of PSAMP and monitor serious network failure affecting service quality. For example, let us assume the following scenario: a packet loss at some point happens continuously at rate 1/1000 affecting the service quality. The measurement system detects the network failure within one minute before several IPTV subscribers inquire about the service condition.

-     Requirement #3: Showing the failure point on the multicast path tree

Showing the failure points on the map visualizing the multicast path tree is required. Hereby, network operators can recognize the failure point and the impact of the failure, such as the number of affected subscribers.

4 Proposal of Measurement Method

As mentioned in Section 2.3, the rule described in [12] related to multicast flow is not suitable for exporting packet-based data because a huge amount of traffic data is generated. The function mentioned in [12] is not a mandatory function to meet the requirements described in section 3. Therefore, we explore the measurement method according to the requirements.

4.1 Visualizing Multicast Path Tree

To visualize a multicast path tree on the network topology, the system is supposed to collect IF-MIB objects via the SNMP of all exporters. Except for the assumption, the collector needs the input and output interface indexes which are entry data in the multicast routing table. To achieve the requirements, we explore an efficient method of collecting them.

Instead of exporting the discrete flow including the output interface, we utilize optional data including a pair of input and output interface indexes. If specified egress interface is added to path tree or deleted, the optional data is updated. This method enables us to reduce the load of exporter and collector. The optional data also includes an eventIdentifier (shown by Enterprise-specific Id = 1 in Fig. 1.) that indicates whether the egress interface is added or deleted, and exporterIPv6Address (Id = 130) as a scope field identifying the router. This optional data structure in the case of IPv6 is shown in Fig. 1.

0		15	16		31
Set Id = 3			Length		
Template Id = 256			Field Count = 7		
Scope Field Count = 6		0	ExporterIPv6Address Id =130		
Field length = 16		0	DestinationIPv6Address Id = 27		
Field length = 16		0	SourceIPv6Address Id = 130		
Field length = 16		0	SourceIPv6PrefixLength Id = 27		
Field length = 16		0	ingressInterface Id = 27		
Field length = 4		0	egressInterface Id = 27		
Field length = 4		1	eventIdentifier Id = 1		
Field length = 4			Enterprise Number		
Enterprise Number			Padding		

Fig. 1. An IPFIX option template structure related to the multicast routing table. The first bit of the each field id indicates IETF-specified or enterprise-specific information element.

4.2 Detecting Service Quality Deterioration

We focus on detecting a packet loss and disorder by keeping track of the sequence number of an RTP header. To achieve an efficient measurement method for multiple IPTV channels in large-scale networks, we can apply sampling functions described in PSAMP to received RTP packets in input interface. Therefore, systematic time-based sampling is suitable for keeping track of the sequence number of an RTP header. This sampling is conducted like the following. In advance, a sampling interval period and a spacing period between samplings are given. Observed packets are selected during the sampling interval period, and then observed packets are ruled out from the end point of the sampling interval to the next start point; that is the spacing period between samplings. Subsequently, the sampling cycle repeats. This outline is shown in Fig. 2.

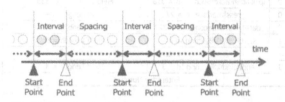

Fig. 2. The sketch of systematic time-based sampling

Prior to systematic time-based sampling, we can extract only multicast packets using the property match filtering. However, in that condition, there are concerns about exporting an extremely large number of IPFIX packets during the sampling interval period. To avoid this issue, IPFIX exporter hosts multiple samplers that independently conduct systematic time-based sampling and allocates the received packet-based data record for the appropriate sampler according to the hash value of a pair of source/destination IP addresses. To avoid synchronization of the interval period on the samplers, the start-up time of each sampler shifts little by little. Finally, selected packets are exported as packet-based data records in IPFIX protocol. In Fig. 3, the components in the IPFIX exporter are shown.

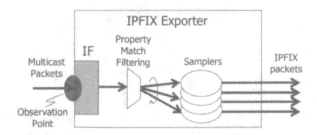

Fig. 3. These are the components of IPFIX exporters

The packet-based data record has a general data structure that is not a multicast-specific structure to be packed into IPFIX packets easily and is widely applied to other applications, such as VoIP RTP packets. Therefore, the data record adopts

IETF-specified information elements described in [14], and contains ipHeaderpacketSection (shown by Id = 313 as variable length field in Fig. 4.) that indicates a series of some octets from the start of the IP header. By extracting a series of octets with maximum of 80 bytes, the element can contain the parts of RTP header.

On the other hand, we add startPointMiliSeconds (Enterprise-specific Id = 2) and endPointMiliSeconds (Enterprise-specific Id = 3) that indicate the start point and end point of a sampling interval period for IPFIX collector to identify a series of packet data in the same sampling interval period. They are exported as enterprise-specific information elements. The data structure is shown in detail in Fig. 4.

0		15 16	31
	Set Id = 2		Length
	Template Id = 257		Field Count = 5
0	ipHeaderPacketSection Id = 313		Field Length = 65535
0	ingressInterface Id = 27		Field Length = 4
0	dateTimeMiliSeconds Id = 323		Field Length = 4
1	startPointMillisecond Id = 2		Field Length = 4
	Enterprise Number		
1	endPointMillisecond Id = 3		Field Length = 4
	Enterprise Number		

Fig. 4. An IPFIX packet-based data template structure. Field length value 65535 means variable length field.

4.3 Showing Failure Point on Multicast Path Tree

Having only one collector gather the packet-based data records from multiple exporters, inspect them, and visualize them seems difficult. To cope with this issue, we adopt an IPFIX mediator to reduce the load of collectors. In that case, a mediator combines a series of received packet data of the same sampling interval period into one flow record. Then, the mediator exports flow records to collectors. The architecture of the measurement system is shown in Fig. 5.

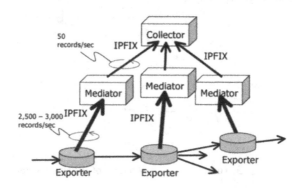

Fig. 5. The architecture of the measurement system

The mediator receives a packet-based data record, as shown in Fig. 4, and then it calculates the byte counter (shown by Id = 1 in Fig. 6.), the packet counter (Id = 2) and the lost packet counter (Id = 133). The values of startPointMiliSeconds and endPointMiliSeconds are copied to the values of flowStartMiliSeconds (Id = 152) and flowEndMiliSeconds (Id = 153), respectively. In addition, the exporterIPv4Address (Id = 130) is also added to prevent loss of the original IPFIX exporter IP address. Thus, collector can recognize the original exporter. The data structure is shown in Fig. 6 in detail. The components in the IPFIX mediator are shown in Fig. 7.

0		15 16	31
	Set Id = 2	Length	
	Template Id = 258	Field Count = 13	
0	Bytes Id = 1	Field Length =4	
0	Packets Id = 2	Field Length = 4	
0	protocolIdentifier Id = 4	Field Length = 4	
0	sourceTransportPort Id = 1	Field Length = 2	
0	ingressInterface Id = 10	Field Length = 4	
0	destinationTransportPort Id = 11	Field Length = 2	
0	sourceIPv6Address Id = 27	Field Length = 16	
0	destinationIPv6Address Id = 28	Field Length = 16	
0	ipVersion Id = 60	Field Length = 1	
0	exporterIPv4Address Id = 130	Field Length = 4	
0	droppedPacketDeltaCount = 133	Field Length = 4	
0	flowStartMilliSeconds = 152	Field Length = 4	
0	flowEndMilliSeconds = 153	Field Length = 4	

Fig. 6. A flow-based data template structure exported from mediators

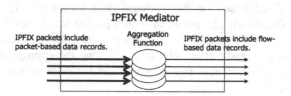

Fig. 7. A basic component of IPFIX mediators. The received IPFIX packets include packet-based data records, and exported IPFIX packets include the flow-based data record.

5 Measurement System Prototype

IPFIX prototype devices were built on Net::Flow module [15] on a PC-based server. Exporters create ten threads in which a sampler conducts, when its own process initializes. After selecting/sampling packets on each thread, an IPFIX packet is encoded sequentially based on the IP header part and then exported.

Mediators create the threads based on the source IP address and port number of IPFIX packets. Each thread gathers a series of packet-based data records and aggregates. Optional data records are directly forwarded to the collector. The following shows the hardware configuration of the mediator and exporter.

Table 1. The hardware configuration of the exporter and mediator is shown in this table

	Exporter	Mediator
CPU/Memory	Intel Quad Core 2.66 GHz /4 GB	Intel Core Duo 2.00 GHz /4 GB
OS	FreeBSD 6.2	FreeBSD 6.2

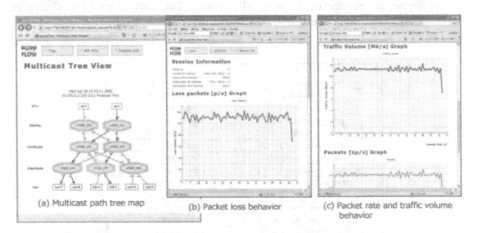

(a) Multicast path tree map   (b) Packet loss behavior   (c) Packet rate and traffic volume behavior

Fig. 8. The visualized multicast path tree map. By clicking a specified router, we can see the time series behaviors of multicast traffic volume and packet loss on the routers.

Collector analyzes and visualizes based on the received records. The multicast path tree map is visualized based on the optional data shown in Fig. 1, using SVG (Scalable Vector Graphics). The router in which packet loss happens is indicated in red on the multicast path tree map. The collector shows the time-series behaviors of packet loss, packet rate, and traffic volume by clicking the appropriate router on the map. A visualized multicast path tree map and the behavior of multicast streaming traffic are shown in Fig. 8.

6 Experimental Results

We evaluate the prototype devices on the following assumptions.

- The traffic volume of an IPTV channel is 12 Mb/s, and 1.2 kp/s indicates the maximum value of the H.264 codec.
- The packets of fifty IPTV channels pass through an exporter at the same time. In the following experiments, the measurement system is required to measure the traffic of fifty IPTV channels at the same time.
- We evaluate the exporter by varying the sampling interval period. The sum of the sampling interval period plus the spacing interval period is kept at a fixed value of 1,000 ms.

Accordingly, we evaluate how much accuracy can be measured by gathering the packet-based data of fifty IPTV channels. Packet loss and disorder is generated by a network simulator.

The volume of exported data records from exporters obtained by changing the sampling interval period from 10 to 100 ms is shown in Fig. 9. According to Fig. 9, the performance limit seems to be 3,000 records/sec at the sampling interval period of 50 ms. According to Fig. 10, we find that packet loss at the observation point happens when the interval period is 50 ms. Figure 10 actually illustrates the load on the exporter. Interval time 50 ms is the performance limit for exporter.

As long as the data volume does not reach the maximum value, the exporting process is maintained in a stable condition. That is, multiple samplers on a thread work to avoid bursty IPFIX packets.

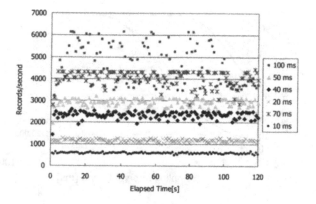

Fig. 9. The volume of exported data records from exporter obtained by changing the sampling interval period

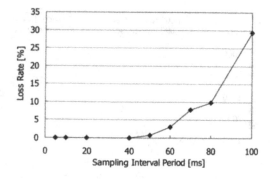

Fig. 10. The packet loss rate at the observation point in exporter

Next, we evaluate how much packet loss can be detected when the sampling interval is 40 ms. Within the given monitoring interval (n), the detection probability for packet loss is shown as follows.

$$1-(1-p)^{r \cdot n \cdot d/1000}$$

- Monitoring interval period: n [min]
- Sampling interval period: d [ms]
- Packet loss rate: p
- IP multicast streaming packet rate: r [p/s] = 1.2 [kp/s]

On the condition that n is one minute, the detection probability is shown in Fig. 11. The above formula and experimental results are shown in Fig. 11. According to Fig. 11, the formula describes the plot of these experimental results. That is, the system can detect failure at a detection probability of 80%, if the sampling interval period is 40 ms and packet loss happens at a rate of 1/1,000 during more than 1 minute. Even if it is prototype version, the result can manage to meet the requirements described in Section 3. However, in actual network operation, more precise accuracy is required.

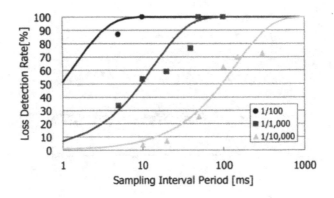

Fig. 11. The packet loss detection probability obtained by changing packet loss rate and sampling interval period

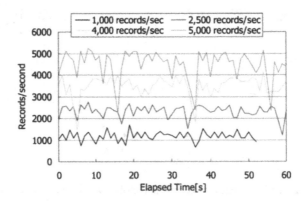

Fig. 12. The volume of exported data records from mediator obtained by changing the volume of received data records

The volume of exported data records obtained from mediators by changing the volume of received data records is shown in Fig. 12. According to Fig. 12, packet loss happens in a mediator when it receives data records at 4,000 – 5,000 records/sec. The performance limit seems to be 2,500 records/sec. In the current prototype version, a one-to-one assignment of the mediator to an exporter is needed.

7 Conclusion

In this paper, we presented a new traffic measurement method of IP multicast streaming services, such as IPTV, and the system architecture. We demonstrated the feasibility of the prototype. The experimental results demonstrated the effectiveness of the new measurement methods. Although there is not enough measurement accuracy in actual networks, building the system to measure QoS performances roughly is feasible. In particular, utilizing systematic time-based sampling and the proposed packet-based data record structure including the start point and end point of the sampling interval period are found to be useful for large-scale networks.

Toward introducing the method to actual backbone networks, much more efficiency and accuracy would be required. Generally, packet capturing without loss is difficult on a PC server. To reduce the load of an exporter, adjusting several parameters is needed, such as the number of threads and interval period. Increasing the number of sampler threads and changing the sampling interval and spacing period to a shorter period might reduce the load of exporters. However, basically, components of exporter are preferably implemented into commercial routers, switches, or network appliance devices, which can handle the huge volume of traffic. If high-efficiency is achieved, network operators would monitor more IPTV multicast channels with more accuracy. In addition, the combination of an estimation model for IPTV service quality would extend this system.

Acknowledgments

This study was supported by the Ministry of Internal Affairs and Communications of Japan.

References

1. McCloghrie, K., et al.: IPv4 Multicast Routing MIB, RFC2932 (October 2000)
2. Claise, B., et al.: Specification of the IPFIX Protocol for the Exchange of IP Traffic Flow Information, RFC5101 (September 2007)
3. Duffield, N., et al.: A Framework for Packet Selection and Reporting, IETF, Internet-Draft (work in progress), draft-ietf-psamp-sample-tech-10.txt (June 2007)
4. nProbe, http://www.ntop.org/nProbe.html
5. B. Lee, H. Son, S. Yoon, Y. Lee.: End-to-End Flow Monitoring with IPFIX. In: APNOMS 2007 (October 2007)
6. Tan, X., Gustafsson, J., Heikkila, G.: Perceived video Streaming Quality under Initial Buffering and Rebuffering Degradations. In: MESAQIN Conference (June 2006)

7. Claise, B., et al.: Cisco Systems NetFlow Services Export Version 9, RFC3954 (October 2004)
8. Phaal, P., et al.: InMon Corporation's sFlow. RFC3176 (September 2001)
9. Kobayashi, A., et al.: IPFIX Mediation: Problem Statement, IETF, Internet-Draft (work in progress), draft-ietf-ipfix-mediators-problem-statement-00.txt (May 2008)
10. Quittek, J., et al.: Information Model for IP Flow Information Export, RFC5102 (January 2008)
11. Zseby, T., et al.: Sampling and Filtering Techniques for IP Packet Selection, IETF, Internet-Draft (work in progress), draft-ietf-psamp-sample-tech-10.txt (June 2007)
12. Quittek, J., et al.: Requirements for IP Flow Information Export (IPFIX), RFC3917 (October 2004)
13. Kobayashi, A., et al.: Multicast measurement with IPFIX/PSAMP. IETF, Internet-Draft (work in progress), draft-kobayashi-ipfix-multicast-measure-01.txt (February 2008)
14. Dietz, T., et al.: Information Model for Packet Sampling Exports, IETF, Internet-Draft (work in progress), draft-ietf-psamp-info-08.txt (February 2008)
15. NetFlow, http://search.cpan.org/~akoba/Net-Flow/lib/Net/Flow.pm

An Enhanced SNTP (ESNTP) Clock Synchronization for High-Precision Network QoS Measurements

Jeong-Ki Park and Young-Tak Kim*

Dept. of Information & Communication Engineering,
Graduate School, Yeungnam University,
214-1, Dae-Dong, Kyungsan-Si, Kyungbook, 712-749, Korea
jk21p@ynu.ac.kr, ytkim@yu.ac.kr

Abstract. In order to assess the performance of QoS provisioning for realtime multimedia services that require end-to-end delay within 100 ms and jitter within 50 ms, the server and client are required to be synchronized with near sub-millisecond clock offset for high-precision QoS-performance measurements. In this paper we propose an enhanced SNTP (ESNTP) that provides sub-millisecond clock synchronization based on the selection of minimum round-trip delay and high-resolution local clock reading with clock drift compensation. Throughout the experiments of varying traffic congestion in public Internet environment, the proposed clock synchronization scheme maintained within 0.5 ms offset between NTP servers and the ESNTP client, where the SNTPv4 maintained 3.7 ms average clock offset in the same environment. The proposed clock synchronization scheme provides higher precision with smaller clock offset error compared to the NTPv4 that is reported to provide clock offset of 10 ms in public Internet.

Keywords: Clock synchronization, performance measurement, QoS, delay and jitter, clock drift compensation.

1 Introduction

Most realtime applications in Internet, such as VoIP, video conference, and IPTV require end-to-end packet delay and jitter within certain limits to guarantee the quality of video and audio play at destination. The realtime conversational services require 100 ms limit of end-to-end packet delay and 50 ms of jitter [1]. In the QoS monitoring of realtime multimedia services in public Internet, the server and clients must be synchronized with limited clock offset for high-precision performance measurement. ITU-T FGNGN specifies the NTP-based clock synchronization to be within 1 ms offset [2].

The popular clock synchronization schemes are based on GPS (global positioning system), NTPv4 (network time protocol version 4), and SNTPv4 (Simple NTPv4) [3]. GPS-based clock synchronization provides high precision clock synchronization, but it is expensive and difficult to install the GPS antenna for in-building multimedia systems. NTP-based clock synchronization can be easily implemented with Internet connection to NTP servers, but the clock offset is reported to be 1 ~ 50 ms in public

---

* Corresponding author.

N. Akar, M. Pioro, and C. Skianis (Eds.): IPOM 2008, LNCS 5275, pp. 91–102, 2008.
© Springer-Verlag Berlin Heidelberg 2008

Internet [4]. SNTPv4 is a simplified subset of NTPv4 protocol for the applications at the extremities of the synchronization subnet. The performance assessment of QoS provisioning in realtime multimedia applications, such as IPTV and video conference, may use SNTPv4 for server-client clock synchronization. Since realtime multimedia applications (e.g., IPTV and video phone) require end-to-end delay within 100 ms and jitter within 50 ms, the server and client are required to be synchronized with sub-millisecond clock offset for correct performance measurements. The clock synchronization precision by NTPv4 or SNTPv4 is reported as 1 ~ 50 ms in public Internet [3], which is mostly not adequate to be used in the high-precision performance measurements of IPTV QoS provisioning.

The major components of millisecond order offset in SNTPv4-based clock synchronization are i) the high Internet packet delay variance (i.e., jitter) between the server and the client, ii) clock drift between the NTP server and local client, and iii) low-precision clock reading at client, especially on MS-Windows environment. In domestic public Internet under light traffic load, the jitter is measured as few milliseconds, but the jitter is increased to few 10's milliseconds when traffic congestion is occurred. Since the traffic congestion status is time varying, the fluctuation of the measured clock offset also increases according to the traffic load.

Another error factor in server-client clock synchronization is the clock drift at client's local clock which is mostly implemented without high-precision oscillator frequency. In usual PC-based client system, the oscillator frequency tolerance is 10^{-4} ~ 10^{-5}, that produce few 10's millisecond drift in few 10's minute period. This local clock drift should be compensated in the virtual clock reading for application programs[6].

In high-precision clock synchronization and virtual clock reading for performance measurements, the high-precision local system clock reading is essential. In Linux environment, *gettimeofday()* API (application program interface) provides a precision of micro-second order that is good enough for measurements in precision of sub-millisecond order. In MS-Windows environments, however, no API is supported for sub-millisecond precisions; *getSystemTime()* API provides clock reading with the granularity of 10 ~ 15 ms [5]. For high-resolution, a synchronized clock reading based on performance counter can be used [5], with periodic re-synchronization[6].

In this paper, we propose an enhanced SNTP (ESNTP) that provides sub-millisecond clock synchronization based on the selection of clock offset measurement with minimum round-trip delay and high-resolution local clock reading with clock drift compensation. The proposed scheme improves the accuracy and stability even under highly fluctuating traffic load between the NTP servers and the ESNTP clients. Throughout the experiments of varying traffic congestion in public Internet environment, the proposed clock synchronization scheme maintained within 0.5 ms offset between server and client. The proposed clock synchronization scheme can be also used in the peer synchronization of NTP (network time protocol) servers to minimize the effect of packet delay & jitter.

The rest of this paper is organized as follows. In section 2, NTP and SNTP are briefly introduced. In section 3 the ESNTP-based clock synchronization by clock offset measurement with minimum round-trip delay, local clock drift compensation, and high-resolution clock reading for Windows applications are proposed. In section 4, the performances of the proposed clock synchronization scheme are analyzed in public Internet environments. Finally, we conclude this paper in section 5.

2 Related Work

2.1 Network Time Protocol (NTP) Version 4 [3]

Network Time Protocol version 4 (NTPv4) is widely used to synchronize the system clocks among a set of distributed time servers and clients [3]. The NTP subnet model includes a number of widely accessible primary time servers synchronized by wire or radio to national standards. The purpose of the NTP protocol is to convey timekeeping information from these primary servers to secondary servers and clients via both private networks and the public Internet.

Fig. 1 shows the major functional modules of NTPv4 implementation model [3]. Two processes are dedicated to each server: a *peer process* to receive messages from the server or reference clock, and a *poll process* to transmit messages to the server or reference clock. The *system process* performs the selection, clustering and combining algorithms which mitigate any possible error in the various peer NTP servers and reference clocks to determine the most accurate and reliable candidates to synchronize the system clock. The *clock discipline process* provides engineered algorithms to control the time and frequency of the system clock which is defined as VFO (variable frequency oscillator). The *clock adjust process* runs once each second to inject a computed time offset and maintain constant frequency.

NTPv4 is mostly used to synchronize the NTP servers from their higher-stratum level NTP servers. The precision of NTPv4-based clock synchronization is reported to be 1 ~ 50 ms in public Internet which is mostly not appropriate for high-precision network performance measurements [4].

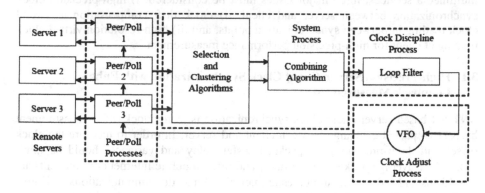

Fig. 1. NTPv 4 implementation Model

2.2 Simple Network Time Protocol Version 4 (SNTPv4) [4]

Simple Network Time Protocol version 4 (SNTPv4) is a simplified access paradigm for servers and clients using current and previous versions of NTP and SNTP [4]. An SNTP client can operate in unicast, broadcast, or manycast modes [4]. In unicast mode, the SNTPv4 client establishes a client-server operation mode with a designated NTP server, sends a NTP mode 3 (client mode) request to the designated server, and expects a NTP mode 4 (server mode) reply from that server. In broadcast client mode, it sends no request and waits for a broadcast (NTP mode 5) from one or more broadcast servers. In manycast mode, the client sends a request (NTP mode 3) to a designated broadcast address, and expects a reply (NTP mode 4) from one or more manycast servers.

In SNTPv4, the client must not under any conditions use a poll interval less than 15 seconds. A client should increase the poll interval using exponential backoff as performance permits and especially if the server does not respond within a reasonable time.

In the performance measurements of QoS provisioning in public Internet, SNTPv4 can be used in server-client mode between the realtime multimedia service server and client. The major limitation of SNTPv4-based clock synchronization for QoS measurement of realtime multimedia service is the poor accuracy on the order of few milliseconds.

In SNTPv4 clock synchronization, the exchanges of NTP request/response messages to/from NTP servers through public Internet experience packet delay and jitter, and in order to minimize the error in clock offset reading by the client, the effect of the packet delay & jitter should be minimized. In this paper, we propose a simple enhancement scheme to select the SNTPv4 response from NTPv4 server, where the round-trip packet delay is the smallest value in the synchronization polling interval (16 s ~ 36 hours in NTPv4).

3 Enhanced SNTP (ESNTP) Clock Synchronization

In the high-precision performance measurements of QoS provisioning in realtime multimedia services, three major issues must be considered: i) high-precision clock synchronization between server and client, ii) clock drift compensation at virtual clock reading in between synchronization points, and iii) high-resolution virtual clock reading at client for high-precision performance measurement.

3.1 High-Precision Server-Client Clock Synchronization with Enhanced Loopback Measurement

SNTPv4-based server-client clock synchronization is using clock offset measurement by NTPv4 packet exchange between client and server. In order to measure the clock offset with high-precision, the packet transfer delay and variance should be minimized. The average packet transfer delay and jitter in public Internet environments are 6 ~ 15 ms and 0.8 ~ 8 ms in domestic inter-city domestic communications in Korea, while 50 ~ 400 ms and 1 ~ 40 ms in international communications across oceans, respectively.

The major delay components in end-to-end packet delivery are packet propagation delay along transmission links, the packet processing time, and packet buffering time at each router. The propagation time and the packet processing time are almost constant according to the physical distance and the hop count, but the packet buffering time is heavily dependent on the traffic load status in the forward and backward path between the client and server. Since the traffic congestion status is time varying, the packet buffering delay becomes also time varying.

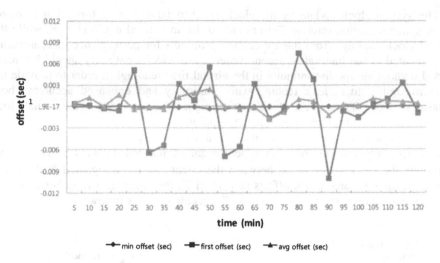

Fig. 2. Example measurements of clock offset: values of first sample, average and minimum in each polling period of 5 minutes

Fig. 2 depicts example measurements of clock offset, the values of first, average and minimum sample in each polling period of 5 minutes. In this example, when only a single sampling is done in each polling period, the clock offset values ranges from - 10 ms to + 8 ms, while the average clock offset values range - 2 ms to +3 ms. These clock offset deviations come from the packet delay jitters where the packet buffering delays are the most significant component.

In order to minimize the impact of packet delay variance, we select the clock offset of minimum round-trip time (RTT) packet delay from the 20 samples in the 5 min polling period. As shown in Fig. 2, the minimum clock offset values at each 5 min ranges within ± 0.1 ms. As a result, the clock offset calculation will be less error prone if the clock offset sample of minimum RTT value is selected from the multiple samples in the polling period. In SNTPv4, the client is constraint to use a poll interval no less than 15 seconds. In the proposed ESNTP scheme, the clock offset polling is done at every 15 seconds, the minimum value is obtained from the samples in 5 minutes, and the virtual clock is adjusted.

3.2 Improvement of Virtual Clock Accuracy with Clock Drift Ratio Compensation

Another important component in the clock synchronization is the clock drift ratio between the NTP server clock and local client clock[6]. From a series of SNTPv4 clock offset measurements between Stratum-1 NTP servers and PC-based SNTPv4 clients, we found the clock drift ratio is $10^{-4} \sim 10^{-5}$ order; for example, after 5 min from the clock adjustment, the clock drift becomes 3 ~ 30 ms. So, if we add only the clock offset that has been obtained in the previous clock synchronization point, without the additional clock drift compensation, the virtual clock reading will contain considerable clock offset error because of the clock drift.

The system clock update by the clock synchronization is performed at a longer clock synchronization interval T, in minute order in general configuration, while the virtual clock readings from the application programs for performance measurements are executed in the interval of second order. Also, clock continuity should be maintained without abrupt discontinuity in the virtual time reading. In order to provide the synchronized virtual clock reading with continuity and enhanced accuracy, both measured clock offset and the clock drift ratio should be included in the virtual clock reading until the next clock synchronization point.

Fig. 3 depicts the virtual clock adjustment with measured clock offset and clock drift ratio compensation. At each synchronization interval T, the ESNTP scheme measures the clock offset δ_{i_min}, between the client and the designated NTP server. Based on the measured clock offsets at T_{i-1} and T_i, the clock drift ratio is calculated, and the amount of clock compensation at T_{i+1} is calculated as follows.

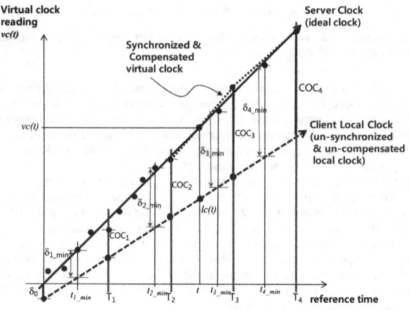

Fig. 3. Virtual clock adjustment with measured clock offset and clock drift ratio compensation

Firstly, at each synchronization interval, the clock offset ratio is calculated from measured clock offsets δ_{1_min} and δ_{i_min}, by Eq. (1).

$$i\text{-th Clock Drift Ratio (CDR}_i) = (\delta_{i\_min} - \delta_{1\_min}) / (t_{i\_min} - t_{1\_min}) \qquad (1)$$

The smoothed clock offset compensation is calculated as follows:

$$(i+1)\text{-th clock offset compensation (COC}_{i+1}) =$$
$$K \times \{\delta_{i\_min} + (T + T_i - t_{i\_min}) \times CDR_i\} + (1-K) \times COC_i \qquad (2)$$

where K is a smoothing factor for smoothed average. Since we do not have enough collected samples to calculate correct clock deviation at the initial synchronization period ($T_0 \sim T_2$), so COC_1 and COC_2 are not calculated, and the clock offset compensation is applied from COC_3. In this interval, the virtual clock reading is simply calculated by the addition of the local clock reading and the minimum clock offset until the moment, δ_{min}. The smoothed average is used in the clock offset compensation in order to minimize the error in the clock offset measurement by occasional & isolated offset surge due to temporal traffic congestion, the clock drift ratio and clock offset compensation are computed as smoothed average with previously computed values. Currently, we set the smoothing factors $K = 1$ during the first one initial calibration interval and $K = 0.8$ afterwards, in our experiments.

The ($i+1$)-th clock offset compensation is used for the virtual clock reading in the period between T_i and T_{i+1} for application programs, such as performance measurements of QoS provisioning. The virtual clock reading at certain time t, $vc(t)$, in the

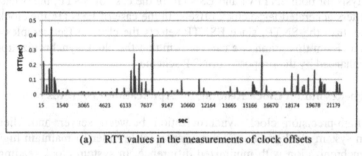

(a)   RTT values in the measurements of clock offsets

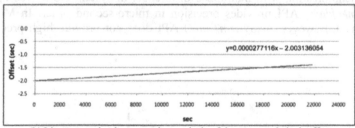

(b) Linear equation by regression analysis of the measured clock offset

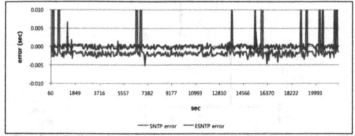

(c) Error from the linear equation by regression analysis of the measured clock offset

Fig. 4. ESNTP clock offset measurements and analysis

interval T_i and T_{i+1} is produced from the local clock reading $lc(t)$, i-th and $(i+1)$-th clock offset compensation, COC_i and COC_{i+1} as follows:

$$vc(t) = lc(t) + COC_i + (COC_{i+1} - COC_i) \times (lc(t) - T_i) / T \qquad (3)$$

The virtual clock reading may have errors from the ideally synchronized clock. The ideally synchronized clock can be estimated by regression analysis of the measured clock offsets. Fig. 4 shows an example of clock offset measurements, linear equation by regression analysis, and the error measurements from the linear equation that represents the ideally synchronized clock.

Fig. 4 (a) depicts the round-trip delay in the measurements of clock offsets, during the working hours when occasional traffic congestions had been generating large packet jitters. Fig. 4 (b) shows the linear equation by the regression analysis of the measured clock offsets by ESNTP. In the linear equation, we can see the clock drift ratio of 2.77×10^{-5}. Fig. 4 (c) compares the errors from the linear equation by regression analysis for both SNTPv4 and ESNTP. In the case of SNTP, the occasional large packet jitters generated large clock offsets; in the case of ESNTP, the clock errors are much less than the SNTP, since ESNTP selects the clock offset samples with minimum RTT. From this graph, we can confirm that the clock synchronization performance is enhanced by the proposed ESNTP scheme.

3.3 High-Resolution Clock Reading for Application Programs

In the high-precision clock synchronization between server and client, higher-precision system clock reading is very important in order to maintain high-precision clock synchronization with minimized difference. In system clock reading in Linux, the *gettimeofday()* API provides precision in micro-second order. In MS-Windows environment, however, *getSystemTime()* API does not provide high precision clock

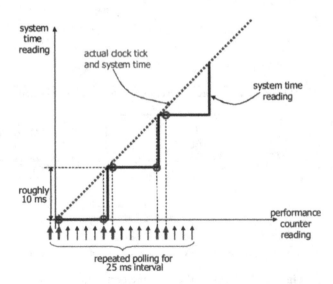

Fig. 5. High-precision system clock reading in MS-Windows applications using performance counter

reading for application programs; it provides clock reading with the granularity of 10 ~ 15 ms [4]. In order to provide sub-millisecond precision of clock reading in MS-Windows environment, we may use *QueryPerformanceFrequency()*and *QueryPer-formanceCounter()* API that provides the performance counter reading which is a high-resolution hardware counter that can be used for measuring brief periods of time with high precision and low overhead. The performance counter value can be mapped to system clock time in the granularity of nano-second order.

The mapping between the performance counter value and the system clock time requires synchronization as shown in Fig. 5. In this scheme, repeated polling of performance counter is performed in the initial synchronization stage for 25 ms period, and the smallest difference of the back-to-back performance counter values at the time value change of system clock reading is used as the initial synchronization point. After the initial synchronization of performance counter and system clock, periodic re-synchronizations are performed at the moments of SNTPv4 server-client clock offset measurements and virtual clock adjustments.

4 Performance Analysis

The proposed ESNTP client program has been implemented on both Linux system and MS-Windows XP system, on desk-top PCs. As explained in section 3, the ESNTP client module contains i) selection the clock offset sample with minimum round-trip delay in the clock adjustment interval, ii) high-resolution local clock reading, and iii) clock drift rate compensation in virtual clock reading for application programs. In this section, we analyze the performance of the proposed schemes.

4.1 Performance of Enhanced Clock OffSet Sampling

Table 1 compares the experiment results of SNTPv4 and ESNTP for clock synchronization performance in Korea domestic Internet environments. The SNTPv4 and ESNTP

Table 1. Measurements of clock synchronizations with SNTPv4 and ESNTP schemes

NTP Server	Average Packet Delay [ms]	Average Packet Delay Variance (Jitter) [ms]	Average Clock Error with SNTPv4 [ms]	Average Clock Error with **ESNTP** [ms]
Pohang, Stratum-1 (ntp.postech.ac.kr)	12.753	3.552	3.607	2.701
Daejeon-A, Stratum-1 (time.kriss.re.kr)	12.759	6.999	3.708	0.450
Daejeon-B, Stratum-2 (noc6-3.koren21.net)	8.118	1.200	1.622	1.491
Seoul-A, Stratum-2 (ntp1.epidc.co.kr)	6.536	0.520	0.524	0.463
Seoul-B, Stratum-2 (time.bora.net)	9.860	3.347	2.676	2.563

clients are located in Kyungsan Campus of Yeungnam University, in the southern region of Korea. The SNTPv4 and ESNTP clients measured their clock offsets with several Stratum-1/2 NTP servers through public Internet. As shown in Table 1, the average clock errors of the ESNTP-based clock synchronization are relatively smaller compared to the errors of SNTPv4-based clock synchronization.

In Table 1, the average clock errors have been calculated from the linear equation by the regression analysis of the clock offset measurements. In the experiments, the stratum-1 level NTP servers provided stable reference clocks, while stratum-2 level NTP servers showed instabilities in some cases. Currently, we are analyzing the relationships between the burst duration of the network congestion and the clock offset jitters. From Table 1, we can see that the proposed ESNTP scheme provides better clock synchronizations with less average clock errors, compared to SNTPv4.

4.2 High-Resolution Clock Reading

Fig. 6 compares the resolutions of virtual clock reading at Linux, MS-Windows environment. In the case of Linux, the *gettimeofday()* API provides high precision clock readings, in the micro-second order. In MS-Windows environment, the *getSystemTime()* API provides poor precision in the order of 10~ 15 ms order, as shown in Fig. 6. We implemented high-resolution clock reading for MS-Windows environment, as explained in section 3.3. The proposed high-resolution clock reading API for MS-Windows environment shows sub-millisecond order resolutions in clock reading, as shown in Fig. 6.

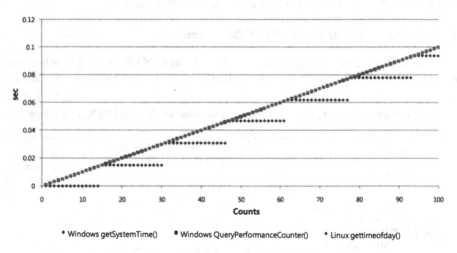

Fig. 6. Comparisons of resolutions of clock reading

4.3 Clock Drift Ratio Compensation

In the measurements of clock offsets between SNTPv4 and ESNTP clients with NTP servers, we found that the clock drift rate is in the order of $10^{-4} \sim 10^{-5}$ when the clients are desktop-PC based computing environment. As a result, the local clock reading will have few milliseconds error from the clock drift from the reference clock, when the clock synchronization & update interval is in the order of few minutes.

Fig. 7 depicts the improvement of resolutions in virtual clock reading with clock drift ratio compensation, between the clock synchronization interval. In SNTPv4, the clock drift is not compensated, and the clock error increases continuously until the next clock offset is measured and updated. In ESNTP, the clock drift rate is calculate by Eq. (1), and it is included in the virtual clock reading, as defined in Eq. (3). In Fig. 7, ESNTP shows very small clock error in the 5 min clock synchronization intervals.

When the clock synchronization interval is increased, considering the processing overhead and traffic overhead, the effect of clock drift error will be larger. So, in order to provide high precision clock synchronization & reading even in longer clock synchronization interval, the clock drift error must be included in the virtual clock reading.

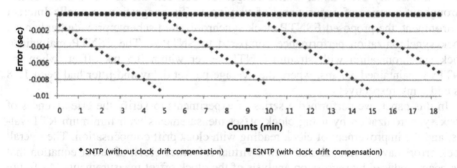

Fig. 7. Comparisons of clock synchronization with/without local clock drift ratio compensation

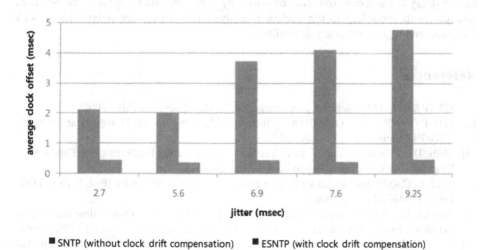

Fig. 8. Clock offset according to network jitter in public Internet

4.4 Stability of Clock Synchronization in Varying Packet Jitter

Fig. 8 compares the stability of clock synchronizations with SNTPv4 and ESNTP, according to packet jitters in the clock offset measurements. The average clock offset by SNTPv4 scheme is gradually increasing when the packet delay jitter is increasing. In the proposed ESNTP, the average clock offset is maintaining almost the same clock offset until the packet jitter is within the range of 9 ms, since it is selecting the clock offset sample with minimum RTT in the clock synchronization interval.

5 Conclusions

In this paper we proposed an enhanced SNTP (ESNTP) clock synchronization scheme based on selection of clock offsets with minimum RTT, clock drift compensation and high-resolution local clock reading. The proposed ESNTP scheme improves the accuracy and stability even under traffic congestion between the server and the client. Throughout a series of experiments of varying traffic congestion in public Internet environment, the proposed ESNTP clock synchronization scheme provided enhanced clock synchronization performance compared to SNTPv4. The ESNTP maintained clock synchronization with stratum-1 NTP server within 0.5 ms offset, when the SNTPv4 maintained 3.7 ms, where the average packet delay and jitter had been 12.8 ms and 7 ms, respectively.

In this paper, we performed a series of experiments to verify the effectiveness of clock synchronization by using clock offset measurements with minimum RTT values, and the improvement of clock reading with clock drift compensation. The overall clock errors have been analyzed with a virtual reference clock of linear equation that has been produced by regression analysis of the clock offset measurements. As future work, we are going to enhance the clock synchronization performance in the high packet delay & jitter environments by carefully screening the samples of clock offset measurements according to the statistical analysis of the network delay, jitter, clock drift rate, and regression analysis results.

References

[1] ITU-T Rec. Y.1541, Network Performance for IP-Based Services (May 2002)
[2] ITU-T FGNGN WG3, OD-00168, Performance Measurement and Management for NGN, FGNGN Meeting (June 27–July 1, 2007)
[3] Mills, D.L.: Network Time Protocol Version 4 Reference and Implementation Guide. NTP Working Group Technical Report 06-6-1 (June 2006)
[4] IETF RFC 4330, Simple Network Time Protocol (SNTP) version 4 for IPv4, IPv6 and OSI, David L. Mills (January 2006)
[5] Nilsson, J.: Timers – Implement a continuously updating, high-resolution time provider for Windows, http://msdn.microsoft.com/en-us/magazine/cc163996.asx
[6] Babu, D.V.S., Pàsztor, A.: Robust synchronization of software clocks across the internet. In: Proc. IMC 2004, Taormina, Sicily, Italy, pp. 219–232 (2004)

Optimum Identification of
Worm-Infected Hosts

Noriaki Kamiyama, Tatsuya Mori, Ryoichi Kawahara,
and Shigeaki Harada

NTT Service Integration Laboratories
Tokyo 180-8585, Japan
kamiyama.noriaki@lab.ntt.co.jp

Abstract. The authors have proposed a method of identifying super-spreaders by flow sampling and a method of extracting worm-infected hosts from the identified superspreaders using a white list. However, the problem of how to optimally set parameters, ϕ, the measurement period length, m^*, the identification threshold of the flow count m within ϕ, and H^*, the identification probability for hosts with $m = m^*$, remains unsolved. These three parameters seriously affect the worm-spreading property. In this paper, we propose a method of optimally designing these three parameters to satisfy the condition that the ratio of the number of active worm-infected hosts divided by the number of all the vulnerable hosts is bound by a given upper-limit during the time T required to develop a patch or an anti-worm vaccine.

Keywords: Worm, detection, sampling, optimum design.

1 Introduction

To find vulnerable hosts to be infected, worm-infected hosts send packets for scanning to addresses generated randomly or sequentially [1]. In particular, when so-called *bandwidth-limited* worms, such as Slammer, are spreading, infected hosts continue to scan by maximally utilizing the available network bandwidth and host CPU power, so this type of worm can spread rapidly [2]. For example, in the outbreak of Slammer, which is a typical bandwidth-limited worm, infected hosts repeated scanning 4,000 times per second on average, and the infection was reported to spread throughout the Internet within just 10 minutes [2]. When a new worm appears, we normally cope with it by developing a patch that fixes the bugs of the OS or application software, or we develop a vaccine program to remove malicious code from infected hosts. Those are distributed to users. However, for worms with a high infection rate, such as bandwidth-limited worms, this solution is not sufficient because the infection will spread over a large part of the Internet until a patch or vaccine is developed.

For worms with a high infection rate, gaining time to develop a patch or vaccine by controlling the speed of worms spreading is important. That is accomplished by detecting the appearance of a new worm as soon as possible, identifying worm-infected hosts automatically, and quarantining the packets sent from

N. Akar, M. Pioro, and C. Skianis (Eds.): IPOM 2008, LNCS 5275, pp. 103–116, 2008.

them. Several authors proposed methods to detect worm outbreaks; T. Bu, et al. proposed detecting a worm outbreak based on a change in the interarrival time of scanners [3], C. C. Zou, et al. presented a detection method based on the trend of an increase in scan counts [4], for example. On the other hand, we have proposed a method of identifying hosts generating many flows within a short time as *superspreaders* [5]. This method, which is called the *superspreader-identification method* hereafter, defines superspreaders as hosts in which $m \geq m^*$, where m is the number of observed flows on the target link generated by a host within a measurement period Φ with a duration of ϕ seconds, and m^* is an arbitrarily defined flow-count threshold. This method explicitly sets the identification probability H of hosts with $m = m^*$ to an arbitrarily defined value of H^*. Using this method, we accurately identify superspreaders by maximally utilizing a limited amount of memory.

However, legitimate hosts generating many flows, such as DNS servers, as well as worm-infected hosts can be superspreaders. Therefore, if we simply quarantine all identified hosts, legitimate hosts are regulated as well. If we regulate important hosts such as DNS servers, we cannot continue stable operation of the Internet. Therefore, we need to carefully regulate identified hosts. Legitimate hosts generating many flows tend to be superspreaders within multiple continuous measurement periods. Hence, we have defined two network statuses, a normal state and a worm-outbreak state, and proposed to store the IP addresses of identified hosts in a white list (WL) in the normal state and to filter legitimate hosts from the identified superspreaders by comparing the identified hosts with the WL after detecting the appearance of a new worm [6]. Hereafter, we describe the *method of identifying worm-infected hosts*, which combines the superspreader-identification method with the extraction method that extracts infected hosts using a WL.

By implementing the method of identifying worm-infected hosts at edge routers, we can accurately identify worm-infected hosts in real time. By regulating the rate at which packets are sent by identified hosts, we can suppress the speed at which infections are spread. Therefore, we can gain time to develop a patch or vaccine for bandwidth-limited worms. However, the problem of how to design parameters, ϕ, m^*, and H^*, remains unsolved. These parameters significantly affect the accuracy of identifying worm-infected hosts and the speed of worm spreading, whereas in general, we cannot predict the scan rate of unknown worms in advance. Hence, adequately designing these parameters in advance for any unknown worm is difficult. On the other hand, suppressing the number of active, i.e., not identified, worm-infected hosts to decrease the volume of abusive traffic caused by scans of worm-infected hosts and reduce the speed of worm spreading is important. In this paper, we propose a method of optimally designing these three parameters with the constraint that the number of active worm-infected hosts is bound below the given upper limit until a patch or vaccine is developed. The approach and framework of the proposed design method can be widely applied to methods of identifying worm-infected hosts.

In Section 2, we give an overview of the method of identifying worm-infected hosts and describe the method of designing the three parameters in Section 3. Section 4 shows the results of a numerical evaluation, and Section 5 summarizes this paper.

2   Method of Identifying Worm-Infected Hosts

In this section, we summarize the overviews of the superspreader-identification method proposed in [5] and the method of extracting worm-infected hosts proposed in [6].

2.1   Superspreader-Identification Method

For a measurement period Φ with a duration of ϕ seconds, we define m as the number of observed flows on the target link generated by a host within Φ. For an arbitrarily defined flow count threshold m^*, we define a superspreader as a host in which $m \geq m^*$. The identification process is executed independently in each continuous measurement period Φ. To identify superspreaders, we need to count the cardinality of flows generated by each host. Therefore, implementing the method on an access router is desirable. In this case, the amounts of available memory and CPU resources are limited, so we need to effectively identify superspreaders using limited resources. This method suppresses the required memory size using a flow-based sampling and limits the required processing time by counting the flow cardinality using a Bloom filter (BF) [7].

Host is identified if the number of sampled flows reaches Y, i.e., the identification threshold, within Φ. Let $H(m)$ denote the probability of a host being identified as a superspreader within Φ. Let us make $H(m) = H^*$ for hosts with $m = m^*$. In addition to m^*, H^* is also an arbitrary parameter set by an operator. We define f_d as the probability that d flows are sampled among m flows within Φ. We have $f_d = {}_mC_d\, r^d(1 - r)^{m-d}$, where r is the flow-sampling rate. Therefore, $H(m)$ is derived as

$$H(m) = \sum_{d=Y}^{m} {}_mC_d\, r^d(1 - r)^{m-d}. \tag{1}$$

In numerically solving (1) by substituting $m = m^*$ and $H(m) = H^*$, we obtain r for a given m^* and H^* when we set Y, or we obtain Y for a given m^* and H^* when we set r.

If we set $Y > m^*$, hosts with $m = m^*$ are not identified at all, so the valid range of Y is $1 \leq Y \leq m^*$. As Y increases, the corresponding r monotonically increases because more flows need to be sampled. When $Y \to m^*$, r approaches 1. As m^* decreases or H^* increases, r increases for the same Y. From (1), we can derive $H(m)$ for a host with arbitrary m, independently of the distribution of m or the number of hosts. We name the curve of $H(m)$ versus m the *identification*

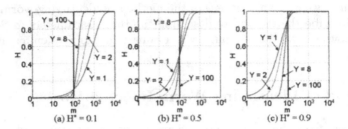

Fig. 1. Identification curves for various Y

curve. The identification curves for some values of Y are shown in Fig. 1, where $m^* = 100$, and $H^* = $ (a) 0.1, (b) 0.5, and (c) 0.9. Although all the identification curves go through the point (m^*, H^*), the slope of the identification curve with larger Y is steeper at $m = m^*$. This is because the flow sampling rate r increases as Y increases. The identification accuracy improves as Y increases. Note that the identification curve and the relationship between Y and r are determined independently of the packet arrival pattern or the distribution of m. This method requires memory device for a host table (HT) as well as the BF, and it optimally sets the identification threshold Y minimizing the number of unidentified superspreaders by optimally allocating the limited amount of memory to the BF and HT.

2.2   Method of Extracting Worm-Infected Hosts

Legitimate hosts generating many flows, such as DNS servers, as well as worm-infected hosts can be superspreaders. Therefore, we need to carefully regulate identified hosts by filtering legitimate hosts from the identified superspreaders. Legitimate hosts generating many flows tend to be superspreaders within multiple continuous measurement periods.

We define two network statuses: (1) a normal state, and (2) a worm-outbreak state. When a new worm is detected in the normal state, the network status changes to the worm-outbreak state. When a patch or vaccine is developed after a new worm is detected, the network status reverts to the normal state. All the superspreaders identified in the normal state are accommodated into the white list (WL). In the worm-outbreak state, on the other hand, the WL is not updated. Instead, the identified superspreaders are compared with host entries in the WL that was updated in the previous normal state. They are regarded as worm-infected hosts and regulated only if they are not matched with any entries in the WL. Legitimate hosts identified as superspreaders in the worm-outbreak state are likely to be identified as superspreaders in the previous normal state as well. On the other hand, worm-infected hosts become superspreaders after being infected, so they do not exist in the WL except those that had already been infected at the instant of worm detection. Therefore, by using the WL, we can effectively extract worm-infected hosts from the superspreaders identified in the worm-outbreak state.

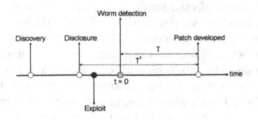

Fig. 2. Vulnerability lifecycle

3   Optimum Parameter Design

3.1   Outline

Figure 2 shows the vulnerability lifecycle of OS or application software [8]. The actions shown in the top, middle, and bottom positions are performed by network operator, software vender, and malicious user, respectively. The time of discovery is the earliest date that vulnerability is discovered by software vender, and the discovered vulnerability is not publicly known until it is disclosed by software vender. A new worm exploiting this vulnerability firstly appears at the time of exploit date. Let us assume that we detect a new worm and begin the identification and quarantine process for hosts infected by this worm at time $t = 0$. We also assume that the time required to develop a patch or vaccine for this worm is T after the worm detection. By identifying and quarantining hosts infected by this worm, we aim to bound the upper limit of the number of active worm-infected hosts, which are making scans, below ϵN when $0 \leq t \leq T$, where ϵ is an arbitrarily given parameter in the range of $0 < \epsilon < 1$ and N is the number of hosts vulnerable to this worm within the network. In other words, we want to satisfy the restriction condition $I_t \leq \epsilon N$ for any t within $0 \leq t \leq T$, where I_t is defined as the number of active hosts infected by this worm within the network at time t.

In [8], it is reported that about 90% worms appeared in 2005 exploited vulnerability in the date of disclosure. Moreover, we can expect to detect worms with high infection rate within a short time after the time of exploit. Hence, we can approximate $T = T'$, where T' is the time required to develop patch after the disclosure. It is also reported that patches for about 85% worms appeared in 2005 were developed in the date of disclosure [8]. Hence, we can roughly set T to 86,400 seconds (one day). In addition to T, we also need to roughly estimate N before deriving the optimum values for the three parameters, ϕ, m^*, and H^*. When network administrators of private networks, i.e., universities or companies, identify and quarantine worm-infected hosts, estimating N is easy. On the other hand, for network operators of large-scale ISPs, it is difficult to obtain the exact value of N. However, in many practical operations, the accurate estimation of N is not necessary, and roughly estimating N is adequate. They can estimate N from the number of subscribers, for example.

The scan rate of worm-infected hosts, η, depends on the worm class. We can afford to develop a patch or vaccine without the identification and quarantine processes for worms with low infection rates. For worms with strong infection ability, i.e., high infection rate, on the other hand, we need to identify and quarantine infected hosts to gain time until developing a patch or vaccine. From this perspective, we focus on designing parameters ϕ, m^*, and H^*, which satisfy $I_t \le \epsilon N$ within $0 \le t \le T$ even when a worm with any scan rate η appears. Note that η^* corresponding to m^* is designed at the same time because $\eta = m/\phi$.

The superspreaders are identified using an integer m^* obtained by $m^* = \phi\eta^*$ from the identification threshold η^*. That is, the identification threshold is rounded at the granularity of $1/\phi$, so the identification accuracy of worm-infected hosts improves as ϕ increases because the granularity of η of identified hosts becomes finer. Moreover, all parameters except ϕ, m^*, and H^* are calculated at each boundary of measurement periods, so more time is allowed to update the parameters as ϕ increases. Therefore, we set ϕ to the maximum value of ϕ satisfying the restriction $I_t \le \epsilon N$.

The total memory size B implemented at the edge router is fixed, so the identification accuracy improves as B_{wl}, the memory size allocated to WL, decreases because more memory is allocated to the superspreader-identification process. As η^* increases, B_{wl} decreases because smaller hosts become the identification target. Moreover, as η^* increases, we can limit the identification and quarantine target to smaller hosts and suppress the influence of incorrectly identifying legitimate hosts. Hence, a larger η^* is desirable. On the other hand, the growth of η^* increases the growth ratio of I_t because worm-infected hosts with larger η are not identified. We also set η^* to the maximum allowable value satisfying the restriction $I_t \le \epsilon N$.

As H^* decreases, fewer hosts are identified, and B_{wl} decreases. On the other hand, the slope of I_t increases as well because more worm-infected hosts are not identified. Therefore, we set H^* to the minimum possible value satisfying the restriction $I_t \le \epsilon N$.

3.2   Assumptions

Here, we summarize the assumptions made in this paper.

- All the hosts infected by the target worm repeat scans at the identical scan rate of η. Define $\widehat{\eta}$ as the anticipated maximum possible value of η that is the scan rate of bandwidth-limited worms. We consider satisfying the restriction of $I_t \le \epsilon N$ against worms with any η in the range of $\eta \le \widehat{\eta}$.
- In the worm-outbreak state, all hosts identified as worm-infected hosts are quarantined. In other words, all the packets sent from these hosts are filtered at the edge routers. The hosts that have already been infected at the time of worm detection ($t = 0$) are never extracted as worm-infected hosts because they are stored in the WL [6].
- Time is divided in discrete time units as long as the measurement period Φ with ϕ seconds length. Assume that hosts infected by the worm within

a certain measurement period start scanning at the beginning of the next measurement period. Moreover, worm-infected hosts identified within a certain measurement period are quarantined from the beginning of the next measurement period.

- We assume that a worm is detected within the measurement period zero, Φ_0. Moreover, we define I_0 as the number of worm-infected hosts at the beginning of Φ_0, J_k as the number of worm-infected hosts at the beginning of the k-th measurement period, and I_k as the number of active worm-infected hosts that are not identified and repeat scanning. Also, we consider satisfying $I_k \le \epsilon N$ for any value of k in the range of $0 \le k \le K$ when defining $K \equiv T/\phi$.
- Worm-infected hosts repeat scanning to randomly generated IP addresses. The number of worm-infected hosts increments by one only under these three conditions: the target host exists, this host is vulnerable to this worm, and this host has not been infected by this worm. Let β denote the infection probability of one scan, so we have $\beta = (N - J_k)/2^{32}$, assuming IPv4 is used. J_k is much smaller than N in the initial phase of worm spreading, so we approximate β to $\beta = N/2^{32}$.

3.3   Preparation

Using the simple epidemic model in [4] and [9], we model abusive traffic generated by scans sent from worm-infected hosts. This is widely used to model the spreading process of infections [10] and gives a good approximation when a geographical uniformity exists in the infection pattern. Although not all worms repeat scans to randomly generated IP addresses, we can ignore the geographical dependence when they scan randomly. Hence, we can apply this model to the spread of work-infected hosts.

Without identifying and quarantining worm-infected hosts, the discrete time model of I_k in the initial phase of worm spreading is given by $I_k = (1+\beta\eta\phi)I_{k-1}$ [10]. Let $H(\eta)$ denote the probability that a worm-infected host with a scan rate η is identified within one measurement period Φ. I_0 worm-infected hosts that have been identified by time $k = 0$ are accommodated into WL, so they are never identified in the worm-outbreak state. Therefore, we have

$$I_k = I_0 + \{1 - H(\eta)\}\,(I_{k-1} - I_0) + \beta\eta\phi I_{k-1}$$
$$= H(\eta)I_0 + \{1 - H(\eta) + \beta\eta\phi\}\,I_{k-1}. \tag{2}$$

By solving this equation, we have

$$I_k = \frac{I_0\left[\beta\eta\phi\Big\{1 - H(\eta) + \beta\eta\phi\Big\}^k - H(\eta)\right]}{\beta\eta\phi - H(\eta)} \tag{3}$$

when $H(\eta) \ne \beta\eta\phi$, and we have

$$I_k = I_0\left\{1 + H(\eta)k\right\} \tag{4}$$

when $H(\eta) = \beta\eta\phi$. The superspreader-identification method proposed in [5] designs the flow sampling rate r and the identification threshold Y so that the identification probability of hosts with $\eta = \eta^* = m^*/\phi$ becomes H^*. Y takes an integer in the range of $1 \leq Y \leq m^*$ and is automatically optimized from the given memory size to maximize the identification accuracy [5]. Hereafter, we investigate the required conditions to satisfy the restriction $I_k \leq \epsilon N$ by separating the range of η into two cases: $\eta \geq \eta^*$ and $\eta < \eta^*$.

3.4   Case of $\eta \geq \eta^*$

From (3) and (4), I_k is maximized for any k in the range of $k \geq 0$ when $H(\eta)$ takes the minimum value. The superspreader-identification method proposed in [5] adaptively sets Y and r minimizing the probability of the failure to identify hosts with $\eta \geq \eta^*$, according to the implemented memory size and the traffic pattern. As shown in Fig. 1, $H(\eta)$ monotonically increases as Y increases when $\eta \geq \eta^*$. Therefore, although $H(\eta)$ depends on Y, we can satisfy the restriction $I_k \leq \epsilon N$ for arbitrary Y only if we satisfy the restriction for $Y = 1$. Hence, we only consider the case of $Y = 1$.

$H(\eta)$ is given by (1) setting $m \equiv \lceil \eta\phi \rceil$, so we have $H(\eta) = 1 - (1-r)^m$ when $Y = 1$. The superspreader-identification method sets the parameters to make $H = H^*$ for hosts with $\eta = \eta^*$, so we have $1 - r = (1 - H^*)^{1/m^*}$. Therefore, we obtain

$$H(\eta) = 1 - (1 - H^*)^{\eta/\eta^*}. \tag{5}$$

When $H(\eta) = \beta\eta\phi$, we have

$$I_k = I_0 + I_0 \left\{ 1 - (1 - H^*)^{\eta/\eta^*} \right\} k \tag{6}$$

by substituting (5) into (4). I_k is maximized when η takes the maximum possible value $\widehat{\eta}$, so we have only to consider the case of $\eta = \widehat{\eta}$.

On the other hand, when $H(\eta) \neq \beta\eta\phi$, we have

$$I_k = \frac{I_0\beta\eta\phi(z^k - 1)}{z - 1} + I_0 \tag{7}$$

by substituting (5) into (3), where $z \equiv \beta\eta\phi + (1 - H^*)^{\eta/\eta^*}$. We assume $H(\eta) \neq \beta\eta\phi$, so $z \neq 1$. When $0 \leq z < 1$, I_k decreases as k increases, so I_k takes the maximum value of I_0 when $k = 0$. Hence, we can satisfy the restriction $I_k \leq \epsilon N$ if $I_0 \leq \epsilon N$.

Next, we consider the case of $z > 1$. We define $f(\eta)$ and $g(z)$ as $f(\eta) \equiv \beta\eta\phi$ and $g(z) \equiv (z^k - 1)/(z - 1)$, and $f(\eta)$ takes the maximum value when $\eta = \widehat{\eta}$. Obviously, $g(z)$ is maximized when z takes the maximum value. We obtain

$$\frac{\partial z}{\partial \eta} = \frac{(1 - H^*)^{\eta/\eta^*} \log(1 - H^*)}{\eta^*} + \beta\phi, \tag{8}$$

and $\partial z/\partial \eta$ monotonically increases as η increases because H^* is in the range of $0 < H^* < 1$. Therefore, z is a convex function of η, and z can take the maximum value at $\eta = \eta^*$ or $\eta = \widehat{\eta}$ in the range of $\eta^* \leq \eta \leq \widehat{\eta}$. To summarize, we only have to investigate the two cases of $\eta = \eta^*$ and $\eta = \widehat{\eta}$.

Restriction Equation at $\eta = \eta^*$ Because we consider the case of $z = \beta\eta^*\phi + 1 - H^* > 1$ and $H^* \neq \beta\eta^*\phi$, I_k monotonically increases as k increases according to (3). Hence, we have to consider satisfying the restriction at $k = K$. By substituting $\eta = \eta^*$, $H(\eta) = H^*$, and $k = K$ into (3), we have the restriction equation,

$$\frac{I_0\left\{\beta\eta^*\phi(1 - H^* + \beta\eta^*\phi)^K - H^*\right\}}{\beta\eta^*\phi - H^*} \leq \epsilon N. \tag{9}$$

Restriction Equation at $\eta = \widehat{\eta}$ η is adequately large compared with η^* when $\eta = \widehat{\eta}$, so we can assume $H(\eta) \geq 1 - \delta$ using a reasonably small positive value of δ. In this time, however, H^* needs to satisfy

$$H^* \geq 1 - \delta^{\eta^*/\widehat{\eta}} \tag{10}$$

according to (5). Hereafter, we consider the case of $H(\eta) = 1 - \delta$ giving the upper limit of I_k. When $\beta\widehat{\eta}\phi + \delta \neq 1$, by subsitituting $\eta = \widehat{\eta}$ and $H(\eta) = 1 - \delta$ into (3), we have

$$I_k = \frac{I_0\left\{\beta\widehat{\eta}\phi\left(\beta\widehat{\eta}\phi + \delta\right)^k - 1 + \delta\right\}}{\beta\widehat{\eta}\phi - 1 + \delta}. \tag{11}$$

I_k monotonically increases as k increases, so we only have to consider satisfying $I_K \leq \epsilon N$ at $k = K$. Hence, we have the restriction equation for ϕ as

$$\frac{I_0\left\{\beta\widehat{\eta}\phi\left(\beta\widehat{\eta}\phi + \delta\right)^K - 1 + \delta\right\}}{\beta\widehat{\eta}\phi - 1 + \delta} \leq \epsilon N. \tag{12}$$

On the other hand, when $\beta\widehat{\eta}\phi + \delta = 1$, by substituting $\eta = \widehat{\eta}$ and $H(\eta) = 1 - \delta$ into (4), we have

$$I_k = I_0\left\{1 + (1 - \delta)k\right\}. \tag{13}$$

In addition, I_k increases as k increases, so the consideration of satisfying $I_K \leq \epsilon N$ at $k = K$ is sufficient. Using $K = T/\phi = \beta\widehat{\eta}T/(1 - \delta)$, we have the following restriction equation:

$$I_0(\beta\widehat{\eta}T + 1) \leq \epsilon N. \tag{14}$$

By numerically solving (12) for ϕ, we obtain the maximum allowable value of ϕ for a given δ. Let I_0^* denote the maximum value of I_0 satisfying (14), and we have

$$I_0^* = \frac{\epsilon N}{\beta\widehat{\eta}T + 1} \simeq \frac{\epsilon 2^{32}}{\widehat{\eta}T} \tag{15}$$

because $\beta = N/2^{32}$. I_k monotonically increases as ϕ increases according to (11). When $I_0 > I_0^*$, I_K exceeds the upper limit ϵN independently of the set values of η^* and H^* if we set ϕ in the range of $\beta\widehat{\eta}\phi + \delta \geq 1$. Hence, we need to set ϕ satisfying $\beta\widehat{\eta}\phi + \delta < 1$ when $I_0 > I_0^*$. When $\beta\widehat{\eta}\phi + \delta \geq 1$, the average number of hosts newly infected by a worm with $\eta = \widehat{\eta}$ within a measurement period is larger than the average number of worm-infected hosts newly identified and quarantined within the measurement period. We can interpret I_0^* as the critical value of I_0 satisfying $I_K \leq \epsilon N$ even in this fatal case of a rapid increase in the number of infected hosts.

To summarize, we can design ϕ by deriving the maximum ϕ satisfying (12), in the range of $\phi < \phi^*$ when $I_0 > I_0^*$ and in the range of $\phi > \phi^*$ when $I_0 \leq I_0^*$, where $\phi^* \equiv (1 - \delta)/(\beta \hat{\eta})$.

3.5   Case of $\eta < \eta^*$

As shown in Fig. 1, the identification accuracy $H(\eta)$ decreases as Y increases when $\eta < \eta^*$. Hence, I_k is maximized when Y takes the maximum allowable value m^*, so we have only to consider the case of $Y = m^*$. Here, we investigate that case by separation into two cases: (i) $\eta \leq (m^*-1)/\phi$ and (ii) $(m^*-1)/\phi < \eta < \eta^*$.

Case of $\eta \leq (m^* - 1)/\phi$:   When $Y = m^*$, $H(\eta)$ is close to the unit step function, which has a discontinuity at $\eta = \eta^*$, and we can approximate $H(\eta)$ as $H(\eta) = 0$ for $\eta \leq (m^* - 1)/\phi$. From (3), we have

$$I_k = I_0 \left(1 + \beta\eta\phi\right)^k. \tag{16}$$

I_k increases as η increases, so considering only the case of $\eta = (m^* - 1)/\phi$ is sufficient. Moreover, we only have to consider the case of $k = K$ because I_k also monotonically increases as k increases. When m^* takes an integer value and (16), we have the allowable upper limit of m^* as

$$m^* = \left\lfloor \frac{1}{\beta} \left\{ \left(\frac{\epsilon N}{I_0}\right)^{\phi/T} + \beta - 1 \right\} \right\rfloor, \tag{17}$$

satisfying the restriction $I_K \leq \epsilon N$.

Case of $(m^* - 1)/\phi < \eta < \eta^*$:   By using a parameter ρ which takes values in the range of $0 < \rho < 1/\phi$, we can express η as $\eta = (m^*-1)/\phi+\rho$. Approximately, we assume that worm-infected hosts repeat scans at a fixed time interval of $1/\eta$. This means that each worm-infected host generates $m^* - 1$ or m^* scans within each measurement period Φ. By regarding that the measurement periods in which m^* scans are observed appear at every continuous x measurement periods, we have

$$\frac{m^* + (x - 1)(m^* - 1)}{\eta} = x\phi. \tag{18}$$

By solving this equation for x, we obtain $x = 1/(\phi\rho)$. Therefore, we can assume that a worm-infected host generates m^* scans in a measurement period with the probability of $\phi\rho$ and $m^* - 1$ scans in a measurement period with the probability of $1 - \phi\rho$. Because we consider the case of $Y = m^*$, this host is identified with the probability of H^* within the measurement periods in which it generates m^* scans and never identified within the measurement periods in which it generates

$m^* - 1$ scans. Therefore, the identification probability of this host over a long time scale is $H(\eta) = \phi \rho H^*$. By substituting $\eta = (m^* - 1)/\phi + \rho$ and $H(\eta) = \phi \rho H^*$ into (3), we have

$$I_k = \frac{I_0 \left\{ (X + H^* \phi \rho - 1) X^k - H^* \phi \rho \right\}}{X - 1}, \tag{19}$$

where $X \equiv 1 - H(\eta) + \beta \eta \phi = 1 + \beta(m^* - 1) + (\beta - H^*)\phi \rho$. X is greater than one, so I_k monotonically increases as k increases. Hence, we consider only the case of $k = K$. When $k = K$, we have

$$\begin{aligned} I_K &= \frac{I_0 \left\{ (X + H^* \phi \rho - 1) X^K - H^* \phi \rho \right\}}{X - 1} \\ &= \frac{I_0 (X - 1)(X^K + H^* \phi \rho)}{X - 1} \\ &= I_0 (X^K + H^* \phi \rho). \end{aligned} \tag{20}$$

By partially differentiating this equation with respect to ρ, we have

$$\frac{\partial I_K}{\partial \rho} = I_0 \left\{ K X^{K-1} (\beta - H^*)\phi + \phi H^* \right\}. \tag{21}$$

Therefore, we have $\frac{\partial I_K}{\partial \rho} > 0$ for any ρ in the range of $0 < \rho < 1/\phi$ when $\beta \geq H^*$, and I_K is maximized when $\rho \to 1/\phi$. When $\beta < H^*$, on the other hand, $\frac{\partial I_K}{\partial \rho}$ monotonically decreases as ρ increases. The solution of ρ satisfying $\frac{\partial I_K}{\partial \rho} = 0$ is obtained by

$$\rho = -\frac{1}{H^* - \beta} \left(\frac{H^*}{K(H^* - \beta)} \right)^{1/(K-1)} - 1 - \beta(m^* - 1) < 0, \tag{22}$$

so $\frac{\partial I_K}{\partial \rho} < 0$ in the range of $0 < \rho < 1/\phi$. Hence, I_K is maximized when $\rho \to 0$.

To summarize, we only have to investigate the cases of $\rho = 0$ and $\rho = 1/\phi$. The case of $\rho = 0$ corresponds to the case of $\eta = (m^* - 1)/\phi$, which we have already investigated. Moreover, the case of $\rho = 1/\phi$ corresponds to the case of $\eta = \eta^*$, which we have already discussed in Sec. 3.4.

3.6   Design Algorithm

Now, we summarize how to optimally set three parameters of the superspreader-identification method, ϕ, m^*, and H^*. We consider satisfying the condition that the number of active hosts infected by the target worm is bounded below the predefined threshold ϵN anytime during $0 \leq k \leq K$ ($K = T/\phi$). The number of hosts infected by this worm at the time of detection $k = 0$ is I_0, the worm has an arbitrary scan rate of η less than or equal to $\hat{\eta}$, and the time required to develop a patch or vaccine against this worm is T.

(i) Designing ϕ:
   Set the maximum value to ϕ satisfying (12), in the range of $\phi < \phi^*$ when $I_0 > I_0^*$ and in the range of $\phi > \phi^*$ when $I_0 \leq I_0^*$.
(ii) Designing m^*
   By substituting the set value of ϕ into (17), set m^*. (Also set η^* as $\eta^* = m^*/\phi$.)
(iii) Designing H^*
   Set the minimum value of H^* satisfying the inequalities obtained by substituting the set values of ϕ and η^* into both (9) and (10), respectively.

4   Numerical Results

In this section, we show an example of parameter settings and investigate how the parameters, ϕ, m^*, and H^* are designed. The scan rate of Slammer was reported to be about 4,000 scans per second, and the number of vulnerable hosts was about 75,000 [2]. Therefore, we set $\widehat{\eta} = 4000$ and $N = 10^5$. Moreover, we set the time required to develop a patch or vaccine, T, to 86,400 seconds, i.e., 24 hours, as mentioned in Sec. 3.1, and the upper bound of the active infected host ratio ϵ to 0.1.

Before designing the three parameters in the manner mentioned in Sec. 3.6, we need to give δ, which determines the identification probability of hosts with $\eta = \widehat{\eta}$. Hence, first, we investigate the influence of δ on the designed values of the three parameters. The designed values of the three parameters versus δ when we set the initial number of infected hosts I_0 to 10 or 100 are shown in Fig. 3. As mentioned in Sec. 3.4, $\phi^* = (1 - \delta)/(\beta\widehat{\eta})$ is the value of ϕ where the average number of newly infected hosts balances with the average number of identified worm-infected hosts within each measurement period when the worm infection rate is $\eta = \widehat{\eta}$. We confirm that the set value of ϕ is close to ϕ^* throughout the range of δ. Therefore, ϕ rapidly decreases as δ approaches unity, whereas ϕ is almost stable when δ is less than about 0.1. Throughout the range of δ, moreover, the influence of δ on η^* is small. Although H^* decreases as δ decreases due to the restriction equation (10), the influence of δ on the identification process of superspreaders is limited because H^* takes a very small value throughout the

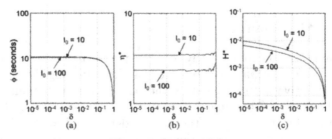

Fig. 3. Influence of δ

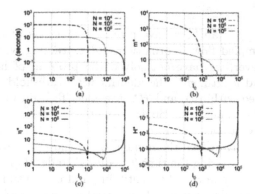

Fig. 4. Set values of parameters

range of δ. Although setting δ smaller than about 0.1 is desirable because a larger ϕ is desirable, we can say that the influence of δ can be ignored when $\delta < 0.1$. Therefore, we set $\delta = 0.01$ hereafter.

The designed values of ϕ, m^*, η^*, and H^* versus I_0 for three values of N are depicted in Fig. 4. I_0^*, the critical value of I_0 in which the number of hosts infected by a worm with $\eta = \widehat{\eta}$ is permitted to increase on average, is independent of N as observed in (15), and we have $I_0^* = 1.243$ in this evaluation condition. Therefore, ϕ is set in the range of $\phi < \phi^*$ in almost all the range of I_0, and $\phi \simeq \phi^*$ except when I_0 is close to ϵN. Although ϕ is designed to satisfy $I_K \leq \epsilon N$ when worms scan at the rate of $\eta = \widehat{\eta}$, this condition is fully satisfied only if the number of worm-infected hosts that is identified and quarantined is slightly larger than the number of hosts newly infected by this worm on average. As N increases, β increases, so ϕ^* decreases. However, when I_0 is close to ϵN, ϕ rapidly decreases as I_0 increases.

On the other hand, m^* and η^* are designed according to the restrictions that satisfy $I_K \leq \epsilon N$ when worms with $\eta < \eta^*$ are spreading without being identified and quarantined. I_K increases as I_0 increases. Hence, we need to lower the threshold defining superspreaders and identify hosts infected by worms with a smaller scan rate when I_0 is large. As a result, both m^* and η^* decrease as I_0 increases. If we can detect the appearance of a new worm earlier, then we can suppress I_0. Moreover, we can set the threshold scan rate to a larger value and suppress the number of legitimate hosts that are defined as superspreaders. We cannot set m^* smaller than unity, so $m^* = 1$ when I_0 is close to ϵN. $\eta^* = m^*/\phi$ and ϕ rapidly decrease as I_0 approaches ϵN, so η^* rapidly increases. Moreover, β increases and the infection rate also increases as N increases, so both m^* and η^* decrease.

The first restriction equation (9) determining H^* is derived from the restriction for worms with $\eta = \eta^*$. We assume $H(\eta) = 0$ when deriving the restriction equation for worms with $\eta = \eta^* - 1/\phi$, so the lower limit of H^* determined by (9) is also close to zero. Therefore, H^* is almost solely determined by the second restriction equation (10) and exhibits a tendency similar to that of η^*.

5 Conclusion

In previous studies, the authors have proposed methods of identifying super-spreaders using sampled flow information and extracting worm-infected hosts using a WL. However, we have not solved the problem of how to set ϕ, the measurement period length, m^*, the identification threshold for m that is the flow count generated within ϕ, and H^*, the identification probability of hosts with $m = m^*$. In this paper, we proposed a method of optimally designing these three parameters with the constraint that the ratio of the number of active worm-infected hosts divided by the number of all the vulnerable hosts is bound by a given upper limit during the time T required to develop a patch or vaccine for the newly appearing worm. By identifying and quarantining worm-infected hosts using the proposed parameter design method, we can adequately suppress the spread of infection even when a worm with an arbitrary scan rate appears, with limiting the number of legitimate hosts that are falsely identified as worm-infected hosts. The approach and framework of the proposed design method can be widely applied to methods of identifying worm-infected hosts.

References

1. Yegneswaran, V., Barford, P., Ulleich, J.: Internet Intrusions: Global Characteristics and Prevalence. In: ACM SIGMETRICS 2003 (2003)
2. Moore, D., Paxson, V., Savage, S., Shannon, C., Staniford, S., Weaver, N.: Inside the Slammer Worm. IEEE Security and Privacy (July/August 2003)
3. Bu, T., Chen, A., Wiel, S.V., Woo, T.: Design and Evaluation of a Fast and Robust Worm Detection Algorithm. In: IEEE INFOCOM 2006 (2006)
4. Zou, C.C., Gong, W., Towsley, D., Gao, L.: The Monitoring and Early Detection of Internet Worms. IEEE/ACM Trans. on Networking 13(5), 961–974 (2005)
5. Kamiyama, N., Mori, T., Kawahara, R.: Simple and Adaptive Identification of Superspreaders by Flow Sampling. In: INFOCOM 2007 Minisymposium (2007)
6. Kamiyama, N., Mori, T., Kawahara, R., Harada, S., Yoshino, H.: Extracting Worm-Infected Hosts Using White List. In: IEEE SAINT 2008(2008)
7. Bloom, B.H.: Space/Time Trade-offs in Hash Coding with Allowable Errors. Communications of the ACM 13(7) (1970)
8. Frei, S., May, M., Fiedler, U., Plattner, B.: Large-Scale Vulnerability Analysis. In: ACM LSAD 2006 (2006)
9. Liljenstam, M., Nicol, D., Berk, V., Gray, R.: Simulating Realistic Network Worm Traffic for Worm Warning System Design and Testing. In: ACM WORM 2003 (2003)
10. Daley, D.J., Gani, J.: Epidemic Modelling: An Introduction. Cambridge University Press, Cambridge (1999)

Session-Based QoS Management Architecture for Wireless Local Area Networks

Badis Tebbani, Kamel Haddadou, and Guy Pujolle

Laboratory of Computer Science
University of Paris 6
104 avenue du President Kennedy
75016, Paris, France
{firstname.lastname}@lip6.fr

Abstract. Growing demands for the public wireless broadband services will require more capacity than the one provided by IP-based service providers (ISPs). The increasing popularity of WLANs due to the use of license-free radio spectrum with low-cost, easily deployable, high-data-rate wireless services, has encouraged service providers to consider their deployment in high density usage areas such us public hotspots to provide complementary broadband access to their networks and services. In order to provide consistent QoS control for multimedia applications (VoIP, VoD,...) over hotspots, a Session Initiation Protocol (SIP) based QoS management architecture is proposed in this article. Performance evaluations are discussed to illustrate the feasibility of the proposed architecture.

Keywords: WLAN, hotspots, SIP, QoS Control and Management.

1 Introduction

Internet Service Providers are strongly interested in extending their networks and services using IEEE 802.11-based wireless technologies to indoor (xDSL) or outdoor (hotspots) areas. WLAN technologies offer services with any time and any where access facilities, and provide nomadic high-speed wireless access to existing wired Internet Protocol (IP)-based networks. However, WLAN environments raise security and quality of service (QoS) issues that current technologies such as 802.11 still do not address properly. Guaranteeing the quality of a delivered service in a shared wireless environment requires an intelligent management of the shared bandwidth.

Management mechanisms are a set of tools enabling efficient network control in accordance with the Wireless Internet Service Provider (WISP) objectives. It implies the following points:

- Access Management: authentication, authorization of users and subscription management.
- Network Provisioning: setting up suitable quality of service (QoS) configurations in order to meet applications needs and users privileges.

N. Akar, M. Pioro, and C. Skianis (Eds.): IPOM 2008, LNCS 5275, pp. 117–126, 2008.

- Adaptation: dynamic network configurations according to user priorities or service level agreement (SLA), and to the network state.
- Robustness and Scalability: in order to provide the same management process to all access points of the WLAN.

These challenges are realizable through some existing service-oriented management systems. In the literature there are several management architectures for the WLAN which allow the provisioning of services and QoS control [1,2]. However, no design proposes an efficient means for the automatic network *adaptation* when a problem like congestion occurs. By congestion we mean that the link is carrying so much data that its quality of service deteriorates. Typical effects include queueing delay and/or packet loss. Since multimedia applications are very sensible to these QoS parameters, they cannot work correctly during the congestion period.

This limit represents a well-known issue for research in the network management field and we can formulate it as follows: when a congestion event occurs, which action to take in order to optimize the use of network resources (bandwidth)? Or fulfill the provider objectives?

To be able to perform a planned action when problems arise, the network will require specific information, whereas monitoring tools used by the majority of management schemes (e.g. SNMP) have only access to data plane information: IP header (Port source, Port destination, Protocol used...) and the queues state. This information helps to know the network state but does not allow acting on a particular flow. Possible actions on this level are service class re-dimensioning (e.g. increase the EF class queue size) or flow re-marking (e.g. change AF flows to BE). There is also lot of works in the literature on these two proposals and it was proven their limit and complexity [3,4]. The main issue in QoS guaranteeing for WLAN users is to knowing exactly at the congestion time the flows of each user, bandwidth allocated for each of their flows and their duration in order to proceed in a way to always respect the user agreement (SLA) and to fulfill the provider (WISP) objectives.

In this work, we focalize on QoS guarantees control for delivered multimedia applications over wireless local area networks. Our proposal is an application-level QoS control mechanism which guarantees the QoS delivery according to user priorities, based on session information (Call_ID, User_ID, Codec_used, Session_duration, ...), our mechanism chooses the application session to be stopped when congestion occurs in order to relax the network and to provide more bandwidth to other user sessions. Moreover, the proposed mechanism is developed over an efficient service provisioning and user sessions management system [5,4], which enforces service access control, and ensures the dynamic network resource configurations defining the network behavior.

Performance evaluations are carried out in order to test the feasibility of our overall architecture. We focalize on delay measurements, the first one is the session establishment delay that must remain always under the recommended ITU-T delay limit of 6s [6], and the second one is the session stopping delay (the reaction time) which must be realistic (<0.5s). Results demonstrate both of the relevance and the efficiency of our solution.

The remainder of this article is structured as follows. Next section presents the design of our solution and some main related features. The Test-bed implementation is presented in section 3 by which we evaluate our solution, while section 4 describes performance evaluation results. Finally, section 5 concludes this work.

2   Session-Based QoS Management Architecture

The main objective of our architecture (Figure 1) is to provide the WISP with suitable tools enabling it to support and control users nomadism, to establish and guarantee their multimedia application QoS.

The session-based QoS management framework of Figure 1 is composed of two levels of abstraction:

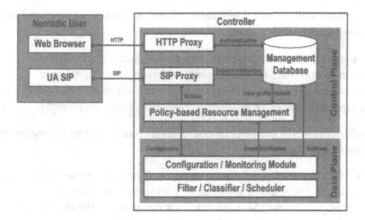

Fig. 1. A Session-based QoS Management Architecture

2.1   Data Plane

The data plane contains the DiffServ router implementation which is based on the Linux traffic control (TC) implementation described in [7,8,9]. It includes:

 – Queuing disciplines: each network interface has a queuing discipline associated with it, which controls how packets enqueued on that interface are treated and determines the order in which data is transmitted.
 – Classes: user flows can be split into classes according to certain rules. Each class sustains a queuing discipline to serve it packets.
 – Filters: or Classifier are used to classify and put packets into classes based on certain properties of the packet (e.g. IP header). Queuing disciplines uses filters to assign incoming packets to one of its classes.

These above elements define for each incoming packet a particular forwarding treatment, which is called Per-Hop Behavior (PHB). In order to control the amount of traffic from and to a given class, we added above this mechanism a Configuration and Monitoring Module (see Figure 1) responsible of the following tasks:

- Traffic monitoring: it analyzes regularly information relating to each class (e.g. Used bandwidth, Loss rate . . .).
- Congestion detection: based on policies which define thresholds, it consider a congestion when a particular class exceeds loss rate threshold.
- PHB re-configuration: it can perform a specific or regular change of configurations (e.g. *Each Monday between 9:00 and 12:00 am, increase the EF class queue size.*).

2.2 Control Plane

The control plane embraces all elements of our architecture responsible of user sessions management, which are:

- Users management: subscription and authentication of users.
- Sessions management: establishment and stopping of sessions.
- Configurations derivation: based on user and application profiles, the material parameter settings (e.g. filter parameters.) are derived [5].

These functionalities are enabled in our design thanks to the following architectural elements (see Figure 1):

- POLICY REPOSITORY: contains user agreements, provider policy rules (e.g. *Promote short communications*) and session information.
- HTTP PROXY: holds the network captive portal. Based on Web, it is in charge for the user authentication and subscriptions.
- SIP PROXY: deals with signalisation, it is responsible for the session establishment of multimedia applications such us the VoIP (Voice over IP) application. In order to guarantee the user service level we have added some functionalities to our SIP PROXY such us the session stopping.
- POLICY-BASED RESSOURCE MANAGEMENT: is the management module, it is responsible for configurations derivation from user and application profiles. It is in charge also to command suitable actions when congestion occurs (e.g. re-configuration, session stopping . . .).

2.3 User Sessions Management Sequence Diagram

In order to illustrate the interaction between all involved components of our architecture, Figure 2 describes the details of user sessions management sequence diagram.

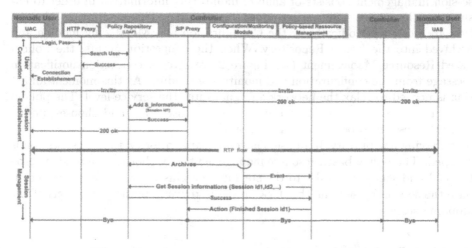

Fig. 2. User Sessions Management Sequence Diagram

2.3.1 User Connection

At the first user connection, it is redirected automatically towards our captive portal in order to authenticate or to sign a new subscription. In general, once the agreement is signed, user information are stored in the Policy Repository. Then, at the user authentication the HTTP PROXY asks the Policy Repository in order to retrieve the user agreement. In the case of the user agreement existence the HTTP PROXY authorizes the user connection.

Note that, before a user is authenticated, none of his (her) generated traffic is allowed through the network. Thus, the connection establishment consists in the derivation of adequate configurations and to authorize his (her) flows to cross the network.

2.3.2 Session Establishment

After the user connection, he (she) can use its subscribed services. At the multimedia application launching, the SIP PROXY receives the 'INVITE' message (from the UAC), it then forwards this message to its destination. By the reception of the favourable response '200 OK'(from the UAS) and before forwarding it to the initiator of the communication like would perform all traditional SIP Proxy, our SIP PROXY stores at first the communication information into the Policy Repository. These information are: a Call_ID, a source address IP, a destination address IP, a Time_Start , a Max_BW (Max_bandwidth) and the communication state. After this, our SIP PROXY forwards the '200 OK' towards the communication initiator (the UAC) to conclude the session establishment. Thus, multimedia application can start.

2.3.3 Session Management:

The beginning of the communication is characterized by the Real-time Transport Protocol (RTP) (or UDP according to the application) flows exchange. The session management consists of analyze monitoring information in order to ensure that flows have sufficient resources (bandwidth). This monitoring information are posted periodically by the Configuration and Monitoring module and archived into the Policy Repository. When the congestion occurs, the Policy-based Resource Management (see Figure 2) receives a congestion notification message from the configuration and monitoring module. At this moment an action is needed to relax the network and guarantee the service level. The policy-based resource management checks the active session list and chooses among them the session to be finished. Based on the user priority, one stops session of users having low priority. If all users have the same priority, the oldest session is stopped. The policy-based resource management only chooses the session to be finished and sends this order to the SIP PROXY. This last is in charge to terminate the session by sending the 'BYE' message towards both applications of the stopping session.

3   Test-Bed Implementation

In order to test the feasibility of our solution we focus in this evaluation on two parameters, which are crucial in the multimedia applications management. The first parameter is the delay of the session establishment that must be under 6s as required in ITU-T recommendations [6]. The second consideration is the delay between congestion detection and congestion fixing which must be realistic.

As we have shown above, there are tasks relating to the session establishment and stopping performed by the SIP PROXY, and separately tasks attached to the resource management realised by the policy-based resource management module. The common element between these two blocks is the Policy Repository, which enables them to communicate.

Preliminary results based on separate experiments of SIP and Resource Management (RM) block give us positive indications on the impact of additional SIP functionalities over the policy-based resource management. Here, we intend to verify the feasibility of our solution. For doing so, an integrated test-bed, containing all SIP and all RM entities, is carried out. The details of our test-bed building blocks are given bellow.

3.1   Resource Management (RM) Building Block

The entire resource management components were realised with Linux bash shell scripting, Java, Servlets and Web applications.

- Policy-based Resource Management: it is completely developed by Java and includes all our management algorithms, it is mainly responsible of translating policies (from the Policy Repository) into network-level configuration commands (DiffServ parameters) [10], reacting when congestion occurs by choosing among active sessions that to stop and posting its information to the SIP PROXY.

- Configuration/Monitoring Module: It is responsible of the network device configurations and is realised by Linux bash shell scripting, which implements a Linux-based traffic conditioning and enforces the QoS decision (Traffic Control 'TC' and 'IPTABLES' [7]). It is in charge to supervise the network state and to archive monitoring information (drop rate, used bandwidth, ...). In addition when it detects a congestion it notifies the policy-based resource management.
- HTTP Proxy: it is developed by Java servlet technology; Apache is used like Web server and Tomcat as servlet container in order to realize the Web-based authentication and SLA negotiations [11,10].

In addition NoCat [12] was used only for the captive portal, which capture all non-authenticated traffic and redirect them to our Web server in order to subscribing or authenticating.

3.2 SIP Building Block

All SIP entities, listed below, have been implemented using the Java-based specifications called Jain-SIP [13].

- SIP User Agent Client (UAC): this component is the one that generates SIP requests and records call set-up delays (from the 'INVITE' message up to the '200 OK'),
- SIP Proxy: in addition to its classical operations defined in SIP [14], it is in charge of: the storage of session information and stopping sessions (generate the 'BYE' message),
- SIP User Agent Server (UAS): this component generates automatically the responses to UAC requests.

3.3 Policy Repository

The Policy Repository is realized as a Lightweight Directory Access Protocol (LDAP) [15] schema, where in the management information are modeled using CIM [16]. When using LDAP we have the ability to access information directly using their distinguished names (DN). Hence, in our architecture, we use, as distinguished names (DN), specific information related to session (User-Login, Call_ID, ...), that are sent as objects of the SIP messages. This allows direct access to the management information that is needed to handle a new media flow and accelerates substantially the delay of each information access and retrieval [4].

4   Tests and Measures

The established test-bed allows us to set up feasibility tests. Demonstrating the feasibility of our solution consists of analyzing the behavior of SIP and RM, and verifying that the delay bound defined by the ITU-T is never exceeded. The test-bed architecture has two main components, wireless access networks through a WLAN network that comprises a number of WLAN access points (APs) and an existing DiffServ-based wired network (backbone). The WLANs are connected to the backbone IP throw a CONTROLLER [17], in order to provide access to external networks (Internet). All access points of the WLAN are connected to the CONTROLLER, which plays a 'gateway' and 'firewall' role. It contains also the core of our solution and all WLAN traffic signalisations were constrained to go through it, before communication beginning in order to control all user sessions.

Lets note that 30 iterative session establishment (respectively session stopping whith 4 active sessions) demands are initiated in order to have statistically acceptable delay estimate.

4.1   Session Establishment Feasibility Test

Table 1 summarizes the main observed delays using our test-bed configuration. First of all, our attention is focused on the small overall measured delays compared to the 6s ITU-T bound. Furthermore, the delays standard deviation is quite low, confirming the accuracy of these experiments.

This Table 1 shows that the simultaneously hold delays for RM are 3% smaller than those of SIP. This is due to the small number of management tasks involved in the session establishment; there is only the session information storage procedure on the level of both SIP Proxies. Moreover, the SIP messages are of text type (said HTTP-like) and need a parser to be interpreted causing the high delay of session establishment processes in contrast with the delay of RM.

Table 1. Session Establishment Feasibility Tests: delay measurements

Delay (millisecond)	Min	Max	Mean	Standard Deviation (SD)
SIP Signalisation	812	1230	915	73.21
RM	17	32	23	6.61
Global	831	1252	**939**	103.41

4.2   Session Stopping Feasibility Test

In order to fulfil the feasibility test of our solution, the application stopping delay that includes: congestion detection, session to be stop selection and 'BYE' message sending must be realistic.

The main result of Table 2 is the overall delay of the session stopping (*the reaction time*) that is always inferior to 0.5s (average delay ≈ 0.4s), with also the low of delays standard deviation (SD), that confirming the accuracy of these experiments.

Table 2. Session Stopping Feasibility Tests: delay measurements

Delay (millisecond)	Min	Max	Mean	Standard Deviation (SD)
SIP Signalisation	109	208	165	17.27
RM	174	222	191	20.23
Global	277	421	**355**	40.09

In opposite to the Table 1, SIP signalisation delays are sensibly smaller than RM delays, because the application stopping process involves mainly the congestion detection, active sessions retrieve and selection among them a session that will be stopped. However, the SIP PROXY have only to send the 'BYE' message towards both applications.

Both Tables 1 and 2 prove the feasibility of our solution. This is very promising because our test-bed is very realistic in currently Information Technology (IT) configurations.

5   Conclusion and Future Work

In this work, we defined a framework for the design of a session-based QoS management solution for nomadic users, which integrates a QoS and service access control management. We defined a session-based dynamic resources management mechanism that deals with user sessions information, by considering user priority (from its SLA) and session duration to guaranteeing certain level of services. It presents a new approach in the QoS assurance that combines the data plane and the control plane to detecting congestion and choosing the suitable action to fix it, in order to provide more bandwidth into the network.

In order to measure the performance of our solution, a complete test-bed has been implemented. It includes all RM, SIP and integration components. The experiments carried out allow us to highlight the feasibility of our solution. Ongoing work will look at the extension of our mechanism to others criterions such that: the used bandwidth per session and the user location. We also consider the roaming and mobility management.

Acknowledgement. The authors would like to thank France Telecom (Orange) R&D, France, for the financial support of this research under C.R.E project Number EB186734.

References

1. Limam, N., Rotrou, J., Loutrel, M., Ouakil, L., Saleh, H., Pujolle, G.: Service Management in Secure and QoS-Aware Wireless Enterprise Networks. IEEE Journal on Selected Areas in Communications 23(10), 1950–1962 (2005)

2. Fodil, I., Pujolle, G.: Roaming and service management in public wireless networks using an innovative policy management architecture. International Journal of Network Management 15(2), 103–121 (2005)
3. Boutaba, R., Polyrakis, A.: Extending COPS-PR with Meta-policies for Scalable Management of IP Networks. International Journal on Networks and Systems Management, special issue on Management of Converged Networks 10(1), 91–106 (2002)
4. Haddadou, K., Ghamri-Doudane, S., Ghamri-Doudane, Y., Agoulmine, N., Pujolle, G.: Designing Scalable on Demand Policy-based Resource Allocation in IP Networks. IEEE Communications Magazine (March 2006)
5. Tebbani, B., Aib, I., Pujolle, G.: SLA-based Dynamic Resource Management in Wireless Environments: An enterprise Nomadism Use Case. International Journal of Internet Protocol Technology (IJIPT), Special Issue on the Management of IP Networks and Services (to appear, April 2008)
6. Union, I.: Network Grade of Service Parameters and Target Values for Circuit-Switched Services in Evolving ISDN. Recommendation E 721
7. Hubert, B., et al.: Linux Advanced Routing and Traffic Control HOWTO, A very hands-on approach to iproute2, traffic shaping and a bit of netfilter, http://lartc.org/; Revision: 1.43, Date: 2003/10/29, 12:33:38
8. Jacobson, V., Nichols, K., Poduri, K., et al.: An Expedited Forwarding PHB (1999)
9. Heinanen, J., Baker, F., Weiss, W., Wroclawski, J.: RFC2597: Assured Forwarding PHB Group. Internet RFCs (1999)
10. Tebbani, B., Aib, I., Pujolle, G.: GXLA a Language for the Specification of Service Level Agreements. In: Gaiti, D., Pujolle, G., Al-Shaer, E.S., Calvert, K.L., Dobson, S., Leduc, G., Martikainen, O. (eds.) AN 2006. LNCS, vol. 4195. Springer, Heidelberg (2006)
11. Brittain, J., Darwin, I.: Tomcat: The Definitive Guide. O'Reilly Media, Inc., Sebastopol (2007)
12. Portals, C.: NoCat, http://nocat.net/
13. Bhat, R., Gupta, R.: JAIN protocol APIs. IEEE Communications Magazine 38(1), 100–107 (2000)
14. Rosenberg, J., Schulzrinne, H., Camarillo, G., Johnston, A., Peterson, J., Sparks, R., Handley, M., Schooler, E.: SIP: Session Initiation Protocol. tech. rep., RFC 3261 (June 2002)
15. C. DMTF: Core Model v2. 5, LDAP Mapping Specification, DSP0123 (2002)
16. I. Distributed Management Task Force: Common Information Model (CIM), Policy Model White Paper, CIM Version 2.7 (June 18, 2003)
17. Tebbani, B., Aib, I., Pujolle, G.: Towards SLA and Location-based Nomadism Management. In: Proceedings of 2nd CoNext Conference, Lisbon, Portugal (December 2006)

Low-Latency Parallel Transport in Anonymous Peer-to-Peer Overlays

Igor Margasiński[1] and Michał Pióro[1,2]

[1] Institute of Telecommunications, Warsaw University of Technology, Poland
[2] Department of Electro- and Information Technology, Lund University, Sweden
{I.Margasinski,M.Pioro}@tele.pw.edu.pl

Abstract. The paper presents a design and discusses configuration aspects of an overlay transport protocol based on an idea of the peer-to-peer direct and anonymous distribution overlay (P2PRIV). We estimate a secure configuration of the protocol and examine a correlation between the P2PRIV's anonymous path lengths and latency. An increase of the path lengths speaks strongly in favor of the parallel solution's anonymity, as in classical cascade networks. In the paper we evaluate the new protocol in a scope of a trade-off between anonymity and traffic performance and show that the presented solution allows effectively increasing anonymity with relatively low impact on anonymous transport latency.

Keywords: Communication system traffic, communication system security, privacy, peer-to-peer overlays, overlay networks management.

1 Introduction

Nowadays anonymous networks impose a trade-off between anonymity and traffic performance. A high level of anonymity can be achieved primarily at a high traffic expense. In particular, the latency constitutes a crucial factor for performance of anonymous networks, as the basic common mechanism used to achieve network anonymization is a traffic forwarding by a set of middleman nodes. Long anonymous path lengths usually speak strongly in favor of anonymity. However, the traffic performance is reduced and a download time elongated by increasing path lengths of the content's transport. Each of forwarding nodes introduces a delay imposed by specific anonymization techniques applied (such as batching and multiple asymmetric encryptions in *Mix-nets* [3]) and bandwidth limitations of routing links. Furthermore, when we consider the environment of peer-to-peer overlays, insufficient throughputs links become an onerous issue while the content relaying by personal or *soho* computers deepen latency of the anonymous transport.

On March 2008, a new anonymous peer-to-peer architecture was proposed by the authors in [12]. In the new solution called P2PRIV (peer-to-peer direct and anonymous distribution overlay) only control messages are sent over anonymous paths, called "cloning cascades" (CC). The P2PRIV uses the well known anonymous techniques for anonymization of a specific management communications adjusted to

N. Akar, M. Pioro, and C. Skianis (Eds.): IPOM 2008, LNCS 5275, pp. 127–141, 2008.

provide further anonymous and direct parallel transport of the shared information content. In this paper we continue the research and present design details of the P2PRIV protocol, and analyze an impact of the protocol configuration, i.e. CC path lengths, on the solution's anonymity and latency. We study the trade-off between anonymity and performance and show that the new solution tolerates an increase of anonymous path lengths with a significant advance in anonymity and with a significantly lower impact on traffic performance.

2 Related Work

A basic common mechanism used to achieve P2P anonymization is the traffic forwarding by a set of middleman network nodes. These peers anonymize a traffic in accordance with various anonymous techniques ranging from heuristics with encryption methods (applied in *Freenet* [4], *Gnunet* [1]) to highly anynymous *mixing* [3] (e.g. in *Free Haven* [7], *Tarzan* [9], *MorphMix* [14]). Mix-net is a network of many intermediate nodes called *Mixes*. Anonymous messages are routed throughout Mixes which aggregate, permutate randomly, and encrypts received messages with public keys of successive nodes. The identity of both a sender and a receiver is never disclosed to any single proxy Mix, and due to specific mixing of asymmetrically encrypted packets an attack based on traffic analysis is unlikely to succeed. Still, highly secure mixing networks impose high latency. Various low-latency – yet less secure – techniques, such as so called *virtual link encryption* (*PipeNet* [5]), *fixed shared routes/cascades* (*JAP* [2]), and *onion-routing* multiple public key encryption (applied in *Onion Routing* [10], [13], and widely used *TOR* [8], [16], [11]), were introduced. Another, simple low-latency technique as involving only a symmetric cryptography, was introduced for *CROWDS* system [15]. CROWDS anonymizes Web traffic and utilizes an idea of *random walk* algorithm by traffic forwarding via a random group of nodes before its delivery. CROWDS member, who wishes to send an anonymous message, selects a random node of the CROWDS network (the so called "Jondo") and then sends the node the message. The message contains a destination address, but the source address is neglected. Then, the selected node flips an asymmetric coin to decide whether to forward the message to the next random node or send it directly do the destination (random walk). All random nodes repeat the same activity and finally the message is sent to its destination (based on the included address). The decision whether to forward the message to a next proxy node or to the message's receiver is random. However, commonly the selection of a proxy is more probable than directing the message to the destination. This probabilistic forwarding assures anonymity, because none of network nodes can ascertain the message's origin. The coin asymmetry is described by a probability p_f. The proxy node forwards the encrypted message to the next random proxy node with the probability p_f and sends it to the destination with a probability $1 - p_f$. Then the mean forwarding path length of network random walk equals

$$P = \sum_{i=2}^{\infty} i p_f^{\,i-2}(1 - p_f) = \frac{p_f - 2}{p_f - 1} .$$
(1)

The P2PRIV system omits the canon of information content forwarding. In P2PRIV only a token is sent over random walk path, called "cloning cascade" (Step 1). The traffic generated by token relaying can be additionally anonymized by Mix-net, as numerous and short messages can be effectively exchanged by the Mix cascades. Then, based on information included in the token and after a random delay, the selected ("cloned") nodes download content data specified by an initiator directly (Step 2). The novel idea of the P2PRIV consists in the parallel content transport separating the anonymization process from the transport function (Figure 1).

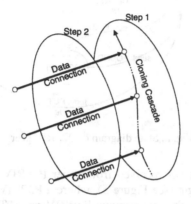

Fig. 1. P2PRIV parallel transport of content

3 Parallel Overlay Transport

Let us describe the protocol design from the point of view of a "cloned peer". Notice that the P2PRIV is a pure P2P overlay, hence all P2PRIV peers are symmetric and represent the same functionality. Figure 2 shows a finite state machine diagram of a single peer. The basic states of the peer are: "LISTEN", "CLONED", and "DATA CONNECT".LISTEN represents an idle operation of a peer waiting for requests (marked on the diagram as "recv:") from other peers or from the user (marked with "user:" symbol). CLONED state is triggered when the peer joins a Cloning Cascade (compare with Step 1 of P2PRIV operation). DATA CONNECT corresponds to the Data Connection step in which P2PRIV node downloads a specified content (Step 2 of P2PRIV operation). The diagram contains also: "COIN FLIP" and "LOOKUP" states. COIN FLIP applies to a decision process based on a binary random selection and LOOKUP initiates a DHT lookup procedure. The P2PRIV communications is based on five messages: "CLONE", "FIND", "FOUND", "GET" and "PUT". The following pseudo-code includes a description of their detail roles (Figure 3, 4, 5, and 6). and is organized as a one infinite loop with three main sections. The first section (starting from the Line 3, Figure 3) refers to a CC joining process and a further contend download. When a peer receives a CLONE message (token) containing a file id it will check whether the message comes from other peer or from a local user. Then it starts a "Clone and Download" subroutine presented in Figure 4. The next section (starting from the Line 8, Figure 3) refers to a reaction of a peer to a content look-up

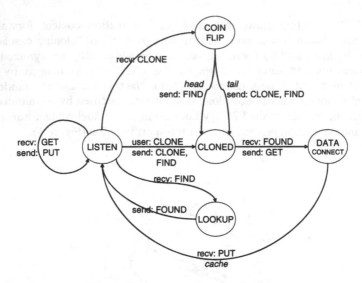

Fig. 2. State diagram of P2PRIV peer

request. If a FIND message is received from other P2PRIV node, then a "Find and Reply" subroutine will begin (see Figure 5), where a P2PRIV node looks for a specified content on behalf of other anonymous P2PRIV node. The last section (starting from Line 11, Figure 3) refers to reaction to an upload request from other node. In this case the node was pointed out by DHT interface as storage of the specified file. If it occurs and a GET message is received then an "Upload" subroutines will begin (Figure 6).

The Clone and Download subroutine describes a process of a CC joining and fulfilling tasks of a clone: a location of a requested content and its download. If the request is originated anonymously (via the Mix-net) from other node, the P2PRIV peer will flip an asymmetric coin to decide whether to forward the token anonymously to the next random peer with probability p_f (Line 5, Figure 4). Otherwise, if the request originates from a user, the forwarding process will surely proceed (Line 8, Figure 4).

```
(1)    while ∞ do
(2)        User_Reqest:=false
(3)        if Mix_Receive (("CLONE", File_Id},Irrelevant_Return_Addr)
(4)        or
(5)        User_Reqest := User_Api_Read (("CLONE", File_Id})
(6)        then Clone_and_Download (File_Id, User_Request)
(7)
(8)        if Mix_Receive (("FIND", File_Id}, Some_Proxy_Addr)
(9)        then Find_And_Reply (File_Id, Some_Proxy_Addr)
(10)
(11)       if Tcp_Receive (("GET", File_Id}, Clone_or_Initiator_Addr)
(12)       then Upload (File_Id, Clone_or_Initiator_Addr)
```

Fig. 3. Pseudo-code description of a P2PRIV single node operation

```
(1)   subr. Clone_and_Download (Download_File_Id, Is_Request_from_User)
(2)       CC_Forward:=false
(3)       if (Is_Request_from_User)
(4)           CC_Forward:=true
(5)       else if (Coin_Flip (pf))
(6)           CC_Forward:=true
(7)       if (CC_Forward)
(8)           Mix_Send ({"CLONE", Download_File_Id}, First_Random_Addr)
(9)
(10)      Mix_Send ({"FIND", Download_File_Id}, Second_Random_Addr)
(11)
(12)      while not
(13)          Mix_Receive
(14)          ({"FOUND", Download_File_Id, "@", File_Owner_Addr},
(15)              Second_Random_Addr)
(16)      do Wait
(17)      after (randomTime) Tcp_Send ({"GET", Download_File_Id},
(18)          File_Owner_Addr)
(19)
(20)      while not Tcp_Receive ({"PUT", File}, File_Owner_Addr)
(21)      do Wait
(22)      Cache (File)
(23)      if Is_Request_From_User
(24)          Alert ("Requested file has been anonymously downloaded!")
```

Fig. 4. Pseudo-code description of the Clone and Download subroutine

Next, the P2PRIV node sends a FIND message to a randomly chosen peer via means of a Mix-net. The selected node will perform a DHT look-up procedure and reply with an address of the peer which stores the file. This reply is sending on a Chaumian untraceable return address allowing a preservation of anonymity of this request. After receiving the reply message (FOUND) with an address of a storage and a file id (Line 13, Figure 4), the P2PRIV peer sends a randomly delayed request for the file (GET) directly to the storage node and waits for PUT reply message (Line 17, Figure 4).

```
(1)   subroutine Find_and_Reply (Lookup_File_Id, Reply_Dest_Addr)
(2)       if File_Owner_Addr:=Lookup (Key (Lookup_File_Id))
(3)           Mix_Send
(4)               ({"FOUND", Lookup_File_Id, "@", File_Owner_Addr},
(5)                   reply_Dest_Addr)
```

Fig. 5. Pseudo-code description of the Find and Reply subroutine

This request can be performed directly as the destination node cannot detect whether this request originates from the real initiation or from one of clones. Finally, the requested file is downloaded and cached (Lines 20-22, Figure 4). If the P2PRIV node is the real initiator, then the user will be informed about the successful download (Line 24, Figure 4). As it was described earlier (compare with Clone and Download

```
(1)     subroutine upload (upload_File_Id, upload_Dest_Addr)
(2)          Tcp_Send (("PUT", Upload_File_Id), Upload_Dest_Addr)
```

Fig. 6. Pseudo-code description of the Upload subroutine

subroutine), the P2PRIV node can send the FIND message to the other P2PRIV node. The "Find and Reply" subroutine describes a reaction to this request. Here the P2PRIV node becomes an anonymizing proxy, which initiates the DHT look-up procedure for a specified file. Additionally, this proxy is reached by means of Mix-net. In the line 2 (Figure 5) a DHT look-up procedure is executed and a result is sent back to an initiator on its untraceable address provided by means of Mix-net.

The last subroutine "Upload" (Figure 6) contains a short reaction to GET request (see Clone and Download subroutine where GET requests are initiated).

4 Path Lengths

In this section we will analyze the impact of p_f configuration on the system's anonymity and estimate secure lengths of CC. The analysis will cover small overlays ($N = 50$ network nodes), where it seems to be more difficult to hide a real initiator, and large networks ($N = 1000$ nodes) – more realistic for open P2Ps. We will analyze static, adaptive, passive, and active attacks using anonymity model of P2PRIV presented in [12]. We will stick to three variants of network collaboration levels:

$C = 10\%$ of colluding nodes, scenario usually considered in the state of the art;
$C = 5\%$:   more realistic collaboration level for large and public access overlays (where, apart from Sybil attack, it is more difficult for the adversary to prevail the level of honest nodes); and
$C = 20\%$: scenario for small overlays (among a small population of honest nodes it is more easy for the adversary to introduce the significant range of colluding nodes).

Let us analyze an uncertainty of finding a real initiator of the content download. The passive-static adversary can distinguish two sets of peers $\{S_1, S_2\}$ among all N nodes and assign their members probabilities of being the initiator $\{p_1, p_2\}$. S_1 consists of peers which are directly connected to colluding nodes C and S_2 are remaining honest nodes. From [12] the sizes of S_1 and S_2 sets equal:

$$S_1 = \frac{C}{N} n = \frac{C(p_f - 2)(N - C)}{(p_f - 1)N^2} \ , \ S_2 = N - C - S_1 \ , \tag{2}$$

and the members of those sets are recognized as the initiator with probabilities:

$$p_1 = \frac{(p_f - 1)N}{(p_f - 2)(N - C)} \ , \ p_2 = \frac{(p_f - 1)N}{(p_f - 1)N^2 - (p_f - 2)C} \ . \tag{3}$$

According to the information theory [18] and ([6], [17]) entropy of P2PRIV for this scenario will be

$$H_{psP2PRIV} = -\sum_{i=1}^{N} p_i \log_2(p_i) = -S_1 p_1 \log_2(p_1) - S_2 p_2 \log_2(p_2) \,, \qquad (4)$$

$$H_{psP2PRIV} = \begin{cases} 0 & p_1 = 1 \lor p_2 = 1 \\ \dfrac{C}{N} \log_2\!\left(p_1^{-1}\right) & p_2 = 0 \\ \left(1 - \dfrac{C}{N}\right) \log_2\!\left(p_2^{-1}\right) & p_1 = 0 \\ \dfrac{C}{N} \log_2\!\left(p_1^{-1}\right) + \left(1 - \dfrac{C}{N}\right) \log_2\!\left(p_2^{-1}\right) & p_1 \in (0,1) \land p_2 \in (0,1) \,. \end{cases} \qquad (5)$$

Figure 7 shows the entropy H of small and large P2PRIV overlays as a function of the parameter p_f.

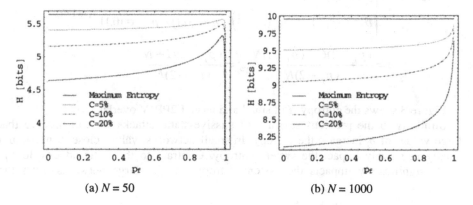

(a) $N = 50$ (b) $N = 1000$

Fig. 7. Entropy of P2PRIV, passive-static attacks

In both cases a p_f increase is in favor of the entropy of P2PRIV system. However, in small overlays (Figure 7a, $N = 50$ nodes) high p_f values (close to 1) eventually degrades the entropy. For $p_f = 0.9$ a cascade mean length reaches value of 6 nodes. This is a relatively large value for small networks. It is significant that in small networks it is easier for the adversary to become a member of CC and degrade P2PRIV entropy (from about 5 bits to even 0). Therefore, when we consider small overlays, p_f configuration should not be close to 1.

The analyzed static attack shows realistic capabilities of the adversary and exemplifies a critical point of view on the expansion of forwarding paths. However, a more pessimistic attack – adaptive observation – is possible. In adaptive attacks it is assumed that the adversary has yet colluding nodes among network nodes, which actively anonymize specified request (e.g., CC in P2PRIV). This scenario shows the effectiveness of the system's anonymity protection among network nodes actively involved in hiding the initiator. If the colluding node belongs to a CC involved in the download of an observed content then based on model from [12] the number of nodes that communicate directly with colluding nodes (S_{1pa}) and the remaining nodes (S_{2pa}) are

$$S_{1pa} = \frac{(N-C)\big((p_f-2)C+(p_f-1)N\big)}{(p_f-1)N^2} \;,\; S_{2pa} = N-C-S_{1pa} \;, \tag{6}$$

with assigned probability of being the initiator p_1 for S_{1pa} and

$$p_{2pa} = \frac{(p_f-1)N\big(N+(p_f-2)C\big)}{(p_f-2)(C-N)\big(C(pf-2)+N(N-p_fN+p_f-1)\big)} \tag{7}$$

for S_{2pa}. Then entropy in this attack scenario is

$$H_{paP2PRIV} = \begin{cases} 0 & p_1 = 1 \vee p_{2PA} = 1 \\ \vartheta \log_2\big(p_1^{-1}\big) & p_{2pa} = 0 \\ \varsigma \log_2\big(p_{2pa}^{-1}\big) & p_1 = 0 \\ \vartheta \log_2\big(p_1^{-1}\big) + \varsigma \log_2\big(p_{2pa}^{-1}\big) & p_1 \in (0,1) \wedge p_{2pa} \in (0,1) \end{cases} \;, \text{where} \tag{8}$$

$$\vartheta = \frac{(p_f-2)C+(p_f-1)N}{(p_f-2)N}, \varsigma = \frac{(p_f-2)C+N}{(p_f-2)N} \;.$$

Figure 8 shows the entropy H of small and large P2PRIV overlays.

Similarly to the previous scenario of passive-static attacks we can observe that large values of p_f increase the entropy. In small networks, values close to maximum finally negatively impact the system entropy. Contrary to the static attacks, low p_f value significantly impacts the system entropy and for large networks gives the

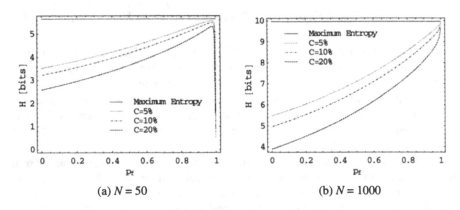

(a) $N = 50$ (b) $N = 1000$

Fig. 8. Entropy of P2PRIV, passive-adaptive attacks

adversary about 5 bits (from a total number of 10 bits) of information about the origin of a specified request.

We will analyze active attacks (static and adaptive) enabling attackers to change protocol operation to disclose more information next. Active attacks, adjusted to the proposed P2P architecture, were proposed in [12]. These attacks allow the adversary to intercept the CC as this action cannot be detected quickly in the new, parallel architecture. Using results from [12] we can stress that the active adversary can distinguish two sets of peer among all overlay network nodes:

$$S_{1as} = \frac{C(N-C)\left(N^3 + p_f^2(C-N)^3 + p_f N(2C^3 - 3NC + N^2)\right)}{\left(N + p_f(C-N)\right)N^4}, S_{2as} = N - C - S_{1as} \quad (9)$$

with probabilities of being initiator, accordingly for static attacks:

$$p_{1a} = \frac{N^3(p_f(C-N)+N)}{(N-C)\left(p_f^2(C-N)^3 + N^3 + p_f N(2C^2 - 3NC + N^2)\right)}, \quad (10)$$

$$p_{2as} = \frac{N^3\left(N + p_f(C-N)\right)}{p_f^2 C(C-N)^3 + N^3(C-N^2) + p_f N\left(2C^3 - 3C^2N - (N-1)CN^2 + N^4\right)}. \quad (11)$$

Taking into account adaptive possibilities of the adversary:

$$S_{1aa} = \frac{C}{N}\left(\frac{(N-C)\left(N^3 + p_f^2(C-N)^3 + p_f N(2C^3 - 3NC + N^2)\right)}{\left(N + p_f(C-N)\right)N^3} - 1\right) + 1, S_{2aa} = N - C - S_{1aa} \quad (12)$$

with probability p_{1a} and

$$p_{2aa} = \zeta\left[N - C + \frac{C}{N}\left(\frac{1 + (C-N)\left(N^3 + p_f N(2C^2 - 3NC + N^2) + p_f^2(C-N)^3\right)}{N^3\left(N + p_f(C-N)\right)}\right)\right]^{-1}. \quad (13)$$

Finally the entropies of P2PRIV for active attacks are

$$H_{asP2PRIV} = \begin{cases} 0 & p_{1a} = 1 \vee p_{2as} = 1 \\ \frac{C}{N}\log_2\left(p_{1a}^{-1}\right) & p_{2as} = 0 \\ \left(1 - \frac{C}{N}\right)\log_2\left(p_{2as}^{-1}\right) & p_{1a} = 0 \\ \frac{C}{N}\log_2\left(p_{1a}^{-1}\right) + \left(1 - \frac{C}{N}\right)\log_2\left(p_{2as}^{-1}\right) & p_{1a} \in (0,1) \wedge p_{2as} \in (0,1) \end{cases} \quad (14)$$

$$H_{aaP2PRIV} = \begin{cases} 0 & p_{1a} = 1 \vee p_{2aa} = 1 \\ \psi\log_2\left(p_{1a}^{-1}\right) & p_{2aa} = 0 \\ \zeta\log_2\left(p_{2aa}^{-1}\right) & p_{1a} = 0 \\ \psi\log_2\left(p_{1a}^{-1}\right) + \zeta\log_2\left(p_{2aa}^{-1}\right) & p_{1a} \in (0,1) \wedge p_{2aa} \in (0,1) \end{cases} \quad \text{, where}$$

$$\psi = \frac{N^3(N+C) - p_f N\left(N^3 - 2C^3 + 3NC^2 - 2N^2C\right) + p_f{}^2 C(C-N)^3}{\left(N^3 + p_f N(2C^2 - 3CN + N^2) + p_f{}^2(C-N)^3\right)N}$$

$$\zeta = \frac{p_f N\left(2N^3 - 2C^3 + 5C^2N - 5CN^2\right) - CN^3 - p_f{}^2(C-N)^4}{\left(N^3 + p_f N\left(2C^2 - 3CN + N^2\right) + p_f{}^2(C-N)^3\right)N}.$$

Figure 9 shows the entropies for P2PRIV static and adaptive attacks against active adversary attempting to intercept the token's random walk.

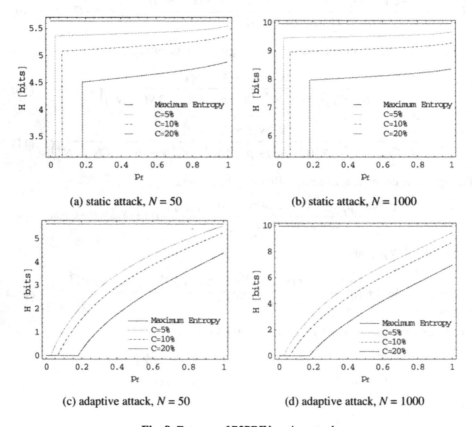

(a) static attack, $N = 50$ (b) static attack, $N = 1000$

(c) adaptive attack, $N = 50$ (d) adaptive attack, $N = 1000$

Fig. 9. Entropy of P2PRIV, active attacks

Taking into account far reaching possibilities of active adversary, which is able to imperceptibly break the cloning cascade, we have observed that P2PRIV can still assure proper level of anonymity. In configuration of high p_f values anonymity of P2PRIV is still close to maximum. However, active-adaptive scenarios show that secure configuration of the system should not cover p_f values lower than 0.5 ($P = 3$). For low p_f the P2PRIV entropy against active-adaptive adversary quickly reaches 0 value, which means that the initiator of the request becomes completely exposed.

Based on realistic assumptions of an adversary capabilities corresponding to the environment of public peer-to-peer overlays, we have observed that the new protocol assures high entropy. Passive attacks reveal that the solution is robust against the specific character of a static attack and that the effective penetration of a proper cloning cascade is difficult to carry out for the adversary. The analysis of active attacks strengthened our pronouncement, obtained by the analysis of passive-adaptive attacks, that p_f configuration should not cover low values (below 0.5) as in this configuration entropy is close to a minimum. Additionally, we have observed that in small overlay networks configuration of p_f close to 1 also negatively impacts the entropy. The overlay is dedicated to public and wide usage; however it should also be able to work under temporal conditions of small number of users.

Serjantov et al. [17] used the entropy measure to calculate the effective anonymity set size of anonymous systems. Let H be the entropy of the system, then

$$S_A = 2^H . \qquad (15)$$

This quantification allows stressing anonymity of a particular system as an equivalent of the perfect system with 2^H users. Table 1 contains a summary of the results obtained throughout analyzed scenarios. For the purpose of results' legibility, we have calculated the effective anonymity set size of the new protocol for characteristic and permissible values of average path lengths P as a function of p_f parameter (compare with equation 1). Here, we can observe how numerous would be the perfectly homogeneous "crowd" of peers surrounding and hiding the initiator of the request for networks of 50 and 1000 nodes.

Table 1. Effective anonymity set size for P2PRIV

p_f P		0.5 3	0.66 4	0.8 6	0.88 10	0.5 3	0.66 4	0.8 6	0.88 10
Attack	C		$N = 50$				$N = 1000$		
Passive-Static		43	44	45	46	750	760	770	790
Passive-Adaptive	5%	21	28	36	42	140	230	380	550
Active-Static		43	43	44	45	740	750	760	790
Active-Adaptive		15	24	32	38	71	160	290	430
Passive-Static		37	38	40	41	550	570	590	620
Passive-Adaptive	10%	18	24	31	38	100	170	290	430
Active-Static		36	37	38	39	540	550	570	590
Active-Adaptive		11	17	24	30	40	92	170	250
Passive-Static		27	28	31	34	300	320	340	380
Passive-Adaptive	20%	13	17	24	30	51	93	160	260
Active-Static		25	26	27	28	270	280	300	310
Active-Adaptive		5	8.5	12	16	11	26	49	74

5 Latency

Based on the previous discussion and results showed in Table 1 we will evaluate latency of P2PRIV with configurations starting from $p_f = \frac{1}{2}$ (3 parallel links) and CROWDS with corresponding configurations $p_f = \frac{2}{3}$ (3 cascade links) and higher.

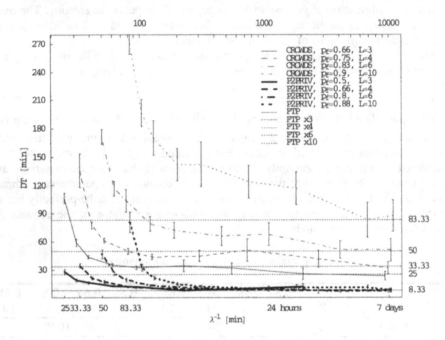

Fig. 10. Number of nodes (*P*) and links (*L*) for cascade (a) and parallel (b) transport

Fig. 11. Latency for CROWDS and P2PRIV

Notice that CROWDS includes one less link (*L*) for the same path length (*P*) because of its cascade transport architecture (Figure 10).

Let us evaluate the latency of the proposed protocol using anonymous traffic simulation model described in [12]. In the peer-to-peer anonymous traffic's simulation environment each peer of the simulated network retrieves the same algorithm suitable to a simulated protocol (for example "Jondo" of CROWDS) and estimates a download time DT quoted as an average time required for a content transport after a submission of the request by the user (initiator). The simulator traces tasks for each symmetric peer independently. We use Poisson distribution to model a request arrival process, where mean request arrival rate λ represent an intensity of requests for a content per single peer. The simulation results are compared to the classical anonymous network CROWDS and analytically calculated DT optimum value μ_{min}^{-1}, referred to as FTP.

$$\mu_{min} = \frac{B}{V} = 0{,}002\left[s^{-1}\right], \tag{16}$$

where average link throughput between peers is $B = 512$ kb/s and average file size of the shared content $V = 32$ MB. Thus, FTP (equaled to 8⅓ minutes) represents a theoretical download time between two directly connected nodes (ratio of average content size to average link throughput).

Figure 11 illustrates latency of P2PRIV and CROWDS. The content transport of P2PRIV is at least three times faster (for $L = 3$ configurations) than CROWDS DT. The observed increase of DT for the close to maximum request arrival rate is lower for P2PRIV. CROWDS introduces multiplications of DT for path lengths increases, while P2PRIV retains the DT level close to optimum regardless of CC lengths for medium- and low-loaded networks.

6 Conclusions

The paper introduces an overlay transport protocol based on a concept of a peer-to-peer direct and anonymous distribution overlay (P2PRIV). The idea of the P2PRIV consists in a parallel content transport instead of the widespread cascade transmission between chaining nodes. This feature allows for a separation of the anonymization process from the content transport function. In the paper we presented a design of the P2PRIV protocol for direct and anonymous P2P download by using a finite state machine diagram and a pseudo-code description. We analyzed the latency of the new protocol and a classical low-latency anonymous network, and compared the results to optimum values. We studied an impact of the protocol configuration, i.e., "cloning cascade" path lengths on the solution's anonymity and latency, and considered an impact of the new solution on a shape of the present-day's trade-off between anonymity and traffic performance. We found that the new solution allows both for increasing of anonymous path lengths and for assuring higher anonymity with significantly lower impact on transport's latency in contrast to the classical low-latency anonymous network (CROWDS). Each successive node from a forwarding path of CROWDS increases anonymity, however, it also considerably increases a latency of the content transport. As one can expect, the average latency imposed by the classical network is at least a multiplication of average number of links between a sender and a receiver, and an average download time of content's portion between two neighbor nodes. P2PRIV dissolve this issue. The impact of anonymization path lengths on the latency of the new parallel transport is significantly lower and in a case of medium- to low-loaded networks it is negligible. We believe that the results bring new possibilities of overcoming borders of existing trade-off between anonymity and traffic performance of anonymous networks.

The proposed solution is dedicated to the transport of a large content. However, it is motivating to analyze its usefulness in a wider range of applications. The vital question is if the new system can assure generic anonymous communications. In this case, it should be studied how robust P2PRIV is against long-term intersection attacks. Having in mind a single access to particular content by a single user, characteristic for a sharing of static, large content, we did not analyze this issue. However, in systems of general purpose, the problem of multiple accesses to the same resource should be considered. In peer-to-peer overlays it is difficult to ensure a long-term availability of individual peers, so the cascade is deemed to change over time (with the exception of the initiator). One direction of solving this issue for the generic purpose anonymous system, based on the P2PRIV architecture, is to allow the initiator to maintain the composition of the cloning cascade for a long period of time.

Our future work will also include analysis of an integration of the P2PRIV with publication of content functions. For a pervasive use of the presented system it is necessary to include in it the anonymous publication service, which together with the described P2PRIV anonymous transport can provide a comprehensive anonymous communications overlay. The publication process can be treated as a separated function of the overlay, however, to achieve a coherent prototype, the publication scheme should be based on a concurrent with P2PRIV set of security primitives. The other motivating goal is selecting such a known anonymous publication system that can share as many security primitives embedded in the P2PRIV as possible.

References

1. Bennett, K., Grothoff, C.: GAP – practical anonymous networking. In: Dingledine, R. (ed.) PET 2003. LNCS, vol. 2760. Springer, Heidelberg (2003)
2. Berthold, O., Federrath, H., Köpsell, S.: Web MIXes: A system for anonymous and unobservable Internet access. In: Federrath, H. (ed.) Designing Privacy Enhancing Technologies. LNCS, vol. 2009. Springer, Heidelberg (2001)
3. Chaum, D.: Untraceable electronic mail, return addresses, and digital pseudonyms. Communications of the ACM 4(2) (February 1981)
4. Clarke, I., Sandberg, O., Wiley, B., Hong, T.W.: Freenet: A distributed anonymous information storage and retrieval system. In: Proceedings of Designing Privacy Enhancing Technologies: Workshop on Design Issues in Anonymity and Unobservability, pp. 46–66 (July 2000)
5. Dai, W.: Pipenet 1.1. Usenet post (1996)
6. Diaz, C., Seys, S., Claessens, J., Preneel, B.: Towards measuring anonymity. In: Dingledine, R., Syverson, P.F. (eds.) PET 2002. LNCS, vol. 2482. Springer, Heidelberg (2003)
7. Dingledine, R., Freedman, M.J., Molnar, D.: The free haven project: Distributed anonymous storage service. In: Federrath, H. (ed.) Designing Privacy Enhancing Technologies. LNCS, vol. 2009. Springer, Heidelberg (2001)
8. Dingledine, R., Mathewson, N., Syverson, P.: Tor: The second generation onion router. In: Proceedings of the 13th USENIX Security Symposium (August 2004)
9. Freedman, M.J., Morris, R.: Tarzan: A peer-to-peer anonymizing network layer. In: 9th ACM Conference on Computer and Communications Security, Washington, DC (November 2002)
10. Goldschlag, D., Reed, M., Syverson, P.: Hiding Routing Information. In: Anderson, R. (ed.) IH 1996. LNCS, vol. 1174, pp. 137–150. Springer, Heidelberg (1996)
11. Loesing, K., Sandmann, W., Wilms, C., Wirtz, G.: Performance Measurements and Statistics of Tor Hidden Services. In: Proceedings of the 2008 International Symposium on Applications and the Internet (SAINT), Turku, Finland (July 2008)
12. Margasiński, I., Pióro, M.: A Concept of an Anonymous Direct P2P Distribution Overlay System. In: Proceedings of the 22nd IEEE International Conference on Advanced Information Networking and Applications (AINA 2008), March 2008, pp. 590–597 (2008) ISSN 1550-445X, ISBN 978-0-7695-3095-6
13. Reed, M., Syverson, P., Goldschlag, D.: Anonymous Connections and Onion Routing. IEEE Journal on Selected Areas in Communications 16(4), 482–494 (1998)

14. Rennhard, M., Plattner, B.: Introducing MorphMix: Peer-to-Peer based Anonymous Internet Usage with Collusion Detection. In: Proceedings of the Workshop on Privacy in the Electronic Society (WPES 2002), Washington, DC, USA (November 2002)
15. Reiter, M.K., Rubin, A.D.: Crowds: Anonymity for web transactions. ACM Transactions on Information and System Security 1(1) (June 1998)
16. Snader, R., Borisov, N.: A Tune-up for Tor: Improving Security and Performance in the Tor Network. In: Proceedings of the Network and Distributed Security Symposium (NDSS 2008) (February 2008)
17. Serjantov, A., Danezis, G.: Towards an information theoretic metric for anonymity. In: Dingledine, R., Syverson, P.F. (eds.) PET 2002. LNCS, vol. 2482. Springer, Heidelberg (2003)
18. Shannon, E.: A Mathematical Theory Of Communication. The Bell System Technical Journal 27, 379–423, 623–656 (1948)

SEM: A Security Evaluation Model
for Inter-domain Routing System in the Internet

Xin Liu, Peidong Zhu, and Yuxing Peng

[1]School of Computer, National University of Defense Technology,
Changsha 410073, China
{xin.liu,pdzhu,yxpeng}@nudt.edu.cn

Abstract. Since the lack of necessary security mechanisms, the Internet's inter-domain routing system, mainly based on the Border Gateway Protocol (BGP), inevitably faces with serious security threats. Although there are many researches focus on the security of inter-domain routing and BGP, few people have quantified the routing security of the current BGP system effectively. Moreover, Internet operators do need useful information to judge security threats of their autonomous systems (ASes) and BGP routers. In this paper, we propose a security evaluation model, *SEM*, to assess security threats of the routing system. The basic idea of *SEM* is simple, namely, the security status of the whole system rests with its parts'. In addition, we quantify security threats status of the routing information from RouteViews using our model. The experimental results show that the model can provide intuitive security threat indices for BGP routers, various ASes and the BGP system respectively, and further more, it can provide valuable, intuitional curve for Internet operators.

Keywords: BGP; Security Evaluation; Security Threat Situation.

1 Introduction

The Internet is made up of many self-governing routing domains called *Autonomous Systems* (ASes), in which network devices share the same routing policies. These independent networks are glued by the Border Gateway Protocol (BGP), a *de facto* standard inter-domain routing protocol, on which the Internet's robustness relies heavily. Since BGP is in lack of security mechanisms, the Internet's inter-domain routing system faces with serious security threats inevitably [1-4]. To build a secure and robust Internet, several solutions have been proposed [5-7], such as S-BGP, soBGP and psBGP etc, and IETF has also established a working group to investigate and recommend requirements of routing security [8].

However, the inter-domain routing system remains at incontrollable risk. On one hand, none of the proposed security solutions have been widely deployed due to the large requirements of modification on BGP, the heavy costs on operation, and the lack of backward compatibilities. Experts, however, are still debating on whether these solutions are feasible. In practice, the difficulties of deploying limit these approaches' usefulness. On the other hand, Internet operators require useful information to judge the security status of their ASes and BGP routers [9].

N. Akar, M. Pioro, and C. Skianis (Eds.): IPOM 2008, LNCS 5275, pp. 142–153, 2008.

How can we know whether the BGP system is safety or not? It is a general, but very difficult problem that needs to be addressed. The difficulties lie in: a) there are very few public efforts on automatic BGP monitoring [10-12]; b) the lack of useful tools for analyzing vast amounts of raw BGP data [13]; c) the issue of detecting anomalous BGP routes is still a tricky problem [14-17]; d) undeniably, the BGP system is very huge and autonomous, and it is not easy to assess it as a whole.

In this paper, we develop an evaluation model for addressing the issue we just described. We call our model *SEM*, which stands for Security Evaluation Model for the inter-domain routing system. Our goal is to provide a methodology to evaluate the security threats of the routing system. Most importantly, coupled with our model, the BGP monitoring system can provide more valuable information, and then Internet operators can analyze the routing security of the BGP system as a whole.

The rest of the paper is organized as follows. Section 2 illuminates a hierarchical architecture of the BGP system and introduces relevant terminologies. Section 3 presents the *SEM* model, which include a route status tree and evaluating algorithms. We demonstrate the efficacy of the model in Section 4. Section 5 describes related work, followed by conclusions in section 6.

2 Analysis of Inter-domain Routing Architecture

There are large numbers of BGP routers, or BGP speakers, in the Internet [18]. Fig. 1 shows illustrative Internet topology at two different levels. At the router level, each node represents a BGP router, and each edge represents a physical link between two routers. At the level of ASes, each node represents an AS, and each edge represents a logical relationship between two neighboring AS, that is, at least an eBGP peering session is in existence. Notice that two neighboring ASes may have multiple physical links. Since BGP paths are represented in the form of AS links, we abstract connections between two AS nodes as a single logical link.

The inter-domain routing system is composed of ASes or BGP routers, so we call them, even the system self, *route entities of the system*, or *entities*. Accordingly, entities of the routing system are of three kinds, AS entities (or ASes), BGP router entities

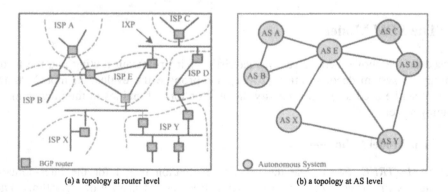

(a) a topology at router level   (b) a topology at AS level

Fig. 1. Illustrative topologies of the inter-domain routing system

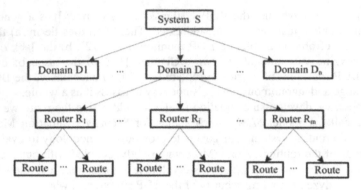

Fig. 2. Hierarchy of the inter-domain routing system

(or BGP routers) and a system entity. Of course, there is only one system entity in the routing system, which includes all autonomous domain entities.

Two entities of the same type may have connective relationship, such as logical link between two ASes. Moreover, dependent relationship consists in two entities of different types. For example, a router entity must belong to a domain entity, and all of them belong to the system entity. Let $X \rightarrow Y$ be a dependent relationship between entities X and Y where X is a *child entity* of Y; conversely, Y is the *father entity* of X. Furthermore, we can give the definitions of *descendant* and *ancestor*. If entities A, B and C satisfy relations, $A \rightarrow B$ and $B \rightarrow C$, then C is an *ancestor entity* of entity A, and A is a *descendant entity* of entity C.

Considering route status of every route entity, i.e. a set of BGP routes totally owned by an entity, we can obtain a hierarchy of the entire BGP system, which is shown in Fig. 2. There are four tiers: a system tier, a domain tier, a router tier and a route tier. In this hierarchy, route status of a father entity is composed by route status of all children entities, or all descendant entities. To evaluate situations of security threats of entities in the inter-domain routing system, we concentrate on anomalous BGP routes at route tier. These routes are inconsistent with routing policies of an ISP or violate involved Requests for Comments (RFCs).

3   The *SEM* Model

Based on the above hierarchical characteristic of inter-domain routing and the technology of system decomposition [20-21], we propose the evaluation model, *SEM*, which can be used to qualify security threat situations of entities in the inter-domain routing system.

3.1   The Model Definition

Let *SEM=(TREE, EA)* denote the security evaluation model for the inter-domain routing system, where *TREE* is a route status tree and *EA* is a set of algorithms. The *TREE* does not only characterize hierarchical relationships of entities of the system, but also stores and expresses security threat status of these entities. Furthermore, an evaluating algorithm in *EA* concretely computes security threat status of every entity. The procedure embodies evaluating the method and policies.

Once Internet operators construct the route status tree completely, they can obtain security threat situations of all the evaluated entities. Next, we will discuss in details the route status tree in Section 3.2 and evaluating algorithms in Section 3.3.

3.2 The Route Status Tree

The route status tree represents a hierarchy that describes the security threat status of entities of the BGP system. Let *TREE=(V, E)* be the route status tree, where *V* is a set of nodes with status information of routing security, and *E* is a set of dependent relationships. The structure of the *TREE* is shown in Fig. 3. Notice that, all leaves in the *TREE* represent BGP routers according to the entity definition in Section 2.

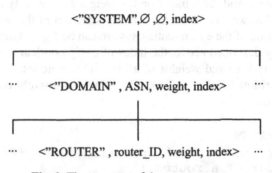

Fig. 3. The structure of the route status tree

In the *TREE*, a node *u*, i.e. an entity of the routing system, can be denoted *<type, ID, weight, index>*. Notice that security threat situation of an entity is characterized by the field of *index*. The meanings of the four fields are listed as follows:

a) The *type* field of *u* is used to express the type of relevant entity. Its value can be "*ROUTER*", "*DOMAIN*", or "*SYSTEM*", which is relevant to BGP routers, ASes, and the system respectively.

b) The *ID* field of *u* is used to identify an entity. When *u.type="ROUTER"*, the value of *u.ID* is the IP address of BGP router. When *u.type="DOMAIN"*, the value of *u.ID* is the AS number (ASN) of AS. In addition, when *u.type="SYSTEM"*, the value of *u.ID* is meaningless, namely, *u.ID=∅*.

c) The *weight* field of *u* is used to describe its importance, that is, relative weight of this entity in all children entities of its father. When *u.type="ROUTER"*, the value of *u.weight* is the weight of the BGP router. When *u.type="DOMAIN"*, the value of *u.weight* is the weight of AS. In addition, when *u.type="SYSTEM"*, the value of *u.weight* is meaningless, namely, *u.weight=∅*.

d) The *index* field of *u* is used to store and express security threat situation (or security threat index) of relevant entity. When *u.type="ROUTER"*, the value of *u.index* is the security threat index of BGP router. When *u.type="DOMAIN"*, the value of *u.index* is the security threat index of AS. When *u.type="SYSTEM"*, the value of *u.index* is the security threat index of the entire system.

3.3 Evaluating Algorithms

According to the hierarchy of the inter-domain routing system, Internet operators can build the *TREE* easily, and determine the fields of *type* and *ID*. Notice that, when the *TREE* is initially constructed, the field of *index* in every node is null. Parameters of the model, i.e. the *severe vector* of anomalous routes and weights of entities, will be discussed in following subsection. In this subsection, we mainly focus on how to obtain index of every entity when the *type*, *ID* and *weight* of each node are known..

Definitely, the goal of evaluating algorithms is to compute the index value of every node in the *TREE*. Since the *TREE* is organized in a hierarchy, a bottom-up process can be adopted. First of all, to evaluate security situations of BGP routers, we can regard anomalous BGP routes provided by BGP monitoring systems as original data. Secondly, analyze the severity of these routes and calculate the amount of these routes for every BGP router. And then, based on the weight and security situation of every BGP router of an AS, we can obtain the security situation of this AS. With the same idea, security situation of the entire routing system can be figured out finally.

Under the policy described above, the index of every non-leaf node in the *TREE* is determined by the indices and weights of all its children nodes. So, we can propose the following algorithm *INDEX*, *INDEX*∈*EA*, which recursively compute indices of all nodes in the *TREE*.

```
INDEX ALGORITHM
Input: TREE and C̄ of all routers, root.index = φ  (C̄ is the
number vector of a router.)
Output: root.index (the threat index value of the root of
the TREE.)
1:  if |TREE|=1 then
2:      if u.type ="ROUTER", u∈TREE then
            // Compute security status according to the
            // amount vector of anomalous routs of a
router
            // and the severe vector.
3:          u.index ← C̄(t)•10^D ;
4:          root.index ← u.index ;
5:      else
6:          error;    // TREE is in error.
7:      end if
8:  else
        // Remove the root node of the TREE,
        // and get a set of sub-tree.
9:      TREE_1,...,TREE_i,...,TREE_m ← TREE - root ;
10:     for each TREE_i do
11:         MI_i = INDEX(TREE_i) ;
            // Get the weight of root node of the TREE_i
12:         Weight_i = root.weight of TREE_i ;
```

```
13:          root.index = root.index + MI_i × Weight_i ;
14:     end for
15:  end
16:  return  root.index ;
```

Although the *INDEX* algorithm computes indices of nodes in a similar way, there are different meanings for nodes of different types. For a node u in the *TREE*:

a) If u.type="ROUTER", then the index of a router is computed with $u.index = f(\vec{C}(t), \vec{D}) = \vec{C}(t) \bullet 10^{\vec{D}}$, where $\vec{C}(t)$ is a router's number vector, in which there are amount of anomalous BGP routes of different types, and it is a function of time; where $\vec{D}$ is the severe vector of anomalous BGP routes, specially, it is a constant. Considering the severity of different anomalous BGP routes, we regard $f(\vec{C}, \vec{D})$ as $\vec{C} \bullet 10^{\vec{D}}$, where the operation, $10^{\vec{D}}$, is defined as $10^{\vec{D}} = (10^{\vec{D}_1}, 10^{\vec{D}_2}, ...)$. For example, one thousand of anomalous routes with level 1 are equal to one anomalous route with level 3.

b) If $u.type = "DOMAIN"$, then the index of a domain is computed with $u.index = f(\vec{W}_R(t), \vec{I}_R(t)) = \vec{W}_R(t) \bullet \vec{I}_R(t)$, where $\vec{W}_R$ is a vector, in which there are weights of BGP routers of a domain; where $\vec{I}_R$ is a vector comprised of indices of relevant BGP routers.

c) If u is the root node of the *TREE* and indices of the others have computed, then the index of the root is computed with $root.index = f(\vec{W}_D(t), \vec{I}_D(t)) = \vec{W}_D(t) \bullet \vec{I}_D(t)$, where $\vec{W}_D$ is a vector, in which there are weights of all domains of the *TREE*, and $\vec{I}_D$ is a vector of indices of relevant domains.

Notice that an exceptional halt condition exists in the *INDEX* algorithm: A node u is a leaf of the *TREE*, but it does not represent a BGP router. A leaf of the *TREE* must imply a BGP router entity due to the definition of route status tree.

3.4 Parameters

Before computing the index of every node of the *TREE* with the *INDEX* algorithm, we must ensure the parameters of the model. First, we start with how to get the *severity vector*, and then we show how we can get weights of entities.

3.4.1 Severity Vector

The impact of anomalous routes on the inter-domain routing system is relevant to the types of these routes. In Table 1, we classify the known anomalous routes as 8 types, and assign a level (0~3) to different type by experience [9]. A higher level implies that a threat is severer. To see this, we specify that the more-specific prefix hijacking is the top level, 3. It is reasonable, because this kind of anomalous routes can influence the connectivity of networks widely.

Table 1. Types of anomalous routes and its severity levels

Type	Priority	Description
Exact-prefix hijacking	2	Exact-prefix is hijcaked
More specific prefix hijacking	3	More specific prefix is hijacked
Less specific prefix hijacking	1	Less specific prefix is hijcaked
Private Prefixes	1	A prefix in the route is private
Routing Black hole	2	private AS existed in AS-Path
Damped routes	2	A route is announced repeatedly
Loop routes	2	An AS-loop existed in the AS-Path
Bogon routes	2	Unallocated prefixes

According to Table 1, the severity vector of anomalous BGP routes is $\vec{D} =< 2,3,1,1,2,2,2,2 >$.

3.5 Entity Weights

As discussed in Section 3.2 (the structure of the route status tree), our model needs to get weights of BGP routers and ASes. To obtain weights of ASes, we adopt a concise method. At first, we use a uniform criterion to estimate absolute importance, *DSI*, of all AS's. Second, we obtain relative importance of an AS, by normalizing *DSI*.

Recall that *AS E* in Fig. 1(b) is situated in a very important position because it has relations with the others. Although the importance of an AS depend on many aspects, such as its role (stub AS, transit AS, or core AS), size, services, and so on, the neighbor number of an AS captures the key part of its importance and it is a reflection of other aspects. As a rule, the more an AS has neighbors the more it can provide good quality of services and has BGP routers. In this paper, we just describe the importance of an AS with its neighbor number.

Thus, the criterion is the neighbor number of an AS, so the absolute importance of AS i, DSI_i, is defined to be $DSI_i =| neighbors_i | =|\{N \mid eBGP(i,N), i, N \in ASN\}|$, where $neighbors_i$ is the neighbor set of AS i, $eBGP(i, N)$ represents an eBGP session between AS E and N, and ASN is the set of all AS's. In Fig. 1(b), we can easily know $DSI_E=6$, $DSI_A=DSI_B=DSI_C=DSI_X=2$, and $DSI_D=DSI_Y=3$. And then, we can obtain weight of AS i by the formula, $weight_i = DSI_i / \sum DSI$. For example, the weight of AS E is 0.3, decrypted in Fig. 1(b). With the similar idea, weights of all BGP routers of an AS can be obtained, so we don't give unnecessary details.

4 Evaluation

In this section we illustrate the usage of *SEM* model and its effect in practice. We first explain data sources and how to determine weights of entities, followed by the main results of our evaluation and the insight behind the results.

4.1 Data Sources

The RouteViews is a project aiming to get comprehensive BGP views from different vantages in the Internet [13]. Through establishing BGP peering sessions with

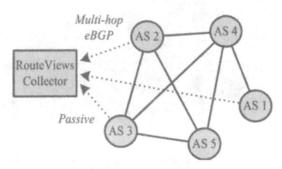

Fig. 4. Collecting method of Route Views project

operational routers, as shown in Fig. 4, the project collect routing data from a few hundred BGP routers around the globe placed in critical exchange points, tier-1 ISPs, and so forth. Furthermore, these collectors don't disseminate any announcements to neighbors. By this means, collectors don't make any impact on the Internet. In experiment, we choose a collector, *route-views.oregon-ix.net*. This collector saves snapshots of its BGP routing table every two hours, and currently peers with 49 BGP routers in 42 ASes in which most of tier-1 domains exist.

ISP-Health, a BGP monitoring system designed in [19], can analyze BGP data collected by RouteViews, and detect anomalous BGP routes that needed by *SEM* model. With BGP data on June 3rd, 2007, we demonstrate how to use the model to evaluate security situation of the BGP system, and analyze the evolution of security situations of BGP routers, ASes and the whole system on that day.

4.2 Weights

To apply the *SEM* model, we had better know topologies of autonomous systems and BGP routers, and the mapping of BGP routers to ASes. The three hard problems have been widely studied in [22-24], and therefore we suppose that this information is already known in the *SEM* model. However, for simplifying this evaluation, we take following approaches: First, we extract AS topology of the Internet only from Route-Views' BGP table. Second, we consider that the BGP routers gathered by the collector represent its AS and overlook physical topology of the AS. Thus, if an AS only has one BGP router peering with the collector, then in the AS the router's weight is 1; if an AS has two BGP routers peering with the collector, then in the AS weights of the both routers are 0.5; and so on. Third, we can directly obtain the mapping of neighboring routers and their AS from RouteViews' data, while the others are disregarded.

4.3 Results

Using *SEM*, we assessed security threat situations of entities of the inter-domain routing system on June 3rd, 2007. The results are shown in Fig. 5, 6 and 7, a higher value of index implies that an entity is confronted with a severer security threat.

Fig. 5. intuitively shows the system's security situation on June 3rd, 2007, and it can provide following useful information for Internet operators: a) Security threats of the system existed on this day, and fluctuated between index 4100 and 4700, which

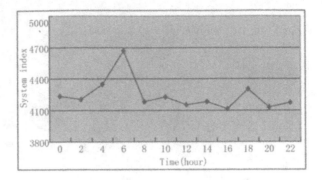

Fig. 5. Security threat situation of the inter-domain routing system on June 3rd, 2007

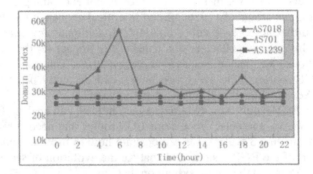

Fig. 6. Security threat situations of ASes on June 3rd, 2007

makes network operators need take precautions and pay attention at intervals. For example, when the security threat is very high, an operator can take rigid safety precautions for security of its routing domain. b) The system's security threat situation tended to peak at 6 a.m.

Then, security threat situations of AS7018, AS701 and AS1239, the biggest three domains in the current Internet, are shown in Fig. 6. From this figure, we can see: a) AS701 and AS1239's situations were relatively calm, but AS7018's undertook a sudden change and its index was higher than others. b) AS7018's index tended to peak at 6 a.m. Compared Fig. 5 with Fig. 6, we find that AS7018 answered for the turbulence of the routing system's situation. AS7018's operators may check its BGP routers over. On the other hand, ASes that neighbored with AS7018 need take relevant precautions.

Since most of ASes collected by RouteViews only have one BGP router that establishes multi-hop eBGP peering session with the collector we choose, security threat situations of these ASes are identical to the corresponding BGP routers' for simplification. For example, security threats of AS7018 and its BGP router (with IP 12.0.1.63) are the same. We notice that, there are three BGP routers in AS4513 peering with the collector. As an example, Fig. 5 shows security threat situations of the three BGP routers of AS4513. We can learn that, not only security threat is in every router, but

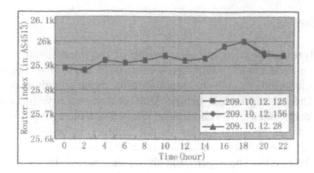

Fig. 7. Security threat situations of BGP routers on June 3rd, 2007

also indices of the three routers are fluctuated lightly and synchronously. We found that synchronous phenomenon existed in multi-routers collected in the same AS, so it seems that a BGP router may reasonably stands for its AS.

These figures show that the model that we provided describe security threat situations of entities of different levels in the inter-domain routing system of the Internet. With these situations, Internet operators can apperceive the security status of the system in time. In addition, Internet operators can find further rules of security and take better safety precautions, when they track changes of security threat situations during long time.

5 Related Work

Since security extensions to BGP are confronted with obstacles of deployment due to requirement of a public-key infrastructure and changes to BGP, a number of anomaly detection solutions have been developed recently [15, 16, 19, 25-27]. A commonality among theses solutions is that they do not use cryptographic-based mechanisms.

Multiple origin AS (MOAS) list [16] and Whisper [25] detect suspicious routes by monitoring the BGP messages exchanged between routers. Both use BGP community attribute to convey extra information. And [16] showed that most MOAS conflicts are short-lived, that is lasting a small number of days. Wang et al. [26] developed a BGP anomaly detector using top-level domain server routes. In order to prevent TLD route hijacks, they suggest filtering out all but the most durable routes. But the anomaly detector cannot be used for all prefixes.

In [15], Kruegel et al. proposed a topology-based method for detecting anomalous BGP messages, which relies on a model of the AS connectivity to verify whether the route advertisements are consistent with the network topology or not. And [19] adopt a method similar to [15], but based on logical topology of ASes. In [27], J. Karlin et al. proposed PGBGP, which identify suspicious routes by consulting a table of trusted routing information learned from the recent history of BGP update messages.

However, there was little work to quantify routing security of the current BGP system, and our study complements all of this work, in particular [15, 19, 27].

6 Conclusion

The paper analyzes a hierarchical characteristic of the inter-domain routing system, and proposes the *SEM* model, which takes anomalous BGP routes as input and produces security threat indices so as to assess security threat situations of entities of the BGP system. The basic principle behind *SEM* is that security threat situation of a father entity is determined by its children's. We validate the efficacy of our model by quantifying status of security threats of the routing information collected from RouteViews on June 3rd, 2007, and discuss the main results of our evaluation and the insight behind the results. The experiment shows that our model can provide an intuitive security threat status for BGP routers, ASes and the inter-domain routing system, and can provide valuable, intuitional curve for network operators.

We plan to provide a public BGP monitoring service and security threat situations. And, in our ongoing research, we will work on finding further rules of security threat situations during long time with our *SEM* model.

Acknowledgments. The authors would like to thank the generous comments from the anonymous reviewers. This research is being funded by the National High-Tech Research and Development Plan of China under Grant No. 2006AA01Z213 and No. 2006AA01Z332, the National Natural Science Foundation of China under Grant No. 60673169 and No. 60433040, and the Research Foundation for Ph.D. Candidates of National University of Defense Technology of China No. B070603.

References

1. Yannuzzi, M., Masip-Bruin, X., Bonaventure, O.: Open Issues in Interdomain Routing: A Survey. IEEE NETWORK 19, 49–56 (2005)
2. Christian, B., Tauber, T.: BGP Security Requirements. Internet-Draft: IETF (2006)
3. Butler, K., Farley, T., Rexford, J.: A Survey of BGP Security (2005), http://www.patrickmcdaniel.org/pubs/td-5ugj33.pdf
4. Nordström, O., Dovrolis, C.: Beware of BGP Attacks. ACM SIGCOMM Computer Communications Review 34, 1–8 (2004)
5. Kent, S., Lynn, C., Seo, K.: Secure Border Gateway Protocol (S-BGP). IEEE Journal on Selected Areas in Communications, Special Issue on Network Security 18, 582–592 (2000)
6. White, R.: Securing BGP Through Secure Origin BGP. IPJ 6, 15–22 (2003)
7. Wan, T., Kranakis, E., Oorschot, P.v.: Pretty Secure BGP (psBGP). In: ISOC. San Diego, CA, USA (2005)
8. Routing protocols security working group, http://www.rpsec.org
9. Popescu, A.C., Premore, B.J., Underwood, T.: Anatomy of a leak: As9121, http://www.nanog.org/mtg-0505/underwood.html
10. Gradus tool, http://gradus.renesys.com
11. Lad, M., Massey, D., Pei, D.: PHAS: A Prefix Hijack Alert System. In: Proceedings of 15th USENIX Security Symposium, pp. 153–166 (2006)
12. Ripe myasn system, http://www.ris.ripe.net/myasn.html
13. Meyer, D.: Route Views Project, http://www.routeviews.org

14. Feamster, N., Jung, J., Balakrishnan, H.: An Empirical Study of Bogon Route Advertisements. ACM SIGCOMM CCR 35, 63–71 (2005)
15. Kruegel, C., Mutz, D., Robertson, W., Valeur, F.: Topology-based Detection of Anomalous BGP Messages. In: Vigna, G., Krügel, C., Jonsson, E. (eds.) RAID 2003. LNCS, vol. 2820, pp. 17–35. Springer, Heidelberg (2003)
16. Zhao, X., Pei, D., Wang, L., Massey, D., Mankin, A., Wu, S.F., Zhang, L.: Detection of Invalid Routing Announcement in the Internet. In: Proceedings of the International Conference on Dependable Systems and Networks (DSN) (2002)
17. Bush, R.: Validation of Received Routes. In: NANOG (2000)
18. Rekhter, Y., Li, T., Hares, S.: A Border Gateway Protocol 4 (BGP-4), RFC 4271
19. Liu, X., Zhu, P.: A Rules-Based Approach to Anomaly Detection in Inter-domain Routing System. Journal of National University of Defense Technology 28, 71–76 (2006)
20. Wang, C., Wulf, W.A.: Towards a framework for security measurement. In: 20th National Information Systems Security Conference, Baltimore (1997)
21. Chen, X., Zheng, Q., Guan, X., Lin, C.: Quantitative Hierarchical Threat Evaluation Model for Network Security. Journal of Software 17, 885–897 (2006)
22. Zhang, B., Liu, R., Massey, D., Zhang, L.: Collecting the Internet AS-level Topology. ACM SIGCOMM CCR, special issue on Internet Vital Statistics (2005)
23. Spring, N., Mahajan, R., Wetherall, D., Anderson, T.: Measuring ISP topologies with Rocketfuel. IEEE/ACM Trans. on Networking 12, 2–16 (2004)
24. Mao, Z.M., Rexford, J., Wang, J., Katz, R.H.: Towards an Accurate As-Level Traceroute Tool. In: SIGCOMM 2003, Karlsruhe, Germany, pp. 365–378 (2003)
25. Subramanian, L.: Listen and whisper: Security mechanisms for BGP. In: First Symposium on Networked Systems Design and Implementation (NSDI 2004) (2004)
26. Wang, L., Zhao, X., Pei, D., Bush, R., Massey, D., Mankin, A., Wu, S., Zhang, L.: Protecting BGP Routes to Top Level DNS Servers. In: ICDCS (2003)
27. Karlin, J., Forrest, S., Rexford, J.: Pretty good bgp: Protecting bgp by cautiously selecting routes, University of New Mexico (2006)

Author Index

Lecture Notes in Computer Science

Sublibrary 5: Computer Communication Networks and Telecommunications

Vol. 4465: T. Chahed, B. Tuffin (Eds.), Network Control and Optimization. XIII, 305 pages. 2007.

Vol. 4458: J. Löffler, M. Klann (Eds.), Mobile Response. X, 163 pages. 2007.

Vol. 4427: S. Uhlig, K. Papagiannaki, O. Bonaventure (Eds.), Passive and Active Network Measurement. XI, 274 pages. 2007.

Vol. 4396: J. García-Vidal, L. Cerdà-Alabern (Eds.), Wireless Systems and Mobility in Next Generation Internet. IX, 271 pages. 2007.

Vol. 4373: K.G. Langendoen, T. Voigt (Eds.), Wireless Sensor Networks. XIII, 358 pages. 2007.

Vol. 4357: L. Buttyán, V.D. Gligor, D. Westhoff (Eds.), Security and Privacy in Ad-Hoc and Sensor Networks. X, 193 pages. 2006.

Vol. 4347: J. López (Ed.), Critical Information Infrastructures Security. X, 286 pages. 2006.

Vol. 4325: J. Cao, I. Stojmenovic, X. Jia, S.K. Das (Eds.), Mobile Ad-hoc and Sensor Networks. XIX, 887 pages. 2006.

Vol. 4320: R. Gotzhein, R. Reed (Eds.), System Analysis and Modeling: Language Profiles. X, 229 pages. 2006.

Vol. 4311: K. Cho, P. Jacquet (Eds.), Technologies for Advanced Heterogeneous Networks II. XI, 253 pages. 2006.

Vol. 4272: P. Havinga, M. Lijding, N. Meratnia, M. Wegdam (Eds.), Smart Sensing and Context. XI, 267 pages. 2006.

Vol. 4269: R. State, S. van der Meer, D. O'Sullivan, T. Pfeifer (Eds.), Large Scale Management of Distributed Systems. XIII, 282 pages. 2006.

Vol. 4268: G. Parr, D. Malone, M. Ó Foghlú (Eds.), Autonomic Principles of IP Operations and Management. XIII, 237 pages. 2006.

Vol. 4267: A. Helmy, B. Jennings, L. Murphy, T. Pfeifer (Eds.), Autonomic Management of Mobile Multimedia Services. XIII, 257 pages. 2006.

Vol. 4240: S.E. Nikoletseas, J.D.P. Rolim (Eds.), Algorithmic Aspects of Wireless Sensor Networks. X, 217 pages. 2006.

Vol. 4238: Y.-T. Kim, M. Takano (Eds.), Management of Convergence Networks and Services. XVIII, 605 pages. 2006.

Vol. 4235: T. Erlebach (Ed.), Combinatorial and Algorithmic Aspects of Networking. VIII, 135 pages. 2006.

Vol. 4217: P. Cuenca, L. Orozco-Barbosa (Eds.), Personal Wireless Communications. XV, 532 pages. 2006.

Vol. 4195: D. Gaiti, G. Pujolle, E.S. Al-Shaer, K.L. Calvert, S. Dobson, G. Leduc, O. Martikainen (Eds.), Autonomic Networking. IX, 316 pages. 2006.

Vol. 4124: H. de Meer, J.P.G. Sterbenz (Eds.), Self-Organizing Systems. XIV, 261 pages. 2006.

Vol. 4104: T. Kunz, S.S. Ravi (Eds.), Ad-Hoc, Mobile, and Wireless Networks. XII, 474 pages. 2006.

Vol. 4074: M. Burmester, A. Yasinsac (Eds.), Secure Mobile Ad-hoc Networks and Sensors. X, 193 pages. 2006.

Vol. 4033: B. Stiller, P. Reichl, B. Tuffin (Eds.), Performability Has its Price. X, 103 pages. 2006.

Vol. 4026: P.B. Gibbons, T. Abdelzaher, J. Aspnes, R. Rao (Eds.), Distributed Computing in Sensor Systems. XIV, 566 pages. 2006.

Vol. 4003: Y. Koucheryavy, J. Harju, V.B. Iversen (Eds.), Next Generation Teletraffic and Wired/Wireless Advanced Networking. XVI, 582 pages. 2006.

Vol. 3996: A. Keller, J.-P. Martin-Flatin (Eds.), Self-Managed Networks, Systems, and Services. X, 185 pages. 2006.

Vol. 3976: F. Boavida, T. Plagemann, B. Stiller, C. Westphal, E. Monteiro (Eds.), NETWORKING 2006. Networking Technologies, Services, and Protocols; Performance of Computer and Communication Networks; Mobile and Wireless Communications Systems. XXVI, 1276 pages. 2006.

Vol. 3970: T. Braun, G. Carle, S. Fahmy, Y. Koucheryavy (Eds.), Wired/Wireless Internet Communications. XIV, 350 pages. 2006.

Vol. 3964: M.Ü. Uyar, A.Y. Duale, M.A. Fecko (Eds.), Testing of Communicating Systems. XI, 373 pages. 2006.

Vol. 3961: I. Chong, K. Kawahara (Eds.), Information Networking. XV, 998 pages. 2006.

Vol. 3912: G.J. Minden, K.L. Calvert, M. Solarski, M. Yamamoto (Eds.), Active Networks. VIII, 217 pages. 2007.

Vol. 3883: M. Cesana, L. Fratta (Eds.), Wireless Systems and Network Architectures in Next Generation Internet. IX, 281 pages. 2006.

Vol. 3868: K. Römer, H. Karl, F. Mattern (Eds.), Wireless Sensor Networks. XI, 342 pages. 2006.

Vol. 3854: I. Stavrakakis, M. Smirnov (Eds.), Autonomic Communication. XIII, 303 pages. 2006.

Vol. 3813: R. Molva, G. Tsudik, D. Westhoff (Eds.), Security and Privacy in Ad-hoc and Sensor Networks. VIII, 219 pages. 2005.

Vol. 3462: R. Boutaba, K.C. Almeroth, R. Puigjaner, S. Shen, J.P. Black (Eds.), NETWORKING 2005. XXX, 1483 pages. 2005.